Irina Gordienko

Sergei O. Prokofieff: Myth and Reality

Irina Gordienko

Sergei O. Prokofieff:
Myth and Reality

Moskau-Basel-Verlag

English translation by Graham B. Rickett, from the German edition "Die Grundlegung der neuen Mysterien durch Sergej O. Prokofieff" (Lochmann-Verlag, CH-Basel, 1998).

Titel of the Russian manuscript:

С. О. Прокофьев: Миф и реальность

Copies of the 210-page Russian manuscript can be ordered from Lochmann-Verlag.

A translation of the only critical review of a work by S. O. Prokofieff to have appeared so far, is given in the Appendix. It was written by Hellmut Finsterlin, the editor of the quarterly journal "Erde und Kosmos", and appeared in Germany (in Nrs. 2 and 3 / 1983 of "Erde und Kosmos") immediately after the publication of the first book ("Rudolf Steiner and the founding ..."). The journal "Erde und Kosmos" appeared from 1976 until the death of its editor in 1990.

Cover illustration:
Fragment from "The Garden of Delights" by Hieronymus Bosch

© 2001 Lochmann-Verlag, Basel
ISBN 3-906712-16-8

Lochmann-Verlag, P. O. Box 231, CH-4009 Basel, Switzerland
Tel. +41 61 3015418, Fax 3013477, Email: lochmann_verlag@gmx.ch

Contents

Author's Foreword

The readers of the works of Sergei Prokofieff fall into three categories. The first (and most numerous) is convinced that his writings accelerate the process of acquiring knowledge in Anthroposophy and, thanks to a more effective method, deepen one's understanding more than does the reading of Rudolf Steiner's own works. In addition they view Prokofieff as being surrounded by a certain aura of spiritual presence.

A second, less enthusiastic, group (numerically smaller) analyzes the texts of Prokofieff, compares his writings with those of Rudolf Steiner, to whose perception reference is continually made.

And finally a third (likewise small) category analyzes in his works the inner structure, the logic, the style, the manner of presentation, the attitude adopted by the author, etc.

In the last two cases the Student makes surprising, nay, shattering discoveries, as a result of which he feels the urge to communicate these discoveries to the readers of the first group and also to those who are still beginners in the study of Prokofieff's works. This was the initial reason why the author decided to write this book.

A second reason was the passage in Herbert Wimbauer's book „The Case of Prokofieff" (1995), in which Wimbauer speaks in connection with Prokofieff of the danger that threatens, from the East, the mission of Middle Europe (Ch. 8), and where he characterizes Prokofieff as, above all, a representative of „this Eastern, Russian Theosophical mysticism" (p. 173).

Without wishing to embark on a discussion of fundamentals with Herr Wimbauer, we would like to affirm that in this particular case neither the East nor Russia itself is to blame, as the Prokofieff phenomenon with its significance as „science" and for the „Society" is a pure product of the West and only of the West. It is there that he was cherished and – with every possible means – supported. His „fame" was – to our great misfortune – re-imported into Russia. This fact cannot be challenged.

Regarding the first motive, the author would like here to raise a central question which she hopes the reader will not overhastily dismiss as a paradox. If that were to happen, then a book of this kind would not need to be written.

Nonetheless the reader will be able to observe quite frequently that many obvious and self-evident facts are not regarded as such within Anthroposophical circles.

Our question is the following: In what we call Anthroposophical „secondary literature" do the sense and content of a work have central significance, or are these only secondary, the essential factors having to be sought elsewhere?

If the latter were to be so, then we would have to confess that in this case we have nothing of real importance to say – indeed, we would feel disinclined to start such an investigation at all. But we are convinced that in the books that are written in the name of Anthroposophy, above all the study of the content is fundamental. If, however, one wishes to form a judgment regarding the content, then the criteria for this must be drawn from the traditional scientific quest for knowledge. And here we have arrived at the point where we would like to make known to the reader our fundamental point of departure, the scientific procedure, with the help of which we wish to analyze the work of Prokofieff.

The path of development of Anthroposophy is usually said to have begun in the year 1902, when the German Section of the Theosophical Society was founded. However, one needs to bear in mind that the foundation for the entire subsequent development of Anthroposophy was laid by Rudolf Steiner in his writings on the theory of knowledge, such as: „Outline of a Theory of Knowledge of the Goethean World-Conception" (1886), „Truth and Science" (1892), „Philosophy of Freedom" (1893), etc.

Special attention should be paid to the fact that, at the time when he was writing these works, Rudolf Steiner had supersensible experience of his own. Before his inner eye the spiritual world stood as a reality that was raised above all doubt. And in spite of this he began his scientific activity not with a description of his occult experiences, but turns his attention to the universal human question of his epoch – that concerning the crisis of knowledge. The essential nature of this crisis – which continues into our own time – consists in the fact that the human powers of cognition, as they have developed in the last few centuries, prove to be unable to answer the question pertaining to the realm of soul and spirit. The consequence of this was that all aspects relating to soul and spirit existence were, on the ground that they were unknowable, consigned to the sphere of religion. The individual thinking consciousness of man was ever more restricted to narrow, purely material interest, leading finally to the complete denial of spiritual reality, which in its turn has resulted in the universal triumph of the materialistic world-view.

For this reason Rudolf Steiner began with a theme that is entirely lacking in interest to popular mysticism – namely, with an investigation of the laws of cognition, in the hope of opening up a possibility of indicating means whereby they can be extended, thus enabling the boundaries of the sense-perceptible world to be crossed. Not until this task had been fulfilled in its most essential elements, did Rudolf Steiner join the Theosophical Society and set up its German Section. The conditions for this step lay in the fact that the Theosophical Society had to fulfil the same task as Rudolf Steiner's theory of knowledge, and this is not surprising, for in both undertakings one and the same spiritual impulse was at work, the same initiators stood. This common task was to overcome the dichotomy between the spiritual world and the consciousness of the civilized man of today, which is sinking ever deeper into materialism.

In the real cultural-historical process, however, things developed in such a way that all that stood at the beginning of the Theosophical activity was taken up by the contemporary mode of thought as something external. This was the Theo-Sophia, the primordial divine wisdom, which had been entrusted at the beginning of Earth-evolution to the leading representatives of the human race, which was guarded in the occult schools, the Mystery centres, and was transmitted by the pupils from one generation to the next. The founder of the Theosophical Society, H. P. Blavatsky, undertook the task of spreading and popularizing this occult knowledge.

In contrast to this, in Anthroposophy the starting-point was taken in what every human being can recognize and observe within himself. For Anthroposophy, from the very beginning, the Anthropos, the human being, stood in the focus of attention – first and foremost the man of the present day; and thereafter the Sophia, that wisdom which he can attain in the process of his becoming an 'I'. In this way, from the moment of its emergence, Anthroposophy is membered organically into the living stream of the general development of mankind. It begins at that point where the human being of today seeks a path into the spiritual world – with respect both to his inner soul-spiritual constitution and to the world around him.

For a while Anthroposophy developed in connection with the Theosophical movement. Later, as a result of Rudolf Steiner's withdrawal from the Theoso-

phical Society, the Anthroposophical movement broke away and became independent; at the same time it represented a direct continuation of the Theosophical Society. But we would again stress that Anthroposophy began, not with the
Theosophy of Blavatsky, but with the theory of knowledge of Rudolf Steiner
which in its turn has deep roots in European Christian esotericism.

What we have just said has significance not merely as history, but rather
with regard to basic principles. Were one to sever Anthroposophy from its actual foundation – the writings of Rudolf Steiner on the theory of knowledge –
one would risk losing sight of that most important aspect which distinguishes it
from other spiritual streams of the past and present, namely the special method
of cognition which is peculiar to it alone. Thanks to this the human being has
the possibility of knowing the spiritual world just as reliably and objectively as
is the case in the physical world with the methods of natural science. When
stressing the possibility of an exact knowledge of the spiritual, Rudolf Steiner
characterized Anthroposophy also as spiritual science or science of the spirit.

Of course there is also a fundamental difference between the spiritually and
the materially-oriented science, which lies not so much in the object as in the
method. The difference becomes particularly noticeable in our time, when sci-
entists are forced, under the pressure of evidence, to acknowledge the existence
of the spiritual and to try to approach it with methodical research; for this purpose special branches of science, such as parapsychology, extra-sensory research, have been developed. As science enlarges its field of research and tries
to advance into the world of the invisible it follows the „extensive" path
through the invention of new technical means of observation which can be employed as a kind of extension of the human sense-organs, but possess an enhanced reliability. Through the technology of the electronic calculators (computer technology) single functions of human thinking can be carried out more
effectively than is possible to the human being. In this way science perfects
both sides of human cognition: perception and also thinking. However, this is
done in an entirely external way, without affecting the human cognitive capacity itself. It merely improves the technical procedures. Materialistic science is
therefore condemned, despite its sometimes fantastic achievements, to gather
knowledge solely within the limits of the physical plane; the kaleidoscope of
so-called paranormal phenomena so far recorded also belongs in this sphere.

Anthroposophy or spiritual science follows a different path. Of almost central importance for it is the development of the cognitive faculty of the human being himself as a subject and object of science. Whereas to materialistic science it is a matter of indifference what inner path of development a scientist is pursuing up to the moment when a scientific discovery is made, this is quite different in spiritual science. The path of cognition here is, at the same time, the spiritual path of development of the researcher. Rudolf Steiner said that spiritual science „strives ... through the strictly-controlled development of purely psychical perception, to obtain objective, exact results with respect to the supersensible world ... [and] recognizes the validity of only those results which are won through a psychical perception in which the soul-spiritual organization is surveyed as clearly and exactly as a mathematical problem. Thus for the [spiritual researcher] ... the scientific method is first applied to the preparation that lies within his spirit-organs" (GA 25, p. 7-8).

The Anthroposophical method of research into the spiritual world comprises the indications given by Rudolf Steiner concerning the esoteric development of the pupil, and is founded wholly on the epistemological principles of his philosophy, in which the nature of human cognition as such is revealed. It consists in the uniting of the percept with the corresponding concept by means of thinking, an activity of the 'I' which is given in experience. In the course of esoteric schooling the human being develops within himself new, spiritual organs of perception, whereby the range of his perceptions reaches beyond the boundaries of sense experience. From the intellectual ability to link together concepts and make logical inferences, thinking rises to a direct beholding of the idea and now begins, in the steadily expanding sphere, to include concepts which can grasp the essence of what is beheld spiritually. Though percept and thinking may qualitatively change, the cognitional character itself permits of no alteration. As the central point of the cognitive process there always remains the self-conscious 'I', in which the percepts – whether they be sensible or supersensible – enter into a union with the concepts that correspond to their essential being.

Thus objective knowledge in the spiritual world has its foundation in the cognitive faculty developed by the human being in the physical world. It is therefore understandable that so stringent demands are made, with respect to his thinking and his general state of psychical health, of the person who wishes to tread the Anthroposophical path of knowledge. And these demands must be met before the student begins the esoteric exercises which lead to the unfolding of the organs of supersensible perception. Thus we see clearly now how mis-guided is the view of those who believe it is possible to carry through serious, independent, spiritual-scientific research without the capacity of logical, conse-quential thinking that remains true to reality, and of objective knowledge in the physical world, but based only on some other kind of soul-spiritual disposition. Hence practical training in the power of thought that is built upon reality is „important, especially for those who are working on the basis of Anthroposo-phy", Rudolf Steiner stresses (18.1.1909, GA 108).

The Anthroposophical path of training is structured from its very first steps in such a way that the student who wishes to follow it can obtain reliable and objective knowledge of the spiritual world. On the Anthroposophical path oc-cult experience as such is not an end in itself, and the satisfaction of curiosity and the leaning of individual personalities towards mystical experiences and ir-regular states of consciousness do not belong to the tasks of Anthroposophy. These tasks stand in connection to the objective knowledge of the spiritual world, and supersensible experience is merely one of the preconditions for this knowledge. The question in what way this experience is attained is of crucial importance in this connection.

A thorough study, a grasp of and strict adherence to all the conditions of the Anthroposophical method of cognition, is thus the prime task (not a matter of personal taste), and is the basic condition to be met if Anthroposophy is to be able to fulfil its mission in the world. Its method was elaborated by Rudolf Steiner in exact correspondence to its task. In Anthroposophy the cognitive process itself becomes a Mystery bearing universal human significance; through it the way is paved for the upward development of human culture as a whole, and this path must be laid correctly and all the laws of the evolution of the World and Man must be observed.

The study of spiritual scientific content on the basis of the cognitive faculty that is the possession of the human being in his ordinary consciousness is the starting-point of the Anthroposophical path and the first stage of esoteric prac-tice. The knowledge that is acquired through thinking, prior to supersensible experience, concerning the beings and lawful structure of the spiritual world, is an absolute precondition for an entry into that world that is rightful and without danger for the human being; while errors on the path of occult development, arising from insufficient or incorrect knowledge, can have the most far-reaching consequence for his destiny, not only with regard to the psychic health of the human being in his present incarnation, but for his entire future destiny. Therefore it is especially important to avoid all distortion of Anthroposophical knowledge. Anyone in the Anthroposophical movement who lays claim to the status of an independent researcher in the spirit-realm, and passes on to other people the spiritual knowledge he has acquired, must first state clearly what method of spiritual research has been applied.

Just as in any other science, not everything can become content of spiritual science without first being tested. Spiritual-scientific research must, in order to be recognized as such, meet certain requirements with respect to method and content. Thus there can be neither internal contradictions nor anything contradicting the communications of Rudolf Steiner or generally accepted and indisputable facts in the outer world; to satisfy this demand alone would substantially reduce the amount of Anthroposophical secondary literature, with its tendency to multiply beyond all proportions, and heads would thereby be less overloaded with all kinds of false and meaningless conceptions. A body (dedicated to this task) would in no way place a limit on individual freedom, any more than this is the case with the activity of scientific panels and adjudication committees. The purpose of such institutions is to protect the branches of science for which they are responsible from false conceptions, distortions, malpractice, wrongful accusations etc., and to guard the scientific associations concerned against the activity of dilettantes and charlatans.

Finally, one must recognize how problematic it is that in the Anthroposophical Society, where people are seeking for the truth in not only practical, but also spiritual matters, the question concerning the credibility of different spiritual contents has, to this day, scarcely ever been asked!

When a false or non-proven assertion appears in the scientific press, this is taken as a signal for the opening of a scientific debate, which continues until the matter is resolved, even if further research has to be carried out. It is quite a different situation in the Anthroposophical media. There one can write whatever one likes, provided no interests are put at risk and the familiar terminology is used. Any attempt to criticize such printed assertions is condemned out of a false ethical principle: tolerance towards a person is confused with tolerance of his mistakes. The ideal of brotherly love comes to mean little more than the maintaining of „diplomatic relations" with one's neighbour, while remaining indifferent to his spiritual destiny.

This situation is, in our opinion, by no means a sign of irresponsibility – this is only secondary – but is rather the expression of a materialism that is deeply rooted in the unconscious, inclining one to experience inter-personal relations in the present as absolutely real, while the working of the counter-forces which stand behind every lie is ignored or is at best passed off as an abstract theory, about which one can hold clever discussions, but which, as soon as one returns to the reality of life, will be forgotten. „An incorrect result of research in the spiritual world is a living being. It is there; it must be resisted, it must first be eradicated" (22.10.1915, GA 254).

Variegated hosts of beings of this kind threaten to engulf the Anthroposophical movement if the contents of books and lectures of the Anthroposophists active today continue to be received in so uncritical a way. Spiritual science risks being overrun by phantasms, personal opinions, subjective experiences and other undigested contents of the conscious and unconscious mind of its present-day „adepts", and thereby losing its scientific character. The 1997 „Easter Conference" in Berlin was a clear illustration of this.

Those people who harbour consciously or unconsciously the desire for an infallible spiritual teacher, those who are lacking strength in their 'I' and who do not have the courage to stand on their own feet; those who are waiting for an opportunity to place the responsibility for their own development on another's shoulders – all these create an atmosphere of devotion and blind trust which surrounds those personalities in the Anthroposophical Society who know how to achieve celebrity and step into the limelight.

The content of this book will demonstrate that these words of criticism addressed to the Anthroposophical Society are not empty and without foundation. We will concern ourselves with a single example only, but one which is weighty and revealing enough to justify what we have said above, and to prompt the members of the Anthroposophical Society to reflect seriously upon the following question: Do they wish to turn their attention to some other content? If the latter is the case, then the Society should be given a different name and the portraits hanging on their walls should be exchanged for others. But if the members wish to remain faithful to Anthroposophy and fulfil their task, then it would now be time to lay aside pseudo-moral prejudices, spiritual passivity and suggestibility, and sentimental impressionability of soul, and ask oneself the serious question: What is the meaning of „truth" from the spiritual-scientific standpoint, and how can it be attained, developed, safeguarded for ourselves and future generations, for at the present time an extremely vigorous and subversive campaign against it is taking place?

In this book we are attempting a critical exploration, minimal in length, (an extensive one would require too many years of work and fill shelves of thick volumes) of the idea-world of Prokofieff – a man whose literary creations have already made him into a kind of Anthroposophical classic, whose lectures attract numerous listeners throughout the world, and whose reputation in certain circles is such that many people see in him the „Guru" and condemn any criticism of him as sacrilege. Finally, his activity determines also to a significant degree the destiny of Anthroposophy in Russia.

We will try to understand what methods he applies in his research, what is the internal logic of his views, and how far these correspond to the facts known to us. We will, as far as is possible, avoid judgments of a personal nature, and try to compare what he presents as spiritual-scientific content with that which is known to us from the communications of Rudolf Steiner. In our study we will only make use of the power of ordinary logic, the hallmark of a healthy human faculty of judgment. We find our standpoint confirmed and corroborated in the following words of Rudolf Steiner: „The healthy human understanding, if it is not misled by erroneous natural or social ideas of today, can judge for itself whether there is truth in what someone speaks. Someone is speaking about spiritual worlds; one only has to take everything together: the way of speaking, the seriousness with which things are considered, the logic that is developed, and so on – then one will be able to judge whether what is brought as knowledge of the spiritual world is charlatanism, or whether it has a foundation. This anyone can decide" (14.12.1919, GA 194).

Our wish is that this work may serve the reader as a stimulus to inner activity, to an independent search for truth and vigilance of thought, to alertness of consciousness and to a further development and strengthening of the sense for truth; that it may also help justice to prevail – that false authorities may be thrown down from their pedestal. We cherish the hope that we may come to a real mutual understanding and productive co-operation with those, in East and in West, who seek with the help of Spiritual Science to make a healing contribution to human development.*

---

* *Translator's Note*: In the following the author I. Gordienko quotes from the original Russian text of a number of published works of Prokofieff:

I   Rudolf Steiner and the Founding of the New Mysteries
II   The Cycle of the Year as a Path of Initiation ...
III   The Twelve Holy Nights ...
IV   The Spiritual Origins of Eastern Europe ...
V   The Occult Significance of Forgiveness
VI   The Karma Research of Rudolf Steiner and the Tasks of the Anthroposophical Society
VII   The Cycle of the Year and the Seven Liberal Arts
VIII The Spiritual Tasks of Middle and Eastern Europe
IX   The Case of Tomberg

We refer to them by means of the Roman numerals. Words, phrases etc. contained in the Russian, that were omitted in the German translations [together with their page numbers in the original text], are here printed in square brackets [...]. Where there is no indication to the contrary, all that is contained in (round) brackets within the quotations is a comment by Irina Gordienko.

1. How the Myth Arose

1.1. The „Lohengrin" of the 20th Century

> *Never shall you ask me*
> *Nor trouble yourself to know*
> *What journey brought me hither*
> *Nor my true name and origin*
>
> R. Wagner, *Lohengrin*, Act 1

S. O Prokofieff made his début as an author on Anthroposophical themes in 1981, when he published his first book under the significant, indeed momentous title „Rudolf Steiner and the Founding of the New Mysteries" (Stuttgart 1982). Despite the youthful age of the author – he was 26 years at the time – it was quite clear from the very first pages: Here was someone who had come to Anthroposophy, who intended to step forward not as a pupil, but as an independent researcher and even as a teacher. It is striking with what pretention, unusual in Anthroposophical circles, he instructs the reader (in magisterial tones) on the task of the Anthroposophical Society and of each individual Anthroposophist. There are a large number of directives that we are urged to follow: what every Anthroposophist must be aware of, what the spiritual mission of the Anthroposophical Society is, what the conditions are for its realization, on what the further development of Christian culture depends, etc. etc. As Prokofieff, already in the foreword, is outlining the theme of his book in so grandiose a way, we discover that it is not based, as one might have assumed in such a case, on a study of the communications of Rudolf Steiner on the subject, but on the contents of lectures of his own whose aim was – no more and no less – „to present the essential meaning of the Christmas Conference … as the culmination (Höhepunkt) of Rudolf Steiner's life-path, and, at the same time, as the most important event to have occurred in the 20th century" (I, p. 12, 375).

It is not unnatural, when one reads such statements, to ask: When and in what way could a human being who has not yet reached the age of the Mindsoul, penetrate so profoundly the significance of this truly remarkable event and presume to „reveal" it to others, first in lectures and then in this book? Reading on, one's astonishment grows still further to hear how the author intends to describe the biography of Rudolf Steiner as an „archetypal image of the modern path of Initiation" (ibid., p. 19), and to explain „the role which the course of this life will play for mankind as a whole" (I, p. 19). Prokofieff goes on to introduce his own concept of the Biography of Rudolf Steiner – and therewith also his own „archetypal image" of the new path of Initiation?!

Looking at the main section of the book, we find that here we are required to divide the course of Rudolf Steiner's life into seven-year periods. Down to the smallest detail we find described how and when which spiritual beings inspired Rudolf Steiner, what processes took place in his „sheaths", and when he attained which degrees of Initiation. And here one cannot help asking: What lofty standpoint of observation has the author attained, enabling him to take in at a single glance the spiritual path of an individuality such as Rudolf Steiner, and with unshakeable certainty to describe the occult background at every stage?

In another part of the book Prokofieff gives an account of his own view of the Christmas Conference, through which its „innermost being" is revealed, and where he tells us, among other things, that the Foundation Stone Meditation is none other than the „[new] Michaelic Grail" (ibid., p. 385), which descended during the Christmas Conference. Here he recommends his o w n imagination of the Grail, when he declares that it – i.e. his imagination – wills to become reality in the souls of human beings! (ibid., p. 381).

In this way Prokofieff obliges not only the Anthroposophists, but human beings in general, to place their confidence in the reliability of his imagination, so that they may take part in the new Grail cult proclaimed by him.

The standpoint adopted by Prokofieff in his perception of events, he describes as „extremely occult" (ibid., p. 491). His thoughts are presented in a manner that can only be termed „dogmatic". He also excludes the possibility that any doubt might arise in the mind of the reader.

With the fervour of a prophet (we take this from the content and do not mean it judgmentally), he proclaims to the Anthroposophists the true sense of their destiny past and future, discloses here and there the as yet unrecognized meaning of some statement of Rudolf Steiner, paints the perspectives of the development of Anthroposophy in connection with the destiny of human culture as a whole.

1. How the Myth Arose

The tendencies indicated here are carried further in other works of Prokofieff. In every one of them he pretends to be in possession of the absolute, all-embracing standpoint, and tirelessly astounds the reader with ever new occult communications, though without informing us of their source or explaining how to gain access to them ourselves.

Thus, in „The Cycle of the Year as a Path of Initiation" (II), which was written shortly after „The Founding ...", he describes to us what happened to the ether-body of Rudolf Steiner after his physical death, and what is supposed to happen to this ether-body in the course of the 20th century (II, p. 259). Proceeding from this he confronts the Anthroposophists with an urgent and [most important] task (II, p. 259 [p. 266]). But how could we take on such a task, or fulfil it, if – we repeat – we do not know how he became aware of these particulars regarding the destiny of Rudolf Steiner after his death?

In Ch. 5 of the same book the reader can find a pointer to the sources of Prokofieff's insights, when he elaborates his view of the events in Palestine and the deeds of the Nathan Soul. He sums up as follows: „This is the [total picture] of these events from the [standpoint of the] Cosmos" (II, p. 188 [p. 196]). How is it possible for the Cosmos which, following Rudolf Steiner's indications, consists of a multiplicity of different spiritual beings – who, according to their position engage in conflict with one another – to arrive at a unified standpoint? – As no answer to this is to be found in Prokofieff's book, we have no alternative but to seek it ourselves. Whatever the case may be: this Cosmos has revealed itself to Prokofieff. And of course one who surveys events from so lofty a standpoint and gives communications concerning the destiny of great initiates after their death, is all the more qualified to make statements about the tasks of ordinary Anthroposophists. Such is the logic of the book.

In the book on Russia „The Spiritual Origins of Eastern Europe and the Future Mysteries of the Holy Grail" (Dornach 1989; IV) Prokofieff takes it upon himself „to explain" the meaning of Russian history „from [the highest and at the same time most spiritual standpoint, namely] from the standpoint of the all-encompassing powers of World-Karma" (ibid., p. 372 [p. 348]). What kind of beings these powers are Prokofieff does not tell us, but the reader who is prepared for the author's exposition will probably not be surprised to learn that the standpoint of these powers is known to him. The question has to be asked: How does the author know what is the „highest" and the „most spiritual"? – This would require the ability to permeate the spiritual cosmos with one's I-consciousness, the ability to assume the standpoint of the Creator Himself. Were this feasible we would have readily concurred if Prokofieff had gone on to inform us what tasks, „the higher guiding powers of Earth evolution" had to fulfil, and at what point in time (ibid., p. 383), without asking, of course, how he came to know that as well.

On what familiar terms Prokofieff stands with the exalted spiritual beings is illustrated in the following statement: „The leading spirit of esoteric Christianity made the decision, at the time when the Spirits of Form were preparing to let their forces flow into a l l human souls around the year 1250, [as an extremely rare exception] to make public a part of the secret knowledge concerning the Mysteries of the Grail" (ibid., p. 109 [p. 105]). So that is how things stand! If a man carries the responsibility for everything that he writes and publishes, then what he writes must be transparent – we can therefore do no other than accept that Prokofieff knows exactly what decision was taken by the spiritual being in question at what point in time; he knows also what activity the Spirits of Form were engaged in at that time. He also knows that someone asked this spiritual being for permission, which was granted, but as an extremely rare exception, from which we conclude that Prokofieff knows the rules normally followed by this spiritual being, and also the exceptions which it sometimes allows. It is also clear that Prokofieff knows who puts the intentions of this spirit into effect on the Earth, and in what way. On p. 103 he writes: „In the strictly-hidden (but accessible to him) circles of esoteric Christianity the decision is taken to make public some of the secrets of the Grail Mysteries in the form of an exoteric legend."

Here one might add that the reader, in connection with the Grail theme brought up by Prokofieff, can learn of further sensational discoveries made by the author. He tells us, for example, that the Russian church cupola corresponds to an astral imagination of the Grail Cup (ibid., p. 71). He refers us here to Rudolf Steiner, who explained that all processes in the astral world occur in mirrored form. Prokofieff concludes from this: In order to obtain an astral imagination of the Cup, it is enough to turn it upside-down! – Prokofieff draws his idea of the cupola as an inverted Grail Cup, from a source known to us, but which he does not mention. This is an article by Nikolai Belotsvyetov about the Russian Grail, which Prokofieff read before the book in question was written. It is also interesting to note that Belotsvyetov was a friend and ardent disciple of

1. How the Myth Arose

Valentin Tomberg, whom Prokofieff has vehemently criticized in recent years. The question arises: How did Belotsvyetov come to grasp the significance of the cupola from of the Orthodox churches? – But as he himself admits – it just seemed to him to be so! And Prokofieff's grounds are shakier still.

The comparison of the cupola with a cup is a harmless and at the same time unscientific expression of artistic liberty; more serious are a number of other assertions of Prokofieff concerning the Grail theme. Thus he writes: „... many of these elected living dead (referring to the chosen souls of the dead as guardians of the Holy Grail) ... [were] incarnated in their former life within the Eastern Slavic people" (ibid., p. 100). One such guardian Prokofieff claims to be Count Yuri Vzevolodovich, whose after-death experience he describes. Already during his lifetime, Prokofieff says, „this Count had, together with his uncle Andrei Bogolyubsky, placed his sheaths at the disposal of Grail knights so that they could work through these Russian nobles" (ibid., p. 101-103).

One gains the impression that Prokofieff is initiated not only into the destiny of individuals, but also into the Mysteries of the Grail. He tells us that „in the Grail Mysteries there are as it were three circles to be distinguished in the spiritual worlds", and gives an exact description of these groups; he also points to concrete individuals who have belonged to this or that group (p. 101), but forgets, here too, to reveal the sources of his information.

Some readers will think, perhaps, that we are falling into an ironical tone. In reality we are merely trying not to lose our sense of humour in the face of what some people allow themselves in their handling of the precious heritage of Rudolf Steiner.

Prokofieff positively asks us to see in him the returning Lohengrin (mention of whose name is clearly not accidental), and thus to believe his every word and recognize him as a spiritual leader; but the essential point is that we are never allowed to ask about his „name and origin" – i.e. the source of his occult knowledge, which is seemingly boundless.

Now a further example to add to our revelations. Here too we do not believe in a miraculous spate of coincidences or acts of Providence, but recognize Prokofieff's intention at the place where – citing a conversation of Rudolf Steiner with Count L. Polzer-Hoditz – he describes in what way Rudolf Steiner intended to set up an esoteric school founded on the Christmas Conference. And then it emerges that this institution corresponds exactly to what Prokofieff – without indicating the source – has described earlier as Grail Mysteries in the spiritual world (ibid., p. 102, 478).

In spite of this, he concludes that the esoteric school is intended as a „mirror reflection", in the Earthly realm, of the Grail Mysteries. This assertion is not new, as already in the 1st book the „Foundation Stone" was said to be the new Grail! As Prokofieff does not reckon with a good memory on the reader's part, he himself emphasizes this amazing correspondence in the occult facts brought forward by him and gives the following reference: Concerning the Christmas Foundation of 1923-24 as a contemporary revelation of the Grail Mysteries on Earth, see – „Rudolf Steiner and the Founding of the New Mysteries" Part III (ibid., p. 478).

In the book on Russia Prokofieff discloses further, hitherto unknown, occult facts, in some cases saying nothing of the sources (meaning very likely that they are his own), and in others proceeding in a similarly unscientific and improper manner; such lapses result not only in a loss of trust, but also of authority. In the course of his exposition Prokofieff occasionally quotes statements of Rudolf Steiner and gives the references in such a way that the reader is led to believe that the rest of the text also comes from this lecture. Possibly he does not want the reader to ask „forbidden questions", which could unmask his – Lohengrin's – incognito.

But on one occasion he did make a slip of the tongue. This happened at the place where the subject was again the Grail stream, which he was then connecting with the working of Skythianos, stating that the most advanced and especially well prepared pupils of Skythianos were Joseph of Arimathia and Nicodemus. He describes in detail the manner of their initiation and the tasks entrusted to them (ibid., Part 3). Here Prokofieff decides to give some clarification, and remarks in passing that „this indication ... is not a direct communication (an 'indication' is not a 'communication'!) of Rudolf Steiner, but the result of meditative work of the author over many years" (ibid., p. 439). Thus we hear that Prokofieff has been active meditatively for many years, so that we can assume that other communications too are the fruit of this work and the result of his independent research in the spiritual world – beginning with the very first lectures and books.

1. How the Myth Arose

In the Anthroposophical Society there is another person who appeared at so young an age as an independent researcher and teacher: Valentin Tomberg. At the time Marie Steiner made the following comment: „Is it conceivable that so young a man as Herr Tomberg, who turned 35 a short time ago, has the necessary maturity for an occult teacher? (We remind readers that Prokofieff held the lectures in which he intended, on the basis of his own research, to reveal the deeper significance of the Christmas Conference, in 1979 – i.e. at the age of 25!). Dr. Steiner often stressed that he himself had not come forward as an occult teacher until the age of 40, and that this corresponds to an esoteric law. The law of gradual maturing outwardly and inwardly likewise calls for this restraint. He indicated as a criterion for the level of maturity of the person who believes he has to present himself as a spiritual researcher, that he should have the patience to wait, and test and test again, and should not assume that before this time he has the capacity to judge his own faculty of knowledge" (Marie Steiner, „Letters and Documents", Dornach 1981, p. 324-325).

We have now reached the point where we have to ask the question: What is the nature of Prokofieff's faculty of knowledge, and what does he himself believe in this connection? Judging by the significance of the facts revealed by him, the breadth of his perspective, the deep conviction resonating in all he says, one could believe that we have to do with an occultist of high degree, an initiate who is fully aware of his rank, and claims the right to work accordingly. If, on the other hand, we examine the fruits – the tree is known by the fruits – i.e. his numerous works, then we are led to the conviction that the expositions, where thinking is concerned, are not worked through clearly, but are inconsistent; there is a great amount of logical absurdity, lack of clarity, and contradiction. These weaknesses of the author on the thinking level stand in striking contrast to his pretentions. As we will be showing in the following chapters of this book, there are to be found in his works contradictions not only to the statements of Rudolf Steiner, but also to historical facts and to healthy commonsense. What, in these circumstances, is the value of his many years of meditative work; on what kind of experience are his communications based; and, finally, what is the nature of his cognitive method? For if in his research he were using the same method as Rudolf Steiner, he could not arrive at results and judgments that contradict those of Rudolf Steiner. Perhaps he doubts the possibility of obtaining objective, reliable insights into the spiritual world through the Anthroposophical method, and does not use it; that this may be the case is

23

suggested by the fact that in his works he gives no sign of having a connection to this method – indeed, there is no mention of method at all; he makes known the results of his occult research as something natural and obvious which must be accepted by the Anthroposophical readership „as is fit and proper".

Our theory has been given added weight, thanks to the circumstance that someone once asked „the forbidden question".

1.2. The Question of Method: the Occult Autobiography of Prokofieff

On the occasion of the 40th Anniversary of the founding of their publishing house the staff of the Verlag Freies Geistesleben approached Mr. Prokofieff with the request for a description of the way in which the content of his first book had arisen. He responded with an autobiographical essay giving an account of his spiritual path of development. This appeared in the Jubilee Volume („Reading the Anthroposophical Book – an Almanac", Stuttgart 1987) under the title „My Path to the Book 'Rudolf Steiner and the Founding of the New Mysteries'".

In view of the fact that the ability to gain knowledge in the spiritual world can, as we have already noted, only be acquired on the path of inner development, this article is of very special interest for us. The path described in it should be considered from the standpoint of the fulfilment of the requirements demanded of the serious spiritual pupil. To these belong above all the acquiring of a balanced, healthy soul-life that remains in touch with reality, the renunciation of idle dreams, false mysticism and fantasies, the development of a logically-structured thinking that is oriented to the real world, and the overcoming of one-sided, overhasty and arbitrary judgments; and also a comprehensive, deepened self-knowledge, the climax of which is attained in the meeting with the Guardian of the Threshold. – This meeting must be borne in mind here, as we will be speaking shortly of independent occult experience.

In this article the impressions (Erlebnisse) of a very young person are described, a fact which might incline the reader to a lenient judgment. But in the case under consideration leniency would be inappropriate, as these very impressions are the way leading to that occult experience which provides the foundation for Prokofieff's entire subsequent work in Anthroposophy. This being so, we are obliged to view them in the light of all the requirements of the inner path. In addition, one should not forget that we are speaking not of youthful diary notes, but with the „Rückschau" of a 32-year-old man who has risen to considerable celebrity in Anthroposophical circles. The way in which Prokofieff evaluates the experiences of his childhood and youth, what conclusion he draws from them, gives us a telling illustration of his relation to the faculty of knowledge, not only with regard to himself, but also in general.

At the beginning of his essay Prokofieff confesses that at first he had wanted to decline the request to write it, as „it has always been my aim to exclude everything of a 'personal' nature from my work" („My Path to the Book …", p. 79). On the other hand the writing of the book was „bound up with certain spiritual-occult experiences which as such cannot be published in an essay" (ibid.).

Regarding the first statement of the author, it turns out that the entire content of the essay serves to refute this, as the most important factors leading Prokofieff on the path to the book prove to be various kinds of secret presentiments, unclear inner feelings, personal impressions and sudden surges of emotion, youthful enthusiasm and mystical communications, in short: all those elements of the subjective, which are the wholly personal content of the inner life of the idealistically-inclined young person. Nevertheless the author proceeds, on the basis of all these experiences, which everyone is familiar with from their youth, to draw far-reaching, all-embracing conclusions, particularly with regard to himself. Here we have to do with a specific personal tendency. But how is one to relate this to the assertion that everything of a „personal" nature must be excluded? In order to understand this paradox a statement of Rudolf Steiner can help us: „A person is working with others in the Anthroposophical movement … but he brings into this work personal ambitions, personal intentions, personal qualities … Most people do not know that these are personal … Most people look upon what they are doing as impersonal, because they deceive themselves as to what is personal or impersonal" (GA 261, p. 306).

With regard to those „occult experiences" of his, which as such cannot be published in an essay, there is a reply to be given, since we are dealing here with a book in which the author is imparting teachings to the reader on crucial matters connected with the development of Anthroposophy. In the course of this he makes a series of statements relating to supersensible facts, whose source, however, is not the results of Rudolf Steiner's research. If, therefore, these statements are based on individual occult experiences of Prokofieff himself, then these must be made known publicly, so that they can be the object of open discussion. Only in this way can the reader acquire a basis for judgment in the question how far these experiences are credible and meet the requirements of objectivity which are placed on supersensible experience by spiritual science. Regarding the task of the Anthroposophical Society which was founded during the Christmas Conference, Rudolf Steiner said the following: „We must be quite clear that our Society in particular will have the task of combining the greatest possible openness to the public (Öffentlichkeit) with true and genuine esotericism" (26.12.1923, 10 a.m., GA 260). Examples of such a combination of these two are found in many lectures of Rudolf Steiner himself, in which, in contrast to Prokofieff, he finds it appropriate to give his listeners not only descriptions of his occult experiences, but also to disclose the method he uses in his research into the higher worlds.

Let us now follow Prokofieff's path further, so as to learn about its characteristics more precisely, and let us try to grasp the quality of his experiences in order to find in them, perhaps, traces of genuine knowledge and self-knowledge; let us also examine his views on occult experience and ascertain how far he possesses the capacity and the inclination to work it through properly. In short: let us compare his path with the demands that are made of a spiritual pupil.

Prokofieff tells us that in his childhood he received profound impressions from Richard Wagner's music, particularly his „Parsifal". In his article he refers to this fact as a part of his path. We cannot expect him to say: „I enjoyed the musical dramas of Wagner, they interested me and left me with this or that impression." – This would have been a gesture of modesty, although many people know the depth of feeling, the variety and sublimity of the characters, the truly exalted inspiration and the stirring presentiments that can be experienced thanks to Wagner's musical creations. Indeed, many people must have these experiences, but the question remains: How does one relate to them? Should one merely acknowledge them as experiences of the human soul, or ascribe to them a significance they do not possess? Prokofieff unhesitatingly speaks of them as a „meeting (Berührung) with the stream of esoteric Christianity … there arose, after this impulse had been received (into him), the question that filled my entire being: Where is to be found today the continuation, in contemporary from, of this spiritual stream?" ("My Path ...", p. 81). Let us not forget that we are speaking here of a child between 7 and 14 years. To say something of this kind about himself would not even have occurred to Richard Wagner in his maturity, although he is not accused of false modesty either; nevertheless he really did take this impulse into himself, and in his creation drew from the source of lofty inspiration, doing so, as he himself testifies, quite consciously.

Thus Prokofieff, when he had barely completed his change of teeth, was able to receive into his soul the impulse of esoteric Christianity. Then his soul was filled with a „new, inner striving" (he says nothing about the previous, old one), which acquainted him with Eastern wisdom. In it he discovered – this, too, in early childhood – „a profound esoteric knowledge", although he continued to feel that in Christianity „still higher and more encompassing treasures of wisdom are contained than in the religious and philosophical systems of the East" (ibid., p. 81-82). Thus it becomes clear that in him the capacity awoke at a very early age to make comparisons between the treasures of universal esoteric wisdom, in respect of their scope and their content.

When Prokofieff was about 14 he came upon Rudolf Steiner's book „Knowledge of the Higher Worlds and its Attainment", and here something peculiar happened. The last two chapters aroused in him „feelings of different kinds". On the one hand „a sense of my own inner imperfection", called forth by „the description of the meeting of the spiritual pupil with the Lesser Guardian of the Threshold" (ibid., p. 83).

How often did Rudolf Steiner point out that the human being who, in one way or another, has penetrated into the spiritual world without the meeting with the Guardian of the Threshold, becomes a victim of his own illusions and of the powers of opposition who lie in wait at the boundary between the world of the senses and the supersensible world. He emphasizes that the meeting with the Guardian of the Threshold is a real, occult fact, a concrete experience in the state of supersensible perception; something of this nature cannot be experienced only in the imagination (Vorstellung). In one lecture Rudolf Steiner says: „The meeting with the Guardian of the Threshold is a tragic occurrence, a life-struggle, with respect to all laws of knowledge, and with respect to all connections of the human being with the spiritual world, with Ahriman and Lucifer. This life-catastrophe must come about, if one wishes to meet the Guardian of

the Threshold. If it impinges upon the human being merely in dreamlike imagination, then this means that one wants comfortably to steal past, in order to
have as a substitute – people are now very fond of substitutes – the dream of
the Guardian of the Threshold" (6.8.1918, GA 181).

As we have seen, in Prokofieff's case we have to do not even with a dreamlike imagination, but with a feeling that arose while the book was being read.
He experiences the meeting – if one can call it a meeting – with the Guardian
only on the level of fantasy (Einbildung). And in this case how can we discount
the possibility that all his later „occult experiences" are products of fantasy
(Einbildung)?

We should bear in mind, of course, that the event described by Prokofieff
was accompanied by a process of self-knowledge. But this process resembled a
tiny cloud passing across the radiant firmament, so insignificant that it can vanish without trace at any moment; thus no mention is made of it again. On the
contrary, in the course of this essay the picture of an ideal human being arises
before our inner eye; one could even say a being who has become ideal already
through inheritance, if one considers how his own family is characterized. Veneration and gratitude towards one's own family are in themselves natural and
praiseworthy qualities, although in the case of the author who grew up in such
privileged circumstances it is unclear what he means to express by saying that
he was born and grew up „in the very difficult spiritual conditions prevailing in
Eastern Europe", but – in spite of all this – „found the way not only to Anthroposophy in general, but to those special questions which are, in a certain sense,
the central ones" („My Path ...", p. 78-80; i.e. the Christmas Conference).
What does he really know of those difficulties of a spiritual, soul and material
nature which his compatriots had to endure at that time? In the autobiographical
essay nothing of this is mentioned at all. Nor is any word spoken indicating a
relation to the situation in the present; there is no suggestion of any life-
experience in this connection, nor even of any interest in the reality surrounding
him.

In Rudolf Steiner's book „Knowledge of Higher Worlds" it is shown how
the spiritual pupil can develop the necessary soul qualities by going through the
trials brought to him by destiny. There have been, and still are, very many people in Russia who have had, or have still today, to go through such a hard
school of life. This cup passed Prokofieff by. But in such a case the pupil must

develop the required soul qualities through conscious work on himself. „It is one of the unavoidable tasks", says Rudolf Steiner, „to be fulfilled by every spiritual pupil, that he must work painstakingly upon himself, so as not to become a fantasist, a person who can fall victim to any kind of deception, self-deception" (suggestion and auto-suggestion) (GA 13, p. 382).

Concerning the steps that are necessary for an occult development that is followed through in full consistency, and lead to the strengthening of a healthy faculty of judgment, feeling and character, Prokofieff has nothing to say. On the contrary, against the background of a lack of life-experience and of any corresponding preparation, he takes up serious esoteric exercises. This happens in the following way:

Likewise around the age of 14 Prokofieff becomes acquainted with the French edition of „Outline of Occult Science". As he does not know this language well enough he does not read the whole book, but discovers in it straight away the description of the Rose-Cross meditation. Its imaginative form makes a deep impression on him – which is quite understandable, considering that at this stage in the child's development those forces especially have a strong influence, on which the faculty of imagination rests. He starts to meditate. Those forces which are needed for the building up of his soul and bodily organization, are diverted in the direction of occult practice.

After this, he obtains „Occult Science" in Russian. Just at this age, after the freeing of the astral body from its connection to the parents, the young person attains a special capacity to relate to figures of an ideal nature (Vorbilder), and also an inclination to fantasy (c.f. 4.1.1922, GA 303): „... the picture of the entire world-evolution beheld in spirit", as described in Occult Science, makes a powerful impression on him. We take him at his word, but we would like to add that he wrote his article, not at that tender age, but after completion of his 32nd year. This does not prevent him from declaring that the most important result of reading of „Occult Science" was the e n t r y – not the acquaintance with, the knowledge or study of, but the e n t r y ! – „into a new spiritual Cosmos, which exceeded in grandeur and sublimity all that I had experienced hitherto" („My Path ...", p. 84; he does not say anything here either, about the „old spiritual Cosmos", or what he had experienced hitherto).

It was not Rudolf Steiner's intention with his „Occult Science" to present the reader with a finished „spiritual cosmos". Later he said of it that it was no more that a „score", and that the reader would have to work through the content in strenuous inner activity in order to arrive at the whole (4.5.1920, GA 334). Prokofieff was content with religious enthusiasm, and passed it by. In later life he never made up for this childhood omission. As we will see later on, „Occult Science" remained an unread book for him.

Let us now make a pause in our critical analysis and reflect upon the uncritical enthusiasts of Prokofieff's occult gift; these admirers are certainly indignant over our „heretical" book. But we would point out the following: If someone writes an autobiography and publishes it, he gives the reader the right to think about the content and thus to try to understand the person who has written it. Only legends of the Saints are approached in a different way – but they are not autobiographies!

But let us continue. After Prokofieff met the Guardian of the Threshold in his imagination, he entered – again in his imagination – the new spiritual Cosmos. In his opinion the process of knowledge is advancing very successfully, as shown by the fact that, when it has hardly begun, it leads swiftly to a resounding climax. And what knowledge? – The knowledge that the „Cosmic Christ is the central point of the spiritual Cosmos. There now grew together with the inner feeling, as it had lived in my soul [since early childhood] (sic!), that this fact is incontrovertible truth ... the sure and encompassing knowledge [of it]" („My Path ...", p. 84). Now we must ask ourselves how many of the great spiritual figures have achieved such outstanding results on the path of cognition – knowledge of the spiritual Cosmos – and that already in their earliest youth (between their 14th and 19th year), and moreover without any special effort or preparation? At this point, so it seems to us, the reader of the autobiographical essay is asked to remain bowed in silent awe.

The feeling for his own lofty calling, which he has no inclination to reflect upon, takes hold of his entire being: „... in the period between my 14th and 19th years [I was able] to get to know the basic works of Rudolf Steiner, and other spiritual-occult works by authors of Eastern, Theosophical, and mystical-ecclesiastical schools of thought. I spent these five years for the most part in spiritual solitude ... In the course of this period, supported only by my own inner forces and by my search for an answer to the life-question that confronted me ... I was to choose Anthroposophy as the task of my entire life, as my destiny in the world" (ibid., p. 86).

1. How the Myth Arose

What „inner forces" can give support to a still immature young person? But let us hear all the same what Rudolf Steiner says about the healthy development of the human being at this age: „At puberty the human being is ejected from the spirit and soul life of the world, and is thrust into the external world, which he can only perceive with his physical, his etheric body" (4.1.1922, GA 303). In Prokofieff's case we hear the opposite: At this age, according to his own words, he enters the „spiritual Cosmos". When the young person in the normal course of development is then cast out of the soul-spiritual life of the world, he compares „the world he enters ... with the world which he had had within him before", and he grows aware of the contrast between them. Therefore the „tumult" is needed, „which arises in the interplay between man and the world in the period between the 14th/15th year and the beginning of the 20's. This tumult must be there ... [must] arise of necessity. People who are perhaps over-inclined to melancholy might imagine it would be a good thing to spare the human being this tumult. But in this way one becomes his worst enemy. One should not spare the human being this tumult" (ibid.). Prokofieff was spared this tumult, this inner upheaval. There did not awaken in him a healthy relation to the outer world, or any living experience of it; hence there are no contrasting feelings, no upheaval. He remains under the spell of his subjective experiences. The new „discoveries" are no more than a „final confirmation" of his „presentiment", which has been living in his soul from early childhood; the world of his dreams flows on in wonderful harmony, and acquaintance with Anthroposophy merely arouses the indistinct feelings that have long been slumbering in his soul.

Against the background of this ever-heightened ecstasy, as the above-mentioned phase in a healthy development is bypassed, the development of an independent power of judgment which is accompanied in the young person by a decided mood of protest against authorities of all possible kinds does not take place and he does not await his coming-of-age, the author comes to the decisive conclusion regarding his higher mission in the world, a world of which, so the account of his life would lead us to suppose, he has very little idea.

„And only ... when I ... could experience", he writes, „that my life had acquired a new meaning and a new goal (and again we must ask: What, then, were previously the 'meaning' and the 'goal' in the life of this young person?), and I had thus begun consciously to serve those ideals which had hitherto lived unconsciously (untergründig) in my soul, and which, thanks to spiritual science, had now become fully conscious reality for me ..." („My Path ...", p. 86).

31

What kind of conscious service can this be, in someone who has not become conscious of himself, in whom (corresponding to his age) the Sentient soul is not yet fully developed?

Here one or another reader might object: Why all this schematic thinking? In the lives of great individualities things can surely follow a quite different course. We are not discussing here how high entelechies, incarnating in a physical body, can bypass the general laws of development. We merely recall that Prokofieff himself in his book brought the life of Rudolf Steiner into a scheme in exactly the same way, placing all the events in his life and his spiritual development into the corresponding 7-year phases, and making no „special allowances" for Rudolf Steiner as an outstanding personality. But nobody has raised any objection against this. If anyone is of the opinion that Prokofieff stands on a higher level than Rudolf Steiner, then he can challenge our right to proceed with him in the same way.

After this Prokofieff gets to know the lecture-cycles of Rudolf Steiner. The following words tell us what significance this had for him: „Through this Cycle a quite new world opened up for me again" (ibid., pa. 87). But how can, yet again, a quite new world open up, and in what way can this „quite new world" be opened up for a man who is already in possession of an „incontrovertible truth" and an encompassing knowledge of the spiritual Cosmos? To this question there is only one answer: the number of worlds that can be experienced subjectively, in the fantasy, is inexhaustible. Here one can even discover a new world for oneself every day. And if we are not right in this, then we can only state the following: Prokofieff does not himself realize what he is writing down, what words he is using etc.

In his thinking Prokofieff follows his soul-experiences, unremittingly and without contradiction – but he has no knowledge of his own motives. On the basis of the enthusiasm and ecstasy he experiences while reading the books and lectures of Rudolf Steiner, he builds up in his fantasy ever new worlds, within which he experiences himself in a special way as a chosen vessel. And for him this is the most important thing. This fact comes to expression most clearly in the following passage: An Anthroposophical friend of Prokofieff recommends to him the three well-known Arnheim lectures from the 6th Karma volume, „remarking with a somewhat mysterious expression that there is something very important in it concerning the Karma of the Anthroposophists, i.e. our own

1. How the Myth Arose

Karma". At this Prokofieff is overcome by an unusual state of agitation, he is gripped – as so often before – „by the abundance of new feelings", and even finds himself „almost speechless" … But he makes no attempt whatever to restore his soul-balance – on the contrary, he justifies and applauds his condition, which he terms „spiritual enthusiasm", the source of which he sees arising „from a memory, hidden in the innermost depths of soul, of the events experienced there" (ibid., p. 89). What is the nature of these events, and what does he „preserve" in the depths of his soul? – After reading the lectures he sees himself as one of those who, in the 15th century, gathered around Michael in his supersensible school, and in spirit he sees how the 1st Hierarchy carries over the cosmic intelligence from the lap of the 2nd Hierarchy into the heads of human beings. With what justification does he come so quickly and with such certainty to this significant conclusion regarding himself? – Here again, the same as before: solely on the basis of the feelings which came to him as he read the lectures.

Here we encounter an amazing quality of this author. He takes into himself the description of the events of world significance, which transcend by far the average human powers of comprehension. But from the point of view of knowledge he shows no interest in it, no questions arise in him, no desire to fathom what happened there and in what way; nor has his soul any wish to bring what he has experienced into connection with what he already knows from Anthroposophy. He simply accepts everything as „his own", and goes on to concentrate entirely on his own person. However, „so long as the human being still has the tendency" – Rudolf Steiner writes in „Theosophy" – „to overvalue himself at the expense of the world around him, he places obstacles on his path to higher knowledge. Whoever surrenders himself to the pleasure or the pain arising for him in connection with every thing or event in the world, is caught up in such an overvaluing of himself. For his pleasure and his pain tell him nothing about the things, but only tell him something about himself" (GA 9, p. 178-179).

Hardly was the sleepless night over, in which Prokofieff had read these lectures, than he came promptly to the conclusion: „Now I knew the spiritual being whom I had always served (when?) and to whom I wished to surrender my entire being" („My Path …", p. 90; he mentions the Archangel Michael). But why „I knew"? In what way was this knowledge acquired? – Here it becomes clear that Prokofieff means by „knowledge" – arbitrary conclusions (also, when such a case arises, in relation to himself), drawn on the basis of indeterminate, but turbulent stirrings in his soul sphere. „For me" – he continues – „this experience represented a kind of inner response to the necessity of which Rudolf Steiner spoke at the beginning of the Arnheim lecture – 'to present oneself in life as a true representative of the Anthroposophical movement', 'to represent Anthroposophy in the world through one's own personality'." (ibid.).

What an opinion of oneself! – Only feelings of uneasiness are aroused in the reader, who begins to experience gnawing shame on the writer's behalf.

After Prokofieff had over-(ful)filled himself with such a feeling of his own importance, there followed another „bold" thought, namely that not even Rudolf Steiner is great enough to make demands of him, Prokofieff. – How else is one to explain the fact that he reduces Rudolf Steiner to the level – forgive me – of a „microphone", for he declares categorically: „I experienced with absolute certainty that this demand [to be a representative of Anthroposophy] does not actually come from Rudolf Steiner, but t h r o u g h Rudolf Steiner f r o m M i c h a e l h i m s e l f, and that in this moment it was directed to me personally" (ibid.; emphasis S.O.P.). What an opinion of himself!

And now, after (in this inspired state) he has heard from spiritual heights the personal call, he feels the irresistible wish to respond as quickly as possible, and so he decides to give expressions to his „inextinguishable" loyalty (Treue) in the form of a vow. How such a vow might look concretely, of this he says nothing. But this does not deter him from drawing a parallel between himself and Rudolf Steiner, and so he writes: „Such occasions in life are moments when an inner vow or 'promise' is made. And we are amazed to hear Rudolf Steiner also speak in this Arnheim lecture of his promise to the spiritual world and the powers guiding him, and also of the 'inextinguishable' loyalty (Treue) towards the obligation he has taken on." (Here it is indicated, as though in passing, that Rudolf Steiner was acting not independently, out of individual freedom, but that he was simply being led by certain „powers". But if this was so, why did he have, in addition, to make a promise to them?) – „At that time I could not yet express in words (meaning: he didn't understand) what Rudolf Steiner meant by this 'promise', but I felt dimly (yet another vague feeling) that my 'vow' was in a mysterious way bound up with h i s ..." (ibid.; emphasis S.O.P.). Thus in a deeply mysterious atmosphere and with vague romantic feelings Prokofieff, yielding to the impulses of his subconscious being, makes a vow whose significance he himself does not understand.

Prokofieff represents this experience „in the night" as being his first meeting with the „essential being" (Wesenskern) of the Christmas Conference. (No wonder this „essential being" is shown in his first book to be an act of initiation performed on the Anthroposophists who were „sleeping" at the time – but more of this later.) And how does he arrive at such a conception? Well, through drawing analogies to himself. – „After the Christmas Conference", he reflects, „everything becomes different in the Anthroposophical movement and the Anthroposophical Society. 'Behold, I make all things new' (Rev. 21; 5) – this theme sounded from the lecture with especial force, and found a powerful echo in my soul. From now onwards, so I felt, everything in my life had to become new, for I had 'made the vow', the first conscious vow in my life" (ibid., p. 91). But what strange things he is saying here! – Firstly, if in the Anthroposophical movement and Society everything becomes different, this means that even Anthroposophy is different after the Christmas Conference; and even the spiritual beings who have guided the Anthroposophical movement hitherto, are replaced by others; and is Rudolf Steiner perhaps no longer himself? ... Or is Prokofieff speaking here of a complicated spiritual metamorphoses whose essential character we are supposed to recognize? If so, we do not need to don the cloak of „unknowability" (behind which Prokofieff takes refuge on his path of knowledge) in order to set a clear boundary between oneself and the intellectual amateurs. Is it possible to express oneself so carelessly in such fundamental questions?

Secondly, Prokofieff tells us earlier that he had already, about one year before the events described here, chosen „Anthroposophy as the task of (his) whole life, as (his) destiny in this world" (ibid., p. 86). How are we to understand his statement to the effect that from then on everything in his life would have to be transformed? If we adopt Prokofieff's standpoint, then the second point arises out of the first. – If, after the Christmas Conference, a completely new and different Anthroposophy arises, which Prokofieff now discovers for himself, then this means that a new vow must be made and everything in his life must be changed! How far this statement is not accidental, is reflected in his further activity. While he is ostensibly serving the impulse of the Christmas Conference, he goes on to develop an Anthroposophy which proves in reality to be something quite different.

A discussion of all these passages in the Prokofieff „Autobiography" from the standpoint of the path of occult schooling is a tremendously difficult undertaking, as there is no such path (as the one described by Prokofieff – Trans.); however, this does not hinder Prokofieff from portraying himself as an esoteric pupil of Rudolf Steiner. And this happens in the following way: After he has made a study of the events of the Christmas Conference he reads a book describing the difficulties that arose in the Anthroposophical Society after Rudolf Steiner's death – and this makes him ill. The reasons for a physical illness can be many and varied, including quite prosaic ones. But he selects the one that allows him to surround the situation with the maximum degree of Romanticism: he connects this illness with the reading of the book in question, giving as a reason that the two events came together in time. It may well be that in the case of an impressionable soul such as Prokofieff (as was seen in the preceding descriptions), something of this kind is possible. But one must have a quite special relation to oneself, and build one's own judgments entirely upon this, to draw such overhasty and far-reaching conclusions from an indisposition lasting only a few days. He describes it thus: „The book made such an impression on me, that for several days I was physically ill. This [difficult] experience conveyed to me, if only in a faint inkling, as I explained, a very real picture nevertheless of what it meant for Rudolf Steiner in 1923 to take on the Karma of the Society. Moreover, I had come to know through my own experience what it means to be a pupil of Rudolf Steiner, in this sphere also. I understood, now that I had experienced this (what, then?) right down into my physical body, that it is not possible to look for an answer to such questions through an external search for those 'guilty' or 'not guilty' with regard to events in the past. The [true] reality of what had happened lay far deeper, and one had to s u f f e r it …" (ibid., 98-99; emphasis S.O.P.).

After a few days of illness Prokofieff believes, without seeking any other reason for it, that he belongs to the community of those who have to bear the Karma of the Anthroposophical Society, and to „suffer" the true reality. He thereby side-stepped the necessity to come to a clear knowledge of it. Is it sufficient, in order to grasp the „true reality" of the problems of the Anthroposophical Society, to read a book on the subject, to „listen in" to one's impressions, and give extra attention to one's own state of bodily health? Prokofieff goes still further, for he believes that this is enough to qualify him as an esoteric pupil. It is possible that all previously valid conceptions of an esoteric pupilship are thereby turned on their heads. We are forced to admit that here we have really to do with something completely new!

And yet we ask ourselves: How does Prokofieff come to such a conclusion about himself? – Well, on the basis, as usual, of subjective feelings: „However, something quite new opened up for me as a result of this painful experience, for immediately afterwards I had the f e e l i n g that the spirit-form of the Teacher had come still closer to me than before, and that o n l y n o w c o u l d I r e - g a r d m y s e l f i n t h e f u l l e s t s e n s e a s h i s e s o t e r i c p u p i l" (ibid., p. 99; emphasis I.G.). Quite clearly he sees himself, in the fullest sense, as one of the esoteric pupils of Rudolf Steiner.

Therefore we would turn to the words of Rudolf Steiner regarding the conditions for esoteric pupilship. „The following rules should be observed in such a way" – he writes in his „Instructions for an Esoteric Schooling" – „that every esoteric pupil so directs his life, that he continually observes himself and checks whether in his inner being he is following the expected requirements. All esoteric schooling, especially when it ascends into the higher regions, can only lead to harm and to the confusion of the pupil if such rules are not observed … Many a pupil deceives himself in this respect. He says: I wish to engage in the purest striving. – But if he were to examine himself more closely he would notice that a great deal of egoism, of subtle self-centred feeling is lurking in the background; it is particularly such feelings that very often put on the mask of selfless striving and mislead the pupil. One cannot too often seriously examine oneself through inner self-observation, to ascertain whether one has not, after all, feelings of this kind hidden in the inner regions of one's soul. One will free oneself of such feelings more and more, through a determined adherence to the rules to be discussed here. These rules are, Firstly: n o u n c o n - t r o l l e d t h o u g h t s h a l l b e a l l o w e d t o e n t e r m y c o n - s c i o u s n e s s" (GA 245, p. 22).

We ask ourselves whether these words of Rudolf Steiner are not a diagnosis of the „Path" of Sergei Prokofieff.

The conceptions (Vorstellungen) formed by Prokofieff on the basis of Rudolf Steiner's books and lectures, he does not question. He might decide to examine them and, for example, compare the new ones with those formed previously; but there is no question of this; rather the contrary: he enthusiastically discovers „new worlds" every time; and the fact that they are always „new" does not disturb him. (Yet another „world of completely new spirituality" – i.e. not that which had revealed itself to him through the books and lectures of Rudolf Steiner – he discovered when he got to know the German text of the Foundation Stone Meditation.) He does not „think through" self-critically the conceptions (Vorstellungen) he has once formed, but after he has, so to speak, appropriated them he straight away turns his attention to the sentiments and feelings they have called up in him. But even the thoughts (Vorstellungen) that arise from the unconscious, and which he accepts without criticism as something natural and obvious, he follows attentively. This tendency, noticeable already in his youth, to follow all the feelings and thoughts (Vorstellungen) that arise in his soul, was allowed to develop because it remained unconscious and bore its fruits in his subsequent work. As we can see in his books, he develops in a narrow and one-sided way the conceptions that have formed in his soul in connection with this or that spiritual-scientific theme, and does not try to ascertain their correctness, either with reference to the facts of external reality, or to the communications of Rudolf Steiner.

Rudolf Steiner cites a further rule: „The necessity must stand before my soul in a living way, constantly to expand the sum of my conceptions (Vorstellungen)" (ibid., p. 24).

Prokofieff's striving for knowledge is confined solely to Anthroposophy. The rare facts that he brings into his books from outer culture and history, do not rise above the level of school textbooks. In Anthroposophy he is only interested in what fits in with his conceptions (Vorstellungen). In this way a science unfolds that is based on the method of Baron von Münchhausen. Prokofieff writes: „Initially with no support from without,* I had the task to find, proceeding only from my inner experiences in connection with the Foundation Stone Meditation and without any outside influence, my own personal relation to the Christmas Conference as the most important spiritual event on the physical plane in the 20th century" (i.e. he even determined in advance what kind of personal relation this must be). And only „after this relationship had been established out of my own cognitive forces (Erkenntniskräfte), and had furthermore been transformed into unshakeable inner certainty (on what basis, one may ask?), did my further searching lead me, in late 1978, early 1979, to the discov-

---

* Here we would inform the reader of a fact of Prokofieff's biography which is not of an intimate nature: his maternal grandfather was an Anthroposophist.

ery, one after the other, of three books about the Christmas Conference" („My Path ...", p. 96).

Yet in these books he only allows those conceptions access to his consciousness, which are in accord with his feelings; all others are of no interest. – The reading of a lecture (the author's name is not mentioned) in which another view of the Christmas Conference is presented, does not give him cause for reflection. But the lecture, he writes, „being based only on speculative and external evidence, could have no influence on what, for me at that time, was already a fact of my own personal experience" (ibid., Footnote p. 96-97).

Prokofieff appeals to his „own personal experience". But experience is not knowledge. Experience – including soul-experiences – is only what is immediately „given". The outer appearance of reality, given to us in experience, is not its true image, as this can only arise on condition that thinking is activated, which brings incomplete experience to completion through the disclosing of its true nature. These are the most elementary truths of Goetheanism.

But Prokofieff does no strive for knowledge, he does not attain cognition; he only takes in experience. The problems of spiritual-scientific cognition, its method, its reliability, its true nature – these things do not exist for Prokofieff. Surprisingly enough, in his first book he mentions the „Philosophy of Freedom". This would indicate that on the „Path to the Book" he at least read it. But after he has portrayed his states of soul-intoxication and enumerated all the texts of Rudolf Steiner that have called forth such states in him, there is no further word mentioned in his autobiographical essay about the „Philosophy of Freedom". One can only suppose that it made no „impression" upon him, left behind no traces in his soul, and did not prompt him to reflection – in short, that it played no part in his spiritual development.

From Prokofieff's reluctance to interest himself in that which flows out of the life in sense-free thinking, there arises the neglect of a further rule, which says: „I am obliged to overcome my aversion to what is known as 'abstract thought'."

With this rule Rudolf Steiner points to the necessity to develop the faculty of sense-free thinking. As can be seen from his autobiographical essay and his book Prokofieff has made no effort to develop this kind of thinking, or thinking at all. Nor has he undergone any higher training to speak of, which could have

fostered the development of thinking; from early childhood he became an Anthroposophist and showed no interest in anything else. But in Anthroposophy
itself he neglects the opportunity for a thorough schooling in thought, which a
study of the works of Rudolf Steiner on the theory of knowledge would have
meant for him. He has no interest in it. In the last resort thinking could also be
trained through a study of other books and lectures of Rudolf Steiner. But these
too Prokofieff does not study, but experiences them on a soul level.

The situation is not different where the theme of the Christmas Conference
is concerned. He believes it is enough to read three books – even if one has
only a fragmentary knowledge of Anthroposophy – in order to understand the
central esoteric truth of the Christmas Foundation and explain it to other people. Without making the effort to acquire further knowledge he rests content
with the first emotional impressions received while reading, and again finds in
it a call personally directed to him:

„Out of this pain (resulting from the indisposition), of which I still felt an
after-trace within me, an all the greater (greater than what?) strength had to
arise for the struggle to realize the impulse of the Christmas Conference, as the
most important spiritual impulse of our time … And this pain must lead us ' t o
take up our task with all the greater strength of will ' –
these words of Marie Steiner (from the Foreword to the proceedings of the
Christmas Conference – I.G.) became a kind of leitmotiv for me in my life …"
(„My Path …", p. 99; emphasis S.O.P.).

Without satisfying a single requirement made of his esoteric pupils by Rudolf Steiner, Prokofieff receives himself into the ranks of the esoteric pupils
and appoints himself as a warrior in the cause of the realization of the Christmas Conference impulses, but in reality for that of his extremely personal, quite
specific, more theological than spiritual-scientific interpretation of it, which he
presented in his 1st book.

In the following text Prokofieff feels that he is already raised above the ordinary human faculty of judgment, and pretends to be receiving communications regarding the Christmas Conference directly from the spiritual world:
„Such an experience of the Christmas Conference" – he writes – „arising out of
its spiritual, one can say esoteric, being, cannot be communicated in an external
way with words, or on paper, to those people who have not had this experience;
still less (can it be communicated) to those who, as a result of differing human

40

opinions, placed insuperable obstacles in their own path with respect to that which Marie Steiner wanted in reality to say to the Members of the Anthroposophical Society when she decided, not long before her death, to publish all the material relating to the Christmas Conference. To let speak, not the differing human opinions, but the Christmas Conference itself – this would mean to let it speak not merely out of the shorthand reports and minutes of the meetings, but, with the help of these, to let it speak as a 'voice from spirit-land' ... that is addressed to all Anthroposophists ..., and then to receive these voices in complete inner freedom from prejudice and in deep reverence, standing truly in this moment only before the spiritual world and the spiritual powers who lead the Anthroposophical movement" (ibid., p. 100; how else then?).

This could be true if it were coming from the mouth of someone who had really fulfilled the demands made of the pupil on the Anthroposophical path of development, who had really experienced the meeting with the Guardian of the Threshold, and had been granted leave by him to enter the spiritual world, in order to rise at least to the level of inspirative consciousness. From Prokofieff's lips, however, all this rhetoric sounds at best like empty phrases. In our circles people often speak in this way, but without at the same time laying claim to the role of esoteric teacher or initiate.

According to his own account Prokofieff did cross the Threshold, but we allow ourselves, in the light of what has been said, not to believe him. But our disbelief is of little consequence to him! He declares that he would have had himself to give a description of Rudolf Steiner's life from the standpoint of the Christmas Conference, „this means in a certain sense (but in what sense, precisely?) from the standpoint beyond the Threshold ..." (ibid., p. 103). Through characterizing the Christmas Conference as an event beyond the Threshold and representing the experience of it as something that cannot be expressed outwardly in words, Prokofieff claims for himself the prerogative of explaining its „essential being"; and this he actually proceeded to do, and in this was aided by the thoughtlessness, passivity and credulity of the Anthroposophists. But to move on to the question: In what way did Prokofieff cross the Threshold to the spiritual world? In this connection we recall the warning of Rudolf Steiner in „Occult Science", where he says: „In the course of a schooling that neglects the development of sureness and firmness of the judgement, and the life of feeling and character, it can occur that the higher world approaches the pupil before he has the necessary inner capacities ... But were the meeting [with the Guardian

41

of the Threshold] to be avoided entirely, and the human being to be led into the supersensible world, then he would be just as little able to come to a knowledge of this world in its true form. For he would be quite incapable of distinguishing between what he 'sees into' the things and what they really are. This distinction is only possible if one perceives one's own being as an image in its own right and thereby frees the surroundings from all that emanates from one's inner being. If the human being, without the meeting with the Guardian of the Threshold, were to enter the spiritual and soul world, he could fall from one deception into another ... But as soon as one enters the imaginative world the pictures in it are altered through the influence of such wishes and interest, and one has before one as a seeming reality, something that one has oneself formed, or helped to form" (GA 13, p. 380-382). Ought we not, from this point of view, to look at the concluding passage of this autobiographical essay, in which Prokofieff speaks of his occult experience, arrived at on a path different from that described by Rudolf Steiner? – „The moment" – Prokofieff writes – „in which, while I was working on my first book, the true nature of the dodecahedral stone of Love revealed itself to me in r e a l s p i r i t u a l e x p e r i e n c e as an imagination of the modern Michaelic Grail, is one of the greatest moments of my life ... Whoever has once seen it [the Grail] in the imaginative form of the Foundation Stone, ceases to have any intellectual doubt with regard to the esoteric significance of the Christmas Conference for our time ..." („My Path ...", p. 104; emphasis I.G.).

Thus Anthroposophy helped Prokofieff to clothe his childhood dreams in imaginative form; it was in this way that he forged himself a path from the enthusiastic experience of the musical dramas of R. Wagner to the experiencing of himself as a Grail Knight of the present day – as the new Lohengrin who brought the message from distant Montsalvat to the Kingdom of Brabant. There lies the origin of his wonderful, romantic „Lebenstraum", which bears no relation to today's reality, and of which he says at the end of his autobiographical essay: „The founding on Earth of a modern Michael community whose mission it is in our time to become a new brotherhood of the Knights and Guardians of the Holy Grail – this seemed to me to be the principal task of the General Anthroposophical Society on the esoteric plane" (ibid., p. 104-105). But here is a case, not of understanding, but of a wishful dream which is in need of clarification. For if one wishes to speak in the present day of the tasks of the Anthroposophical Society, and that in connection with the Grail Mysteries, then it is necessary to fulfil a number of extremely difficult conditions: to bring the will into the thinking, to develop the Consciousness-soul, to understand thoroughly the time in which one is living, and to have mastered moral technique. Only when all this has been accomplished, and not before, can the human being come to objective imaginations, which presuppose the development of the lotus flowers, a heightened control of consciousness, and much more. But even the objective imaginations are, according to Rudolf Steiner, no guarantee of an objective supersensible knowledge. Of the qualities enumerated here, which are absolute requirements on the path of esoteric schooling, Prokofieff possesses, as is clear from his autobiographical essay, not a single one. Rudolf Steiner had to work consciously for their attainment.

Prokofieff's fame rest upon a myth which was able to arise out of the longing of many Anthroposophist for radiant representatives of the „self-revealing" spirit, and which paralyzes the faculty of discrimination. The triumphal entry of Prokofieff into the Land of the Anthroposophists recalls the story of the Trojan Horse. The „innards" of the „horse" disgorged themselves in the form of countless lectures, brochures and thick volumes (produced by the metre), as though from a horn of plenty, into the heads of the Anthroposophists, in their virginal innocence in matters of spiritual knowledge (if they were not virginal the things we have described could not have come about).

In the chapters to follow we will examine what some of these „gifts of the Danaans" really mean.

2. Prokofieff's Concept of Evolution

The science of initiation, which forms the central core of all the Mysteries, is elaborated in strict correspondence to the laws of development of the human being. The character assumed by the Mysteries in the one or the other epoch is determined by the level of development attained by the human being, his consciousness, and also by the future tasks of evolution. Thus any account of the Mysteries and of initiation must presuppose a deepened understanding of the human being and of the evolutionary laws. Thus it comes as a great surprise to us to find that when Prokofieff in all his books takes up the theme of initiation and the new founding of the Mysteries he ignores the theme of evolution (with the exception possibly of the Sixth epoch, propagated by him with „endless re-currence"). But we would not be devoting an entire chapter to this fact if there were not a special reason for it. In Prokofieff's books there are, scattered over many pages, a great number of individual statements which, seen as a whole, indicate a kind of concept of evolution, which is fundamentally different from the Anthroposophical one, although outwardly there is a certain resemblance between them. Prokofieff's view of evolution is nowhere formulated openly and clearly, and is thus not easily recognized, but its effect is all the more damaging, as the reader takes it up only by degrees and thus almost unnoticed; it appears as a fragment, occurring singly and often in a secondary context and, without being perceived, calls forth a confused state of mind. The main feature of this concept is the exclusion of the principle of the individual 'I' from the general picture of human evolution, in favour of a higher principle, that of the Spirit-Self. We will try in this chapter to reconstruct this fictitious evolutionary theory and bring it into the light of day; as to Prokofieff's conception of the new Mysteries, which is based on this theory, we will undertake a more exact analysis of it towards the end of the book.

2.1. The New „Task" (Mission) of the Earth

Prokofieff's mistaken view of the evolution of man was formulated already in his first book and appears in concentrated form in a paragraph in Chapter 4; because of the importance of this passage we will quote it in its entirety:

„[Thus humanity truly stood, in the epoch immediately preceding the 'turn-ing-point of time', at the beginning of the path that would have led it inexorably into the realm of death, with the result that it would not have been possible to reach through to the higher 'I', the complete development of which in the individual man is the mission (the principal task) of the Earth]. In other words, humanity as a whole stood before the real danger that the meaning of Earth development might be lost. Only one thing could rescue it: the introduction of the Mysteries, through which the mystery of the transformation of the lower, mortal 'I' into the higher, immortal 'I', i.e. into the Spirit-Self, is revealed" (I, p. 152 [p. 171]; emphasis I.G.).

Very deftly and inconspicuously Prokofieff carries out this deception. His statement seems barely noticeable in the chapter devoted to the Goetheanum, where the reader's attention is directed to quite other matters. – In the reading of Prokofieff one must exercise an unrelenting wakefulness in order not to be caught up in a tissue of false conceptions that are foreign to Anthroposophy. Thus he says, for example, instead of „the development of the individual 'I' in the human being": „the development of the higher 'I' in the individual human being". One is tempted to think that one has to do with a mere change in the word-order. But what it really is one can only discover through closer examination. Prokofieff's approach is to tell one, not straight away, but only several lines later, and then only by the way, that by „higher 'I'" he means the Spirit-Self. And to this he holds unwaveringly in this and all his subsequent books. We have to conclude from this that the principal task of the Earth aeon is the complete development of the Spirit-Self in the human being; and not merely the development, but the transformation, by which is meant the process of transubstantiation.

It is amazing that Prokofieff does not realize the obvious consequence of his thesis, namely, that the Earth in an occult sense is void of human beings; „man" on this planet is that being who is developing here his individual 'I'. Thus, for example, the Angels of today were the „human beings" of the Moon aeon, where they developed their 'I' and became individual beings; and from their standpoint the main task of the Earth aeon is indeed the „complete development" of the higher member, the Spirit-Self, „in the individual Angel being". In Prokofieff, however, it would appear that on the Earth both human beings and Angels are evolving the Spirit-Self! – As a result the actual „human" species is lacking on the Earth.

The incompatibility of this thesis of Prokofieff with the spiritual-scientific concept of development requires no lengthy demonstration. One only needs to be able to count up to five, in order to grasp the following basic principle of evolution. Putting it simply, one could say: In each aeon of the sevenfold planetary sequence – from Saturn to Vulcan – a new member is added to those that have been attained on the previous planetary stages. In the unfolding of this new member and its working together with those already present, consists the evolutionary task of the aeon in question. The Earth aeon continues the development of Saturn, Sun and Moon as the fourth member in this series. Accordingly, the fourth member or principle is incorporated into the human being on the Earth, through which for the first time he is given the possibility to unfold his individual 'I'-consciousness and realize in himself the free spirit. This fourth principle, which was originally bestowed, as group-'I', upon the whole of humanity by the Spirits of Form, came into interaction with the three bodily sheaths of man developed in the previous aeons, and works now at the unfolding of the threefold soul. It attains final individualization in its highest soul-member, the Consciousness-soul. The development of the threefold soul, and the 'I'-consciousness which unfolds on the foundation it provides, together constitute the principal task of the Earth (from the standpoint of man). But what about the fifth principle, the Spirit-Self? This will only become the possession of the individual human being in the following aeon, that of Jupiter. The task of the human being in that aeon – and not at all on the Earth – will be the complete development of the Spirit-Self.

Rudolf Steiner stressed that one should distinguish this great evolutionary stream of the planetary incarnations from the more intimate one, which takes its course in the period of the post-Atlantean Earth development and is connected with the finer elaboration of the different members of human nature. – Prokofieff is unable to grasp this distinction. In the course of the post-Atlantean period the human being, out of his own 'I'-forces, carries his development forward as far as the consciousness-soul. According to Rudolf Steiner this development would not be complete unless in the 6th post-Atlantean epoch a higher principle, the Spirit-Self, were to enter the human being. Earthly man, however, cannot develop this alone; he needs the help of higher beings. Rudolf Steiner expresses it thus: „Up to the end of Earth-evolution the human being should be developing his 'I'. He would have the opportunity to accomplish this within the realm of Sentient, Rational and Consciousness soul. But the actual Spirit-Self is only to become the possession of man on the later Jupiter; only then will it really belong to the human being. On Jupiter the human being will stand in relation to the Spirit-Self, in approximately the same way as he stands on Earth towards the 'I' ... We say of our 'I': that is what we are ourselves ... When in the next, the 6th post-Atlantean epoch, the Spirit-Self will come to expression, we will not be able to address this Spirit-Self as our Self, but we will say: Yes, our 'I' has developed itself to a certain stage, so that, as though from higher Worlds, our Spirit-Self can shine down as a kind of angel-being, which we are not ourselves ... And only on Jupiter will it so appear, that it is our own being, like our 'I'" (9.1.1912, GA 130).

Let us leave this problem for the moment and return to the statement of Prokofieff we quoted above. Is it really the case that in the period preceding the „turning-point of time" the event happened that he describes? It turns out that this paragraph in his book is nothing more than the re-wording of a statement of Rudolf Steiner, but with a shift of meaning. To enable the reader to convince himself that this is so, we quote Rudolf Steiner in full: „... at the time when the events of Palestine were taking place, and the human race moving over the Earth had arrived at the place where this decay of the physical body had reached its climax, and where for this reason there was a danger for the entire development of mankind that the 'I'-consciousness, the central achievement of Earth-development, might be lost. If nothing further had been added to what was there up to the events of Golgotha, the process would have continued – more and more the destructive element would have entered the physical being of man, and the human beings born after the event of Golgotha would have had to live with an ever more dimmed feeling of their 'I'. That which depends on the perfection of the mirroring by a physical body would have grown ever more dull" (11.1.1911, GA 131).

The reader can now compare the two texts and reflect upon the validity of such „interpretations" of statements of Rudolf Steiner. He speaks here of the extinction of individual 'I'-consciousness and not of the „impossibility of reaching through to the Spirit-Self". What Spirit-Self could this be, and that for humanity, at a time when it had not even developed the Mind-soul, and the way to the Spirit-Self will only be opened up for it in the 6th cultural epoch? Why does Prokofieff not speak also of the impossibility of reaching through to Life-Spirit and Spirit-Man, as this would not have been significantly further removed from reality?

He also maintains that it had been possible to rectify the situation through the revelation of the Mystery of transformation (Transsubstantiation) of the lower 'I' into the Spirit-Self. If, as he claims in his autobiographical essay, he has read „Occult Science", then he should be aware that the Spirit-Self is the astral body that has been taken possession of and transformed by the 'I' (GA 13, Chapter 2), i.e. an astral body that has been transformed through 'I'-activity, and not an 'I' that has undergone T r a n s s u b s t a n t i a t i o n. Or could Prokofieff mean by the lower 'I' the astral body? What right has he to call it an 'I', albeit a lower one? From this it would follow that human beings already in the Moon aeon possessed an 'I'!

Why in this case could one not equally well call 'I' etheric or even physical body? And where is, then, the individual 'I', the fourth principle of man? – Prokofieff is silent on this question. The lack of a concept of the individual 'I' does not disturb him in all his constructions; for him the dichotomy of l o w e r and h i g h e r 'I' is quite adequate, whereby the h i g h e r 'I' always stands for the Spirit-Self, and the lower for heaven-knows-what (this problem will be dealt with in more detail in 2.2.). The 'I' as such is nowhere to be found!

But what really happened through the Mystery of Golgotha? Rudolf Steiner's explanation sounds quite different from that of Prokofieff. Rudolf Steiner says that the germ of the 'I' was laid into the human being already in the Lemurian period, but that the possibility of taking hold of the 'I' consciously only arose towards the end of the Atlantean period and gradually developed from then on. – „In order that we can acquire the 'I'-consciousness on Earth, our physical body with the brain-organization has to function as a mirroring apparatus" (11.10.1911, GA 131). The Luciferic working had a certain destructive influence upon the phantom (the spiritual form-body) of the human physical body. And this phantom was rescued by the Christ. After the Mystery of Golgotha „the spiritual bodies, the phantoms of all human beings, have their source in that which arose from the tomb ... And it is possible to establish that relation to the Christ through which the earthly human being infuses into this otherwise disintegrating physical body this phantom which arose out of the tomb of Golgotha ... Through the process of infusing into himself this inde-structible body he will come, over the course of time, to make his 'I'-consciousness ever brighter and brighter ..." Thus the Mystery of Golgotha is the „salvation of the human 'I'" (ibid.). We have therefore to do with the 'I' and 'I'-consciousness, not with the Spirit-Self.

2. Prokofieff's Concept of Evolution

But as Prokofieff speaks of the „introduction of new Mysteries for mankind, which contain the mystery of the transformation [Transsubstantiation] of the lower 'I' into the Spirit-Self", let us compare with this what Rudolf Steiner says about the changes in the life of the Mysteries after the Mystery of Golgotha: „... The essential nature of the Christ-event is the following: That human development to which we have referred as the living ascent (Hinaufleben) of the soul to the realms of the spirit, which in pre-Christian times could only be achieved within the Mysteries, and by virtue of the fact that the 'I' in a certain way – to the extent that it was developed in the normal human consciousness – was dimmed down; that human development was to receive such an impulse that – though for the most part this belongs as yet to the future – c a n p r e - s e r v e for the human being t h a t ' I ' - c o n s c i o u s n e s s w h i c h i n o u r t i m e h e o n l y p o s s e s s e s f o r t h e p h y s i c a l s e n s e w o r l d . This progress in human evolution, which came through the Christ-event, is at the same time the greatest progress that has ever been made, and will ever be made, in Earth-development and human evolution" (9.9.1910, GA 123).

Here again reference is being made to the 'I'-consciousness as it unfolds in the normal human life, to that 'I' which Prokofieff calls, in contrast to the Spirit-Self, the „lower I". This individual 'I'-consciousness which the human being possesses on the physical plane, had the possibility, after the Mystery of Golgotha, of upholding itself in the spiritual worlds, and this represents the greatest progress in the Earth-development. What Prokofieff ought to know already, is the fact that in the Mysteries the most important aim was the development of the 'I'-consciousness. The only rational sense that can be found in Prokofieff's statement concerning the transformation (Transsubstantiation) of the lower 'I' into the Spirit-Self, lies in the fact that the human being begins to experience the Spirit-Self as his 'I'; but this, as we said, leads him beyond the limits of Earth-development. This condition will be a hallmark of the normally-developed Jupiter man, but on the Earth this only applies to the high Initiates, not at all to mankind as a whole.

The degree to which Prokofieff's interpretation of the Mystery of Golgotha diverges from a true understanding of its meaning for Earth-development; how far removed he is with his untimely „Spirit-Self" from reality, and from an understanding of the meaning of the Earth-development, can be illustrated by a statement of Rudolf Steiner concerning the Christ-being: „Thus Christ is a being with a fourfold nature – just as the human being is, on the microcosmic level. When He descended to the Earth everything in His being was brought to bear in such a way that His fourth principle came to expression in the most perfect possible form. Now within the macrocosm and microcosm there is a deep inner relation between every numerical principle and that which corresponds to it, bearing the same number, on the other side. The fourth macrocosmic principle in the Christ corresponds to the fourth microcosmic principle in man, and the fifth in the Christ will correspond (on Jupiter) to the Spirit-Self in man. The Christ is a being who had developed himself macrocosmically as far as the fourth principle, and who during the passage through Earth will develop his fourth principle through giving everything in order that man may develop his 'I' … It will not be the Christ who, let us say, will encourage human beings to bring to expression in the future anything other than the actual 'I', the innermost essence of the human being, to an ever higher and higher level …

… the Christ comes to the Earth with something that is closely related to man's fourth principle. – It does not lie within His nature to lead the human being beyond himself, but only deeper into his own human soul-nature … The progressive inwardizing of the human soul into unbounded depths, that will be the gift of the Christ-impulse" (9.1.1912, GA 130).

Thus we see that already in his first book Prokofieff departs radically from esoteric Christianity in his view of the aim of Earth-development. It is without doubt unprecedented to speak of the development of the fifth principle as being the p r i n c i p l e   t a s k   of the fourth, the Earth aeon; yet another reason why he should found his own occult school, which differs greatly, however, from the school of Anthroposophy.

2.2. The Five-Membered Superman of the Earth Aeon. From Individual Death to Group Freedom

Prokofieff is in a great hurry to incorporate the fifth principle into the human being; in his opinion the Earth mission is the complete development of the Spirit-Self – half the Earth aeon is already past. Now it is really interesting to note that his striving coincides with the interest of a number of Luciferic beings who remained behind in the Moon aeon; Rudolf Steiner speaks of them in the lecture we have already quoted (9.1.1912), where he says that they implant into the human being, in a parasitic way, their not yet fully evolved, higher microcosmic principle (fifth, sixth or seventh, according to their stage of development), and use the human beings who are thus possessed, for their own further development under Earthly conditions. And whereas the Christ encourages the human being only to unfold his own 'I', these beings strive in an unnatural way to lead human beings beyond themselves, to inspire them suggestively to become a superman, to reach as far as the seventh principle already during the Earth development (GA 130).

And now we discover that in Prokofieff's book „The Spiritual Origins of Eastern Europe and the Future Mysteries of the Holy Grail" (IV), the five-membered Earthly man appears in his completeness. The author enumerates the following five [main] members of man's being: physical body, ether-body, astral body, the 'I', and Spirit-Self (the higher 'I') (IV, p. 53 [ibid.]). Where did he find such a human being? Earthly man has four members, and that until the Sixth post-Atlantean cultural epoch. Shortly before, Prokofieff writes that in the 6th epoch „the fifth member, Manas or Spirit-Self, will be awakened in the human being" (ibid.), but this is not correct. The indication of Rudolf Steiner relating to this we have already quoted: In the sixth culture epoch the Spirit-Self is not awakened in the human being, but it overshadows him like an angel-being, and cannot therefore be spoken of as a [principal] member of man's being.* In the Jupiter aeon the Spirit-Self will indeed be awakened in the human being, but not merely as an addition to the members already developed. In that period the human being will pass through a fundamental metamorphosis. The 'I'-Consciousness will indwell the astral body. In proportion as the 'I' with its self-consciousness transforms and takes hold of the astral body the latter will change into Spirit-Self, not suddenly, but through the course of the entire Jupiter aeon. Prokofieff's book, however, is describing the Earth aeon and not that of Jupiter.

One of the main weaknesses of Prokofieff's thinking is that it is neither analytic nor synthetic, but „affirming", „showing the way", i.e. Prokofieff is not so much a thinker as an ideologue. Thus, not only is the concept of method in science foreign to him, but he has no sense for the nuances and reciprocal relations which are of special importance in Rudolf Steiner's communications. If one now tries to fathom why Prokofieff places such emphasis on the development

---

* He even quotes a statement of Rudolf Steiner which is in obvious contradiction to his own thesis: „... if [the Spirit-Self in the 6th cultural epoch] can only descend into a human community that is permeated by brotherhood" (IV, p. 94; quote from lecture of 15.6.1915, GA 160).

of the Spirit-Self in the Earth aeon, one might recall a place in the lecture of Rudolf Steiner held on 16.5.1908, where he says: „The human beings, however, who have not taken the opportunity on the Earth to develop the fifth member, will appear in their development on Jupiter as nature-spirits" (GA 102). No doubt Prokofieff has read this lecture, but has not noticed that this quotation anticipates another: '... The human being will have developed the fifth member of his being, Manas, on the Jupiter stage."

It was our aim here to show that the elements of evolution are revealed within a coherent whole, whereby a clear distinction must be made between what is still at a stage of preparation, and what is yet to be brought to completion. It is clear that if the human being does not create the necessary condition for the development of the Spirit-Self on Jupiter, he will appear there as a retarded being. And in the present case the pre-condition lies in the development of the autonomous 'I' in the threefold soul, and in this the experience of moral intuitions as a result of its being overshadowed by the Spirit-Self. It is an undeniable fact that Rudolf Steiner characterized, with the entire content of spiritual science, the development of the 'I' in the Earth aeon as a task of the highest significance. Why Prokofieff does not understand this is a complete riddle.

But let us move on to a further hypothesis. Could it be that Prokofieff wishes to present the human being as a whole, corresponding to his archetype which is revealed in stages and in the most diverse aspects through the course of all seven aeons, from Saturn to Vulcan? In this case, however, the human being would have, not five, but seven members, as the seeds for the three highest spiritual members were laid in his three bodies in the three previous aeons. Why then does he pay no attention to Life-Spirit and Spirit-Man? Why this continual stressing of the Spirit-Self?

This is a fanatical and blind fixation on the fifth principle of man's being, which occurs in all his books and is quite inappropriate in our time. He calls the Spirit-Self the [highest spiritual] ideal (IV, P. 113 [p. 119]), thereby devaluing the two still higher spiritual members. In so doing he forgets that for the ordinary human being the h i g h e s t   s p i r i t u a l   i d e a l is Christ Himself, and not an abstractly understood fifth microcosmic principle. How can one not recall Rudolf Steiner's warning in the lecture quoted above, where he says that in the not too distant future there will be human beings who, in short-sightedness, will heed those Luciferic beings who wish to endow them with the higher principle prematurely, because they believe that these are more important spiritually than the macrocosmic Christ-'I'. Prokofieff speaks continually of the Christ, but, as we have seen from one example (para. 2.1.), he develops a one-sided and tendentious Christology of his own, which he puts together out of Rudolf Steiner's Christology and places entirely in the service of the Spirit-Self.* Moreover, he develops it in an extremely inconsistent, chaotic way, even in „The Spiritual Origins of Eastern Europe [Russia] ...", where he postulates a five-membered human being. Here he declares with no explanation: „T h a t the Spirit-Self principle is still in the higher worlds and is not attainable in full consciousness by any of those incarnated in a physical body" (p. 123); that the real entry of the Spirit-Self into the evolution of humanity will only take place in the Jupiter aeon (p. 122), meaning, therefore, after the human being has c o m p l e t e l y d e v e l o p e d this in the Earth aeon – but not in full consciousness, only in a sleeping or, perhaps, trance condition. One gets the impression that Prokofieff's own consciousness splits into two parts: all that he derives from Rudolf Steiner on the one hand, and what he says himself on the other, though the irreconcilable nature of both – we are forced to conclude – remains unnoticed by him.

In order to gain a glimpse of the peculiar conclusions to which the inconsistency of Prokofieff leads when he is setting out his views, we feel the moment has come to ask: what does he mean by the „lower I"?

We have already alluded to this problem with an ironical observation (para. 2.1.). In Prokofieff's opinion the principle task of the Earth consists in the complete development of the individualities who are already highly developed, and also of the angels. In other words, the Earth thereby becomes the planet of

---

* Prokofieff's wish to renew spiritual science under the banner of the Spirit-Self is all but insatiable. In his book „Spiritual Origins of Eastern Europe ..." he writes the following: „Looking at this 'Pietà-Motif' Parzival has a first inkling of the fact that (now Prokofieff quotes Rudolf Steiner) '... if he had asked about the wonders of the Holy Grail, he would have experienced in the new form the connection that exists between Isis and Horus, between Mother and the Son of Man', or, in the terminology of modern spiritual science (now Prokofieff's own formulation): the mystery of the interaction between the spiritualized Consciousness-soul and the Spirit-Self" (p. 135). We would compare this passage with the statement of Rudolf Steiner: „Son of Man is 'I' and astral body as they have emerged in the course of Earth-evolution ... For this, there is in occult language the technical expression 'Son of Man'." (25.5.1908, GA 103).

the superman, which was already asserted by Nietzsche's well-known hero Zarathustra – and yet how many times falsely interpreted! – But let us take one point at a time.

For the sake of orientation we will take that definition of the „lower I" given by Prokofieff in „The Occult Significance of Forgiveness" (V), where he says: „... only out of [the forces] of the fully-developed i n d i v i d u a l ' I ', w h i c h u n f o l d s w i t h i n t h e C o n s c i o u s n e s s - s o u l, and from there seeks the way to the higher 'I' [can] the true deed of forgiveness ... be accomplished ... This relation of the lower to the higher 'I' in the act of forgiveness is indicated by ..." (p. 17 [p. 13]; emphasis I.G.).

Here we have the assertion: the lower 'I' is the fully-developed individual 'I', which unfolds in the Consciousness-soul (higher 'I' = Spirit-Self).

Elsewhere in the same book Prokofieff attaches baseness and bad qualities to the lower 'I', and admonishes us to overcome them. Evidently he now longer means that 'I' which, at the beginning of the book (as quoted above), he refers to as individual and as possessing a moral will of its own. Or is it the same after all? As Prokofieff employs an unclear terminology the impression might arise in the reader that he is describing different nuances of the self-revealing human 'I'. However, when one looks more closely one discovers that he is leading the reader – and perhaps himself – by the nose. He uses four different terms to refer to one and the same concept. Sometimes he speaks of the 'I', then of the lower 'I', of the normal everyday (gewöhnliche) 'I', and of the individual 'I' – for him these are all synonymous. But if he uses them in alternation with one another, they end up by cancelling each other out, thereby leaving the human being without an individual 'I'.

On the one hand Prokofieff borrows the concept of the 'I' from Chapter 2 of „Occult Science", where we read of the fourth principle, endowed with the faculty of memory which provides the actual foundation for waking 'I'-consciousness. This fact is cited in Chapter 4 of the above-mentioned book (V), in order to build up on this basis his theory of forgiveness. But the 'I' remembers, and interruptions in the memory entail interruptions in the 'I'-consciousness. In his search for a way out of this dilemma Prokofieff arrives at the conclusion that an interruption brought about through the agency of the Spirit-Self does no harm to 'I'-consciousness: „Thus only the higher 'I' of man, or his Spirit-Self, can work upon the everyday (gewöhnliche) 'I' without harming it – on the contrary, it thereby promotes its further growth and development" (p. 55).

As we see, he calls the 'I' an everyday 'I'. A few lines further on we read: „The human being can in reality only forgive, i.e. of his own free will and without the least harm to himself interrupt the stream of memory which bears his individual 'I', when he lets the radiance of his higher 'I' light up within him ..." (p. 56) – here he calls the same 'I' – „individual"; and further: „... in the question of forgiveness as such the mutual relation of higher and lower 'I' is already contained" (ibid.); here it has become „lower". In the following chapters he reverts finally to the term „lower I" (or „everyday I"), stressing repeatedly as he does so, that its most important feature is the lust for revenge (such is the metamorphosis undergone by the „capacity for forgiveness" in the course of his exposition).

We will look at this question in more detail in para. 4, but affirm for the present that we have sufficiently proved that Prokofieff means by the „lower I" the fourth principle of the human being. For him there is a lower and a higher 'I', and thereby he has said everything about the individual 'I', the development of which is the central mystery of the Earth aeon. But anyone who does not possess at least elementary, genuine spiritual-scientific knowledge of this Mystery should abstain from the wish to do independent research in Anthroposophy. It is as though someone should wish to practise chemistry without knowing Mendelev's periodic system, or to compose a piece of music without a knowledge of notes.

„I am the Alpha and the Omega, the beginning and the end" (Rev. 1, 8), said Christ, the 'I' of the Macrocosm and the God of the human 'I'. If one does not know what an 'I' is, if one only studies it in trite ambiguity rather than in the many-facetted nature of its concrete manifestations, then this means that one does not understand the Christ – or, by implication, the Earthly evolution. It should therefore not surprise us to discover that the primitive scheme set up by Prokofieff, which has a religious-dogmatic rather than Anthroposophical character, and in which an earthly, fallen, lower, mortal human 'I' stands in opposition to a higher 'I', can lead us nowhere.

We recall what Prokofieff has written about the transformation of the lower, mortal 'I' into the higher, immortal 'I', i.e. the Spirit-Self (cf. Para. 2.1.). One would be forced to conclude from this that the Spirit-Self is the first immortal member of the human being, while the lower 'I' is mortal – and meanwhile we have discovered the nature of this 'I'. This would mean, according to Prokofieff, that Earthly man, who is a four-membered being, cannot attain individual immortality! From this we conclude that towards the end of the Earth aeon all human beings, with the exception of the few select supermen, will die; contrary to all laws of development these will gain control of the fifth principle, and renounce the fourth. For the sake of these lone and reckless figures – the race of mortal men has toiled and suffered.

Anthroposophy gives us a quite different perspective on individual immortality. According to Rudolf Steiner the 'I', and also in part the astral body of the human being, passes from one incarnation to another. Although the astral body leaves behind a great deal in Kamaloka, it preserves all that has been attained morally, intellectually and aesthetically in a given incarnation. „That which is true progress is held together through the power of the astral body, is carried from one incarnation to the next, and is as it were grafted into the 'I' which passes, as the fundamentally eternal in us, from incarnation to incarnation" (9.10.1911, GA 131). We take note of Prokofieff's attempt to do away with the human 'I', which has always been an obstacle in his path, but in the light of the facts we must admit that, in the absence of any foundation, this attempt is doomed to fail.

But we would like to bring a further argument. In his book „The Spiritual Origins …" (IV), Prokofieff writes entirely in the spirit of his doctrine that the „first of the 'divine' members of the human being" is the Spirit-Self, „which is to descend to Earth (in the 6th cultural epoch), and in it there will be a microcosmic reflection of the World-Creator-Spirit" (p. 135). This means that earthly man is mortal and has nothing in him of the Divine. Here we realize that Prokofieff has not read „Occult Science", despite his frequent references to it in the autobiographical essay and a quotation from Chapter 2. For in this very Chapter 2 we read the following: „Here [in the Consciousness-soul] is the 'hidden sanctuary' of the soul. Only a being can seek entry to it, with whom the soul shares a common nature … The God who lives in the human being speaks, when the soul knows itself as 'I'. As the sentient and rational souls live in the outer world, so a third member of the soul is absorbed into the Divine when it comes to a perception of its own essential being … the 'I' is of a single nature and being with the Divine … As the drop is related to the ocean, so is the 'I' related to the Divine. The human being can find a divine element within himself, because

2. Prokofieff's Concept of Evolution

in his deepest, original being he is descended from the Divine ... in the Consciousness-soul the true nature of the 'I' is first revealed" (GA 13, p. 67, 69).

Just as Rome denies the spirit of man, but concedes to the soul a few spiritual characteristics, so Prokofieff's spiritualism denies the soul; not the soul as such, but as a revelation of the spiritual and the Divine in the Earthly aeon. Although outwardly they stand in opposition to one another, both directions are pursuing the same distant goal: to lead the human being astray with regard to the true nature of his 'I' and lead him on to a false path of development.

But what are the prospects held out by Prokofieff for the „mortal", four-membered human being? – To renounce his own will and entrust this to the higher, hierarchical angel being: „For the human being is free only when his will proceeds entirely from his higher 'I', and is led by it"* (V, p. 122). In other words: „Not I, but the Spirit-Self in me" are the words of St. Paul, revised by Prokofieff in the spirit of Lucifer.

We will not dwell on such obvious details as the question: How can „his will" proceed from something that lies outside him, and what kind of freedom can we speak of in this situation? Now Prokofieff is no friend of logic, but in the case in question not even that is essential. – The Angel of regular development will not accept from man the sacrifice of his will, because He leads to independence, to freedom of will – „... owing to the fact that the hierarchy of the Angeloi works into our soul-spiritual being (our 'I' and our astral body), we feel ourselves to be a free personality" – says Rudolf Steiner (7.9.1918, GA 184).

By contrast to this, the Luciferic angels strive to extinguish the 'I' and the individual will in man. In addition they wish to throw him back into earlier conditions, when his actions were inspired from above and he was guided by the hierarchical beings. Concerning those times Rudolf Steiner says: „The human being had no will of his own. What he did was an expression of the divine will. Step by step ... we have acquired a will of our own, whose time began about five centuries ago" (GA 26, p. 82). The religious surrender to the higher spiritual being, as preached by Prokofieff, does not correspond to the evolutionary task of the fifth cultural epoch, in which the human being must learn to

---

* „... in our age the higher 'I' of man (Spirit-Self) is borne in the spiritual worlds by the guardian angel" (V, p. 56).

act „entirely out of his own forces". The state of possession by higher powers resulting from such surrender is not the ideal of human freedom. „... Everything that the human being encounters in this fifth post-Atlantean period must be tested by the yardstick of human freedom. For if the forces of the human being were to weaken, everything could take a turn for the worst. The human being in this fifth post-Atlantean period is not in a position to be led like a child" (19.11.1917, GA 178).

Through development of the Consciousness-soul the human being gradually acquires the capacity to receive from the Angel (the Spirit-Self) the moral intuitions which can inspire his deeds. „The free thoughts must ... animate (impulsieren) the will, then the human being is free" (17.2.1924, GA 235). But when this is the case, his will proceeds from his own 'I', it is the activity of the 'I' and not of the Angel. Not the denial of the lower 'I' and of one's own will – to which Prokofieff admonishes us in his book of „The Occult Significance of Forgiveness" – nor the quest for guidance from above, are the task of the 5th epoch – quite the contrary: purposeful, conscious work at an all-round development, and that is the strengthening of the 'I'. The renunciation of one's own will is merely the line of least resistance; it means a return to the past, and is thus all too easy a solution. If people were to follow this path, as recommended by Prokofieff, the sixth epoch too would be for them an epoch of retrogression, of the „abolition of the I". „In the 5th epoch", says Rudolf Steiner, „human beings have had the task of raising themselves to an 'I'. But this 'I' could be lost again if they were not really to seek it through inner effort" (8.2.1916, GA 166).

We are led precisely in the direction of the „abolition of the I" through this turning of the attention away from the 'I' and the Consciousness-soul towards the Spirit-Self – which Prokofieff is continually preaching. His conception, with respect to the tasks of evolution, is not merely an abstract-theoretical error, but contains a real force of disintegration; for if it were to be accepted it would be a temptation to abandon the path of evolution – to return to group-soul consciousness and „eternal childhood". This statement is confirmed with especial clarity when we consider what Prokofieff says in another of his books – „The Spiritual Tasks ..." (VIII). Here he asserts that the Folk-soul is the sum of all the guardian angels contained in a given people. The direct conclusion to be drawn from this would be: human beings would have, in the name of freedom, to give up their individual will, and again become group beings who are guided from the spiritual world by the totality of their guardian angels.

2.3. Dawn of a Light-filled Future

In this study we have set ourselves the task of analyzing the worst and most striking of Prokofieff's errors. Where he is dealing with the subject of the 6th culture epoch we see at first „only" his one-sidedness. But it must be realized that this „only" is relative. „What can most harm a spiritual movement is one-sidedness" – says Rudolf Steiner (GA 284, p. 154).

Because in Prokofieff's view the development of the Spirit-Self is, to all intents and purposes, the most important task of the Earth aeon, he focusses his interest on the 6th cultural epoch. He proclaims and extols it in every imaginable way, devotes many pages to it with enthusiasm, while the actual tasks of the 5th epoch scarcely interest him at all. When he does speak of them, he does so only in general terms and confines himself to a few commonplaces. He manifests a one-sidedness, therefore, in that he regards the 5th epoch as being no more than a kind of prelude, a preparation for the sixth; the emphasis of the entire post-Atlantean development is shifted on to the 6th epoch, and he sees in it the imminent culmination of the highest strivings of humanity. Moreover, if Prokofieff is to be believed, then not only the 5th epoch would be a preparation for the sixth. The deliberate and purposeful preparation for the 6th cultural epoch, bypassing the 5th, began much earlier. Back in the days of the Mongol-Tartar invasion of Russia – i.e. in the fourth cultural epoch – the people who had suffered death by martyrdom united „... with those who (already then) are working (this he knows from personal experience) in the supersensible worlds at the preparation of that which is to become earthly reality for mankind as a whole in the 6th cultural epoch" (IV, p. 117-118). Even the authors of the old Russian legend of the „City of Kitesh" were well-informed about the 6th cultural epoch. Prokofieff claims that they were preparing it consciously. He tells us that „... the path to the 6th culture-epoch – according to the deep conviction of those in Eastern Europe who had once in spiritual vision, created the Kitesh Legend – can only be found if all human beings succeed in entering the hidden City" (ibid., p. 123).

The present, 5th, epoch is characterized by Prokofieff as the epoch which is to prepare the Spirit-Self principle (I, p. 371). He says that already now, or more precisely, since 1879 (ibid., p. 408) „… the transition from the Consciousness-soul to the Spirit-Self was to be accomplished (ibid., p. 371); then the goal set for the 5th epoch by the divine-spiritual powers who direct Earth-development – the complete spiritualization of the Consciousness-soul – will be attained" (IV, p. 373). Mankind as a whole, starting in our own time, is crossing „the threshold that lies between the highest soul-member [the Consciousness-soul] and the lowest spiritual member [the Spirit-Self]" (V, p. 124 [p. 99]) etc. Prokofieff is especially keen to find, also in the lectures of Rudolf Steiner, indications of „possibilities for preparation" of the Spirit-Self epoch „already in our own time" (V, p. 162). No-one will question that there might exist such a possibility, and there are „already in our own time" people who are even preparing the seventh epoch, or to be more precise, a particular aspect of that epoch, namely, the „war of each against all". The question is, i n w h a t w a y the 6th epoch is to be prepared. Is it at all possible, so long as the tasks of the 5th epoch are not fulfilled? Rudolf Steiner, in any case, speaks of this with unmistakably clarity: „The summit of the post-Atlantean culture is to be attained already in the 5th post-Atlantean cultural epoch. What is to follow in the 6th and 7th cultural periods will be a development in decline" (15.6.1915, GA 159). We cannot determine precisely what is valid for whom, but for Anthroposophists this is without doubt a basic truth.

But who can explain to us how far Prokofieff's assertion that mankind as a whole is already crossing the threshold between the Consciousness-soul and the Spirit-Self, differs from the ideology of those occult brotherhoods who, through the medium of the most varied outer institutions, wish to impress upon the world the idea that the Age of Aquarius is about to begin?

It is known to us from Anthroposophy that so far only one quarter of the fifth culture-epoch has passed, and that its principal goal will be realized only when, in science and culture, Goetheanism comes to expression, the further development of which will be accompanied by the individual u n f o l d i n g of the Consciousness-soul in the human being – not by its complete spiritualization – what would there be to spiritualize in this case? Prokofieff sees it quite differently; he says: „The only correct transition can be found to the Spirit-Self when the stage of the spiritualized Consciousness-soul is attained (preceded of necessity by the full development of the rational or mind-soul) – there is no other way" (IV, p. 124). Here he is putting forward a thesis that is true, but which, coming from his pen, sounds untrue. For in the case of Prokofieff this is

2. Prokofieff's Concept of Evolution

no more than an abstract phrase. Let us examine it more closely. In his works a concept of the development of the Consciousness-soul as such is entirely lacking. He makes a leap from the rational soul to the s p i r i t u a l i z e d Consciousness-soul. And what can this Consciousness-soul be, which is to take up the impulse of the Spirit-Self – i.e. that which will only be appropriate in the 6th epoch?

In continuous repetition, without sense or content, Prokofieff uses the words „spiritualization of the Consciousness-soul" and prompts us to ask: what is it actually that has to be spiritualized? Rudolf Steiner spoke of the spiritualizing of t h i n k i n g . This means the development of clearly cognizable ideas and concepts, free of all sense-reality, but which in their unfolding prove capable of grasping a spiritual content. With the help of these the human being can rise from the comprehension of the facts and laws of the physical world to an equally clear and concrete understanding of the laws of the spiritual world. This is a rightful development, an organic component of the Consciousness-soul development in the 5th epoch, and it is brought about, not in a religious striving towards the spiritual heights, which we encounter on literally every page of Prokofieff's books, but on the path of a planned and systematic study of spiritual science, and the development of social understanding. He would like to reach over directly from the rational soul of the 4th epoch to the completely spiritualized Consciousness-soul of the 6th epoch. Such a „flight without stop-over" is, however, only possible to a thinking that is far removed from reality.

If, as Prokofieff claims, we are already standing at the threshold of the Spirit-Self epoch, then we would ask what took place in the first quarter of the 5th epoch. „The unfolding of materialism", Prokofieff replies. And thus „… the [accumulated] negative karma of materialism so grew in extent … that, as a result of this karma, humanity at the end of the dark period of Kali Yuga in 1899 and at the beginning of the new, light epoch would not be able to fulfil the tasks of the 5th post-Atlantean epoch to the degree that was necessary" (IV, p. 378). What attitude are we to adopt, in this case, towards Goetheanism? – we would ask. What do we say about Goethe, Schiller, Hegel, Fichte etc.? What significance do we attach to them?

If we now listen to Prokofieff's answer, we will realize that humanity has started to address the tasks of the 5th epoch only now that he, Prokofieff, has begun to proclaim the 6th epoch and the ascent to the Spirit-Self. But this is not the main task of the 5th epoch; this consists in the strengthening of the 'I'-consciousness on a new and higher level, which can only be achieved in the process of development of the Consciousness-soul. For only here „does the 'I' become, as it were ... pure, can it become fully aware of itself" (8.2.1910, GA 116). This development begins with the elaboration by the human being of an independent thinking. „We cannot develop the Consciousness-soul in the 5th post-Atlantean period, without developing the power of understanding" (24.10.1920, GA 200). Rudolf Steiner indicates this, and what follows: „The reasoning faculty must, in concrete development in the 5th post-Atlantean period, bring the 'I' into the Consciousness-soul" (21.8.1917, GA 176). In our age the required mode of thinking is developed in the process of grasping the laws of the material universe. Equally in accordance with law and in harmony with the task of evolution, the materialistic world-view also comes into its own. It is recognized by the divine-spiritual powers, to whom Prokofieff continually refers. Rudolf Steiner says: „Since the 16th century we have a new time-spirit (Zeitgeist). This time-spirit has its own quite definite task. Its task is to add to the earlier impulses of development the entirely materialistic skills (Können) and understanding of the world. This is why the materialistic element in the world has made such great strides since the 16th century. We do not therefore need to look upon the materialistic understanding of things as inferior to the earlier mode of understanding, so long as we do not identify with it in a one-sided way" (13.5.1915, GA 159).

To identify with something in a way that is not one-sided is a problem which Prokofieff is clearly unable to comes to terms with: thus he identifies with spiritualism. In intellectual development he only sees the negative side, the intellect itself he sees as merely Ahrimanic; the spiritual approach favoured by him – one that is diametrically opposed to the intellect – draws him away from the Earth into the expanses of the cosmos. In order not to come into open confrontation with Rudolf Steiner he recognizes the objective inevitability of the emergence of materialism, but is unable to overcome a deep antipathy towards it, and characterizes it without qualification as the „mass l i e " that has been spread most widely and in the most radical way, which sees the physical sense world and its laws as the sole reality and regards everything spiritual – Prokofieff here uses a Marxist expression – as an unreal „superstructure" (IV, p. 378; emphasis S.O.P.).

2. Prokofieff's Concept of Evolution

Here too Prokofieff slips up, confusing the sociological teaching of Marx, his „h i s t o r i c a l materialism" which speaks of „basis" and „superstructure", with the natural-scientific materialistic view of the world. But within the context of this world-view (which, incidentally, was inspired by the brotherhood of Christian Rosenkreutz), a natural science has developed that is entirely valid in its own sphere, and whose profound knowledge in the realm of sense-reality can in no way be spoken of as a „mass-lie". It did not occur to Prokofieff with his militant spiritualism, that „through the course of four centuries the best training for spirituality was that which forced human beings into natural-scientific thinking" (1.6.1913, GA 146). Materialism is not a lie, although it is mistaken with regard to the world-order. Thus Rudolf Steiner warned the Anthroposophists: „Materialism cannot be refuted" (5.5.1923, GA 225).

The tasks of the 5th epoch were taken hold of before our own time. The rightful development of the Consciousness-soul in the 5th epoch depends upon the attainment of two faculties in the human being. One is a really pure perception of the sense-world – a task fulfilled by Goetheanism. The other is characterized by Rudolf Steiner as the capacity for „free imaginations, within which one moves as freely as one otherwise moves only in one's power of understanding". To this we are led by spiritual science (17.9.1916, GA 171).

For Goetheanism Prokofieff shows no interest. He appears, at least so far as the fruits of his own research are concerned, to have no idea of the existence of a spiritual-scientific method which fosters the development of free imaginations. He loses sight of the Consciousness-soul altogether. It separates into two extremes – one that is spiritualized, and one that is demonized (through materialism) (IV, p. 126), similar to the 'I' which he loses in the unresolved dualism of lower and higher 'I'.

Pushing with his oar from this unsteady dual ground he steers towards the 6th culture epoch, where „the light of an early dawn" shines towards him „from the depths of an as yet indistinct future" (ibid., p. 125). And what rises before him from that „indistinct" but unquestionably shining future, on whose threshold he already stands? He repeats it again and again: „the conscious connection of an ever growing number of people with the Sophia realm" (ibid., p. 134); the opening up of the possibility of finding the way to the cosmic sphere of Maria-Sophia (ibid., p. 139), etc. But why the c o s m i c sphere? In the statements of

Rudolf Steiner quoted by Prokofieff in support of his claims there is no mention of „cosmos".

The Gospel of St. John tells how Christ, when he saw his mother standing with John before the cross – according to Rudolf Steiner she was the bearer of the divine wisdom, the Sophia – says to his mother: „Woman, behold your son. And then he spoke to the disciple: Behold your mother. And from that hour the disciple took her to him" (John 19, 26-27). Have these words no significance for Prokofieff? Only in the distant 6th epoch, he maintains, will „… for the first time in the entire Earth development the possibility be given [to the forces of the cosmic Sophia] to incarnate on the Earth" (IV, p. 94). And only then will „the Christ impulse work within humanity with the help and by means of the cosmic Sophia forces" (ibid.). With blind persistence Prokofieff continues to search for wisdom, as in pre-Christian antiquity, out in the cosmos.

Knowledge of the truth is, from Prokofieff's standpoint, the same as „consciously uniting with the Sophia sphere" (ibid., p. 133). – Only after the triumphal union of all mankind with „… the cosmic sphere of the Sophia" in the 6th epoch will the possibility be given to know the truth. For this reason not only materialism but much more agreeable things too – nearly everything, in fact, which our time has brought forth, however hard one may try to find an exception, will in the end prove to be lies, whether of a collective or an individual nature. Perhaps it is just because Prokofieff is initiated into this shattering secret, that he is so lax in the question of the truthfulness of his own literary creations, which aim to meet one requirement only: namely, that they should sound sublimely lofty, and encourage people to direct their gaze into the light-filled future and thus forget the present as far as possible.

The truth is that, with the coming of Christ, the divine wisdom also descended to the Earth and drew close to man. The entire situation of human knowledge changed decidedly for the better, and it is unfortunate that Prokofieff has not been able to realize this. Because the „Fall into sin" stands in a connection with knowledge, it is through knowledge that it will be overcome. However, this task of the overcoming of the „Fall" by way of knowledge must be fulfilled, not by the 6th post-Atlantean epoch, but by the 5th, through spiritual science.

A mighty impulse of ascent to a spiritual – but now individualized – wisdom took place through the Mystery of Golgotha, already in the 4th cultural epoch. Rudolf Steiner says that the initiates of pre-Christian times, although they could penetrate into the spiritual worlds, „[had] within [their own] 'I' … no ability to judge, no understanding of, the higher worlds … With all the forces belonging to the 'I', the human being before the Mystery of Golgotha was unable to unite with the spiritual worlds. This was the secret that was to be made clear to people through the Baptism by John, that the time had now come where the heavenly kingdoms should radiate down into the 'I', should come right down to the 'I', the earthly 'I'" (21.9.1912, GA 139). This secret has not become clear to Prokofieff. He does not see how the Christ impulse is active in the development of the 4th and 5th epochs, how individual human wisdom gradually matures, stage by stage, in these cultures. In his view of things everything of the highest and best strives across into the 6th epoch – including knowledge of the truth and the experience of freedom.

„You will know the truth, and the truth will set you free" (John 8, 32). These words of Christ are quoted by Prokofieff, with the following commentary: „And this means that k n o w l e d g e   o f   t h e   t r u t h (emphasis S.O.P.) o r ,   w h a t   i s   t h e   s a m e (emphasis I.G.), the conscious union with the Sophia-sphere, so purifies and spiritualizes the Consciousness-soul, that the human being becomes able really to experience within himself the impulse of freedom, which always has a moral character" (IV, p. 133). Thus he tries to give reinforcement to his own fixed idea by quoting the texts of Holy Scripture and making use of the circumstance that no-one will dare to call this in question. And there is scarcely anyone able to unravel the demagogical subtleties into which these texts are woven, for we have here to do, not with logical errors, but with an absence of logic, an accumulation of arbitrary associations which he succeeds in bringing together only in an external fashion, with the aid of grammar and of easily-overlooked expressions such as „what is the same thing"; the assertion thus takes on the appearance of being obvious and universally recognized. This is one of the simple but highly effective means used by Prokofieff to fool the reader. Thus we find him skilfully combining quotations from the Gospel with statements of Rudolf Steiner, and thereby subtly suggesting to the reader that human beings will have to wait for knowledge of the truth, and thus for an experience of the impulse of freedom, and finally for the founding of communities according to the principle of ethical individualism! – until the 6th epoch, in order then to unite themselves with the sphere of the

Sophia (ibid., e.g. p. 133). And this entire construction is supported on a single „hook" – the expression „the same".

Knowledge of the truth enables us to become free. But to be free is not identical with the experiencing of the impulse to freedom. Coming to know the truth (and also becoming free) is a complex process which unfolds in the course of time and is connected inseparably with the course of human evolution, and does not begin and end simultaneously with the outpouring of the „Water of cosmic Wisdom" at the beginning of the 6th epoch. But with regard to the impulse to individual freedom, the experiencing of this must, as we know from Anthroposophy, take place in the period of the Consciousness-soul, and, moreover, under the conditions of the separation of the human being from the cosmic spheres – normally referred to as the spiritual hierarchies – and the development of „dead", abstract thinking, which becomes object-related (gegenständlich) in the process of cognizing the material world – and, only after this, is spiritualized.

„My effort in the development of natural-scientific concepts" – Rudolf Steiner says in his „Autobiography" – „had finally led me to see in the activity of the human 'I' the only possible point of departure for genuine cognition" (GA 28, Chapter 3). Through losing sight of the human 'I' Prokofieff has lost „the only possible point of departure for genuine cognition", and finds himself with no choice but to seek this „genuine (wahr) cognition" in the distant cosmic spheres.

Rudolf Steiner gave expression to the secrets of the coming 6th cultural epoch in the language of the Rosicrucian Temple Legend (GA 93). This legend has remained incomprehensible to Prokofieff. The spiritual Temple of humanity envisaged by him is created solely out of the [heavenly] Sophia-forces, the forces of the cosmic, feminine, priestly Abel-wisdom (IV, Ch. 14 and Note 233 on p. 482). From Rudolf Steiner's lecture of 22.5.1905 he carefully selects only those passages which have to do with the feminine principle and with divine wisdom (IV, p. 134), and patently ignores what is said in this lecture about the work of the Sons of Cain, through whose forces the Temple is built f o r the heavenly wisdom of the Sons of Abel. In the Golden Triangle, which symbolizes Atma-Buddhi-Manas, is contained the higher 'I' of man, knowledge of which „will be the content of the renewed Christianity of the 6th sub-race" (i.e. the 6th culture-epoch; 4.11.1904, GA 93). Of this triangle Prokofieff recognizes one angle only – namely Manas. In his „bronze sea", out of which „a combination is to arise, which can be carried into the ages to follow" (ibid.), there is only the Water, the old inspired wisdom of the Sons of Abel, but not the Fire, the elementary forces of the Sons of Cain, the fire of cognition and of the mastery of the earthly plane. In this regard it is symptomatic that Prokofieff, in his book on Novalis („Eternal Individuality", Dornach 1987), characterizes the 6th epoch as the time whose beginning is marked by „the outpouring for humanity of the W a t e r of the new cosmic wisdom" (p. 216; emphasis I.G.). – How can one not recall here the journeymen in the Legend, through whose intrigues water is mixed into the casting of the bronze sea, which nearly brought everything to ruin?!

Can Solomon alone, without the help of Hiram, construct a temple? Is Prokofieff not afraid that there might remain of the Temple no more than a cosmic project, of which hardly a memory will survive to the time of the 6th epoch if he expels the Temple-builders?

If we wish to form a judgement of this depressing picture of human development, the following words of Rudolf Steiner can help us. He says: „The Luciferic beings" hate the Earth, „they strive to cast it aside, to cast aside the Earth, to cast aside everything earthly from the human being, and to spiritualize the human being completely, so that nothing earthly works upon him, so that he is not permeated and strengthened by the earthly. They would wish only to have in him a cosmic being ... In order to achieve this the Luciferic beings try continually to make automatic the intelligence which we have as human beings, and they try to suppress the free will in us ... Then we would be able to do what we need to with automatic intelligence, and act, not out of our own will, but out of the will of the Gods. We would be able to become pure cosmic beings ... Their striving is, as it were, to make us into pure spirits, endowed not with an intelligence of our own, but only with cosmic intelligence; beings with no free will of our own, but in whom everything in the nature of thought and action functions automatically, as is the case with the hierarchy of the Angeloi, and in many respects in the hierarchy of Luciferic beings themselves ..." (21.9.1918, GA 184).

Does Prokofieff too want to deprive the human being of a will of his own (cf. Para. 2.2., 4.1.), endow him with cosmic wisdom in the place of his „lying thoughts" (cf. V, p. 66) which cannot know the truth; implant in him the f i f t h principle instead of the individual, lower 'I'; make the human being moral in a Luciferic fashion? That such intentions are proclaimed t h r o u g h Prokofieff – in the name of Anthroposophy – with the approval of the overwhelming majority of Anthroposophists, is a truly remarkable fact – „So woe betide, if we do not keep in mind the words (from Goethe's „Faust" – Trans.): 'The common folk can't see the Devil – even if he has grasped them by the collar'" (17.6.1912, GA 130).

3. The Spiritual World and its Beings in the View of S. Prokofieff

In the spiritual world there is no distinction between beings on the one hand and nature-processes on the other. Rudolf Steiner explains this as follows: „In the spiritual world we are only confronted by Beings, and over against these Beings there is nothing that could be called a nature-process. Everything one encounters is Being ... and one cannot say as in the sense-world: There is an animal, and those are outer substances which are eaten by it. This duality is not to be found there ..." (29.8.1912, GA 138).

For this reason one cannot abstract the relation to the spirit world from the relation to its Beings; here the laws of being, of development, of the activity of Beings, are at work, and cognition of the spiritual world is always as concrete as are the spiritual individualities who become the object of cognition.

Prokofieff's works have surprises in store for the reader, in this realm too. In this chapter we will analyze a few examples and show by means of them how arbitrarily and irresponsibly he operates with those concepts which relate to Beings of the spiritual worlds. This kind of treatment of them is only possible if they are regarded as purely nominal concepts devoid of all real content; knowledge of the spirit world is here replaced by abstract constructions of schemes and definitions, which create the outer impression of spiritual scientific research.

3.1. Which Folk has the Larger Soul?

At first sight, this appears to be a strange and unanswerable question. In order to be able to determine what is bigger or smaller, measure, number and weight are required. A whole palette of possibilities is conceivable: from simple calculation to the precise quantitative methods of natural science, and the impressive methods of calculation used by applied mathematics; from the most primitive scales to the most precise electronic measuring instruments – they are all achievements of science. However, there is something lacking in all these methods and instruments which are developed for research into the material world: namely, they are not applicable beyond the confines of this world.

Rudolf Steiner's Anthroposophy has extended the sphere of cognition, and has shown that cognition is also possible beyond the limits of the sense-perceptible world. But in order to gain knowledge of the spiritual and remain within the bounds of what is scientific a method must be devised which is just as precise as, even if fundamentally different from, the methods of the material-istic sciences. But now a new generation of researchers appears on the scene, foremost among them Prokofieff, and it turns out that not only through cogni-tion but through quantitative methods of the sciences – starting with the most simple, namely statistics – boundaries can be crossed. A quite ordinary calcula-tion is enough to establish the size of the various „Folk-souls", and compare them with one another. It is all extremely simple: The more populous a nation, the larger is its „Soul"; the size of any Folk-soul is dependent on the size of the population. But a theory underlies every method, and we will now inquire what this is.

The basic outlines of this theory are formulated in his book „The Spiritual Tasks of Middle and Eastern Europe" (VII).[*] The most important is the follow-ing: „ T h e i r (the angels') t o t a l i t y ... c o n s t i t u t e s w h a t c a n b e t e r m e d ' F o l k - S o u l ' . Hence there belong to this, in the first place, all the guardian angels of the human beings who are members of the Folk in ques-tion; that is to say, who constitute its physical (earthly) body" (p. 118; emphasis S.O.P.). Prokofieff derives his theory from the „universal law of the correspon-dence of Micro and Macro-Cosmos" (ibid.), and adds the following reflection: The soul of the human being acts as a mediator between his spirit and his body. If, therefore, according to Rudolf Steiner, the angels act as mediators between the archangels – the Folk-spirits – and the human beings who constitute the Folk, then – so Prokofieff concludes – the totality of the angels is the Folk-soul.

Why only the totality of the angels? One can prove to oneself that this asser-tion does not correspond to the truth. For example: When a leading politician is inspired by the Folk-spirit, then he too acts as a mediator between the Folk-spirit and the Folk. Following Prokofieff's theory one would therefore have to include amongst the constituent parts of the Folk-soul not only the angels, but

---

[*] The author refers to an extract from the book, which was published in the Russian journal „Anthroposophical Messenger", Nr. 10, June 1996. We are therefore unable to indicate page numbers (Ed.).

also prominent human beings such as state functionaries or personalities in the armed forces.

Moreover, he applies the law of the correspondence between Micro- and Macrocosm in an arbitrary and false manner, as he has not taken the trouble to reflect on the relation between part and whole. The human being as microcosm is a „miniature version" (a mirror image) of the Macrocosm, and there is thus a similarity between them. But this does not mean that the Microcosm is similar to any arbitrarily chosen part or fragment of the Macrocosm; if this were so one might compare the human being with any conceivable thing.

There is no rationally plausible analogy to be made between the spirit, soul and body of the human being, on the one hand, and the Folk-spirit, the totality of the angels, and the Folk itself on the other. The human soul mediates between the spirit and the body, behind which the spirit is also present. But the physical bodies of the human beings who, in their totality, constitute a Folk, cannot constitute the body of the archangel, however firmly convinced Prokofieff may be of this.* The archangelic body is spiritual in nature. „The entire Folk", says Rudolf Steiner, „[is] as it were embedded as a whole within a spiritual substance, and this spiritual substance is the body of a Fire-spirit [an archangel]" (6.8.1908, GA 105). Thus the angels mediate between the archangel and the Folk, not between the spirit and the body of the archangel - hence their totality is not comparable to the human soul as Prokofieff maintains.

The totality of the angels consists of a multiplicity of a u t o n o m o u s s p i r i t u a l   i n d i v i d u a l i t i e s , which cannot be said of the human soul. Prokofieff has realized this fact, only it does not disturb him. He says that, as in the Folk-soul, there is multiplicity in the individual human soul also, expressed in the three basic forces of thinking, feeling and willing, „each of which comprises a multiplicity of complex processes" (VIII, p. 121). Something analogous to this „applies also to the Folk-soul ... The Folk-soul is always a multiplicity, but it can nevertheless be summed up as a threefoldness ... constituted by the three principal groups of angel-beings" (ibid., p. 122). Then, in order to demonstrate the importance of his analogy, he goes on to describe those three groups, unaware of the fact that in the case in question the analogy does not apply. Al-

---

* In „The Spiritual Origins of Eastern Europe" he also speaks of „Archangels who are i n c a r n a t e d   completely or partially in the earthly bodies of the peoples" (p. 128; emphasis S.O.P).

71

though the human soul is differentiated it lives as a single whole; its parts have no individual being of their own; the Folk-soul, as described by Prokofieff, would be split up into a multiplicity of independent spiritual individualities. Prokofieff speaks of an „infinite multiplicity of soul processes" (ibid., p. 121) in the human being on the one hand, and a multiplicity of angels in the Folk-soul on the other (ibid., p. 122). But how can he compare undefined processes taking place within a single individual being, with the independent angelic spirit beings? This can only apply if the individuality as such is left entirely out of account.

If, for example, large-scale migrations of a population were to take place, then Prokofieff's Folk-spirits would continually have to exchange the members belonging to them. When have human beings ever exchanged amongst themselves parts of their own souls? If the reader reflects on these questions, he will be able himself to find enough arguments to demonstrate the untenability of Prokofieff's analogies.

But Prokofieff also has something of a problem with the archangel of a people. He says: „The totality of the guardian angels of the human beings who belong to the Folk in question [constitutes] as it were a part of the supersensible soul-body of the archangel who guides this Folk" (ibid., p. 120). But, as Rudolf Steiner tells us, some human beings can also have guardian angels of a Luciferic nature. As a result of this, the leading archangel of the Folk would be involuntarily Luciferized, as his soul-body would be permeated by Luciferic spirits. A human being, through the exercise of free-will, can resist the temptation of Lucifer, but the archangel, as distinct from the human being, would come into a difficult position in such a case. As we know, the human being proceeds from one incarnation to the next with the same guardian angel, and once he has incarnated into a given Folk his angel must also be accepted. The archangel cannot dismiss the angel of a human being through a command from above! – So we see that Prokofieff needs to work at this question a bit further. Assuming that, for some reason, migrations to another land by human beings with Luciferic guardian angels were to take place on a larger scale, what consequences would this have for the archangel of that land?

Now some readers will perhaps reply that logic is one thing, but supersensible experience must also be considered. And Prokofieff does indeed appeal to this. He says: „And when their (the guardian angels') united working takes a harmonious course ... then spiritual perception can see the Folk-soul merging into one with the Folk-spirit to some degree, becoming an integral part of it" (ibid., p. 120). From the point of view of content this assertion is an example of what one is not permitted to do and say in Anthroposophy, and also in occultism in general; in this particular instance the statement also has value in that it gives an indication of Prokofieff's „spiritual perception" and of the source of his „knowledge" of the so-called „Folk-soul".

In the following paragraph he repeats what we have just quoted, brings forward the same analogies with the individual human being, and says that, just as in clairvoyant observation the human aura presents the picture of a unity of soul and spirit, so this is also the case with the „angel-soul and the archangel Folk-spirit, which, for the spiritual perception of their combined working, form an indissoluble whole" (ibid.). Here he forgoes the demand for a „special harmony"; there is also no „integral part", but only an „indissoluble whole"; however, the „spiritual perception" is the same, namely Prokofieff's own. He has „perceived" all this „spiritually". This is confirmed by the following words: „Such a picture is presented to the eye of clairvoyance when it beholds these processes more from the standpoint of the archangel as he incarnates into the Folk-soul. From the standpoint of the angels who constitute this (Folk-soul), it appears somewhat different" (ibid., p. 121). To judge by the context, the first sentence of the passage quoted above could refer to an indication of Rudolf Steiner mentioned earlier, which does not, however, confirm in any way Prokofieff's assertion. In the second sentence Prokofieff presumes to correct Rudolf Steiner, through observing these things from his own standpoint, namely that of the angel.

In order not to tire the reader any further with the casuistry of Prokofieff's clairvoyance, we will not, in what follows, take account of his „spiritual perception", which is supposed to lend support to his theory. There are statements of Rudolf Steiner from which one can infer that the Folk-soul is definitely not the totality of the guardian angels of the human beings who constitute a Folk. In the daytime, says Rudolf Steiner, the Folk-soul is united with the human soul. „Every time we fall asleep we leave, as it were, the habitation of the Folk-soul to whom we belong" (27.11.1914, GA 64). „In waking consciousness we exchange our forces with our own Folk-soul" (12.12.1914, GA 156). The relation between the human being and his guardian angel is built up in a contrary way in the rhythm of sleeping and waking. „So long as the human being is awake, the

73

angel is in the lap of ... the higher spiritual beings" (17.7.1921, GA 205). But when the human being leaves his physical and etheric bodies during sleep, he is accompanied by his angel (if the materialistic outlook of the human being concerned does not prevent this). „... The Archangeloi principle is [connected] with the etheric nature, ... the Angeloi principle must as it were accompany the human being from one state to another and back again. This Angeloi principle, this essential being of the Angeloi, must accompany the human being on his way into the sleeping state and on his return from the sleeping state" (ibid.).

Now this should suffice to lead Prokofieff's theory „ad absurdum". In the waking state the Folk-soul is united with the human soul, whilst the angel is resting in the lap of the Hierarchies. Conversely, in sleep the human being leaves the physical and etheric body – the dwelling-place of the Folk-soul – and unites with the angel. Thus the Folk-soul is connected with the physical and etheric body of man, so that the angel cannot be a part of it. The angel works within the human astral body and, in contrast to the Folk-soul, accompanies the human being through sleep. There is yet another interesting and unambiguous statement of Rudolf Steiner regarding the Folk-soul: „The Folk-soul is a real Being, but it has no physical body; its lowest member is the ether-body ... it spreads itself out like a body of mist, and all the ether-bodies of individual human beings of a given Folk are embedded within it, and its forces flow into the ether-bodies of the human individuals" (21.6.1907, GA 100).

3.2. Mental Arithmetic as a Means of Bringing Order into the Angelic Worlds.

How can the spiritual tasks of Middle and Eastern Europe be fulfilled if one is not clear on the question of what the Folk-souls actually are? Prokofieff is accustomed to resolving spiritual-scientific questions speedily and without effort, but here his ideas become unexpectedly complicated. His Folk-soul has grown too many-layered and many-facetted. But things may have grown uncomfortable for the archangel too, as he now possesses a soul-body which consists of a multiplicity of the most varied and continuously changing individualities. As Prokofieff is considering things from the standpoint of the archangel, then from the standpoint of the cosmos, and finally from the standpoint of the spiritual beings who guide humanity, contradictions appear. And in order that no anarchy should arise in the Folk-soul as he has conceived it, he decides to create order in the angelic realm (and thus also in the Folk-soul) through arranging the angels according to various spheres of responsibility or more or less easily surveyable „categories". (Something of this kind was undertaken by Swedenborg, of whom we know that he was the reincarnated Ignatius de Loyola.)

First, he envisages three stages in the evolution of the angels (VII, p. 123). The principle whereby the stages arise – they are categories – is amusing. To the first category belong the angels of „ordinary human beings in all their different gradations" (ibid.). Here Prokofieff ought to have asked himself the question: what, from the standpoint of spiritual science, is the meaning of „ordinary human beings in all their different gradations"? He is doing nothing less than to set up a classification according to rank within the angelic realm! What gradations are meant here? Has it to do with social status, doctor's degree, or military rank? Such concepts have no place in Rudolf Steiner's Anthroposophy.

To the second category belong the angels of „prominent" human beings (ibid., p. 124). And even the concept of a prominent human being is unknown to spiritual science. Though it may deserve mention that Otto Weininger wrote a book entitled „Genius and Mental Confusion"!

To the third category belong, according to Prokofieff, the angels of the Initiates. „Among these most highly-developed angels" – he informs us – „are to be found, for example, the guardian angel of Rudolf Steiner, and also the guardian angels of the other leading initiates of Mankind" (ibid., p. 123). In order that the third category should not coincide with the second (or the first), the Initiates should not be counted among the prominent – and still less among the ordinary – people. That Prokofieff knows so much about the Initiates of humanity should no longer be any cause for surprise.

The question might be asked: what is the value of such an abstract scheme whose concepts are completely lacking in contour? Is the progress made by the human being to be determined, not by himself, by the efforts of his individual 'I', but by the level of his angel in the order of rank set up by Prokofieff? – Or, conversely, is it the case that the angel on the ascending ladder rises higher when the human being entrusted to him has worked his way up from the category of „ordinary" to the category of „prominent" people? What kind of criteria determine whether a human being has become prominent, or whether he is still ordinary? Is it the number of books the person has written, which is the decisive factor, or is it their thickness? In this question Prokofieff gives no concrete recommendations to the heavenly guiding powers, and allows them room – within the framework he provides – to act at their own discretion. In this respect Prokofieff differs from the Catholic clergy, who decide such things themselves, even if the process of deciding may extend over a matter of centuries.

According to Prokofieff the first category of angels is still „at the beginning of its development" (ibid., p. 124), while the angels of the Initiates are preparing „to ascend to the next higher rank, that of the archangels" (ibid.). According to Rudolf Steiner's research into karma, human beings who, in one incarnation have undergone an initiation, do not necessarily incarnate thereafter as „prominent human beings" – to use Prokofieff's expression – but sometimes as „ordinary" ones, because they have to fulfil certain tasks which have no direct connection with their past incarnation. But what happens to the angels? – Are they, after having almost attained the rank of archangel, made to return to the beginning of their development?[*]

Prokofieff says to this: „In individual development, and also in the general historical development of mankind as a whole, these three groups of spirits of the angelic realm correspond a p p r o x i m a t e l y to the developmental stages of sentient-soul, intellectual or mind-soul, and consciousness-soul" (ibid.). One can find no fault with this statement, because it is without content. It arises on the basis of the trivial fact that between two quantities consisting of the same number of elements there exists a numerical correspondence. One can maintain with equal validity that there is a correspondence to these three angelic groups in: head, rhythmic and metabolic system in the human being; Atma, Buddhi, Manas in relation to the human spirit; June, July, August in relation to the summer months of the year. And why the formulation „approximately"? Is an approximation needed when one is counting up to three?

If we consider his last assertion from the aspect of the d e v e l o p m e n t o f t h e i n d i v i d u a l, are we to take it that „ordinary" people develop the sentient soul; the particularly „prominent" ones - such as Goethe and Schiller, through whose work the Folk-spirit was able to speak to human beings (ibid., p. 123) – develop the intellectual soul; and the Initiates the consciousness-soul? According to Rudolf Steiner this is not the case, for the o r d i n a r y h u m a n

---

[*] Here again we remark that it is impossible to work through these things without humour. Let the reader try to imagine how terrible it would be if we were to carry out our analysis with a long face and a deadly serious expression!

b e i n g s of the 3rd post-Atlantean epoch develop the sentient-soul, those of the 4th the intellectual soul, and the ordinary human beings of the 5th epoch develop the consciousness-soul. The Initiates develop still higher members.

Let us now try to examine the above statement from the aspect of the „historical development of mankind as a whole" (ibid., p. 124). When Prokofieff maintains that the three post-Atlantean epochs in question correspond to his three angelic groups, to whom (or what) do the 1st, 2nd, 6th and 7th post-Atlantean epochs correspond? If there are correspondences between the epochs of human development and the g r o u p s within the Hierarchies, then a certain lawful structure is to be expected in these correspondences, and all the Hierarchies of an epoch should be assigned their place. But this is not the case.

We conclude that Prokofieff's attempt to introduce a new order in the angelic world is unsuccessful. Pursuing the investigation still further one realizes that, within the second category, there is yet another second category, consisting of angels „who are not the guardian angels of individual human beings" (ibid.). This second s e c o n d c a t e g o r y is again divided into three categories: messengers, leaders of (human) communities (ibid.) and – let us call them for brevity's sake – „Folk-Gods". Thus we have as a third s e c o n d c a t e - g o r y : the angels of the communities. So as not to tire the reader with the verbal, hair-splitting account of Prokofieff's categories, we will attempt to bring order into his categories by means of a diagram:

THE ANGELS

First Category: GUARDIAN ANGELS

1st Category	2nd Category	3rd Category
Angels of ordinary human beings	Angels of prominent human beings	Angels of Initiates

Second Category: ALL OTHER ANGELS

1st Category	2nd Category	3rd Category
Messengers	Leaders of Communities	„Folk-Gods"

How many categories of angels has Prokofieff „found" altogether? His answer is: seven, for he says: „in all the s e v e n angelic categories described ..." (ibid., p. 125).

Is he leaving out the larger „categories" and counting only the small ones into which they are divided? But there are only six. What ought to be included as the seventh category he calls, not category, but „group". This consists of beings who actually „belong to the hierarchy of archangels"! Thus the seventh group of angels consists of those archangels who are „willing in a spirit of sacrifice to work in the spiritual world bordering on the Earth, on the same level as the angels" (ibid., p. 124). Consequently the angelic realm in Prokofieff's scheme is divided into six (small) „categories" of angels and a „group" of archangels – not into seven categories of angels.

Let us see what he understands by the remaining approximately three or four (or whatever is needed to bring them up to the number seven) categories of angels: „The angel-messengers carry out the instructions of a Folk-spirit in relation to various human beings belonging to the Folk" (ibid.) – i.e. they are something like cosmic postmen. Or could the guardian angels also take on this task, perhaps? Why does the separate institution of angelic messengers need to be set up? Rudolf Steiner does not mention them. He says only that the angels have an affinity with the human soul-life, because they are „engaged in the transformation of their astral body into Manas ... but have not yet completed this work. The human being stands at the beginning of this work ... Thus they understand fully all that the human personality can experience through sorrow and joy" (9.6.1910, GA 121). And this applies to the angels in general, not only to a special group. But as the angels also reach up with their consciousness to the sphere of the archangels they serve as mediators between the human being and the Folk-spirit: „They receive the instructions of the Folk-spirits" – says Rudolf Steiner – „and carry them into the individual souls ..." (ibid.). Nowhere does he speak of a division according to which some angels serve only as messengers, and the others as guardian angels.

To the third „second category" of angels in Prokofieff's system belong the „leaders or 'group-souls' of individual human communities or associations w i t h i n the sphere of activity of a given Folk-archangel" (VIII, p. 124; emphasis S.O.P.). The regular angels work together with individualities, and it is their task to work with the aim of individualizing. The angel-being works in the astral body of the human being; if the angel were to work as a group-spirit, this would give him the possibility of working for the development of group-soul qualities, thereby creating a dominance of the group-soul consciousness in relation to the individual. However, this would conflict with the task of our epoch. Only the Luciferic angels work in this way. Are they the ones Prokofieff meant, perhaps?

To work with groups is the task of the archangels, whose sphere of activity is the human etheric body. In our time only the retarded spirits are concerned with the development of the group-soul nature. (There are exceptions; but one would have to deal with these separately, and they are unrelated to Prokofieff's theme.)

To a further third category in Prokofieff's system belong „those angels whose working reaches across the boundaries of the sphere of activity of a Folk" (ibid.). From spiritual science, however, we know that we have here to do with neither angels nor archangels, but with Archai. What kind of activity does Prokofieff ascribe to the „angels"? He says: „These angels bring about the connection between the various peoples on the level of the angels" (ibid.). What could the meaning of this be? „On the human level" connections of this kind are realized through diplomatic representatives – i.e. through embassies. Perhaps „embassies", modelled on the earthly ones, arise also in the angelic realm, and Prokofieff's angels of the third category are appointed as their staff?

We arrive at an interesting observation if we compare these „calculations" of Prokofieff with what he says about himself in the book „The Spiritual Tasks of Middle and Eastern Europe". In the Foreword he says: „The book can [also be regarded] as a task assigned to me by Destiny, which has made me into a mediator between two peoples. The mutual understanding of these peoples I see therefore as one of my most important tasks" (p. 12). Here one would wish to ask Prokofieff: Would it not have been simpler to say quite straightforwardly – „My guardian angel is not just an angel like other people's (the ordinary, the prominent, and the initiated), but an angel of the (second) third category, whose activity reaches across the boundary of a people – in other words, an Archai"? Indeed, something comparable to this regarding his relation to the Spirit of the Age, Michael, was already expressed in his autobiographical essay (cf. § 1.2.).

Might there not, we ask, in addition to Prokofieff's personal „Archai-guardian-spirit", also exist other „angels" of this kind? Yes, of course. And Prokofieff tells us about them: „To this group belong many of the gods, known to us in the different mythologies, who were revered by various peoples in antiquity. (Thus the Egyptian god Thoth was revered in Greece as Hermes and in Rome as Mercury" (VIII, p. 124). We gather from this that one and the same Being was known in Egypt as Thoth, in Greece as Hermes, and in Rome as Mercury, i.e. this Being „brought about the connection between the various peoples", and does so to this day. According to Rudolf Steiner, Hermes – or Thoth, as the Egyptians called him – was an individuality who was once a pupil of Zarathustra, and received from him the Sun Wisdom and the power of judgment, and later appeared in the realm of science. Thereafter this pupil appeared in the astral body sacrificed by his teacher, as Hermes, the great teacher and sage of the Egyptian Mysteries (cf. 15.2.1909, GA 109 and 2.9.1910, GA 123). That Hermes is an angel who brings about the connection between peoples – of this Rudolf Steiner said nothing, it was „discovered" by Prokofieff. But Rudolf Steiner did speak in unmistakable terms about the hierarchical Being who in the ancient religions was also known as Hermes or Mercury (cf. 4.1.1918, GA 180). He says: „The god Mercury is an Archangelic being" (1.6.1924, GA 236).

Thus Prokofieff's scheme of the angelic realm has, on closer inspection, dissolved into nothing.

3.3. From Arithmetic to Algebra. The Spiritual Beings as Variable Quantities.

The spiritual world as it is described by Rudolf Steiner presents considerable difficulty to anyone who wishes to grasp it with a simplistically dogmatic and schematic understanding. There are spirit beings who express themselves through other beings; relationships reproduce themselves in different forms on different levels of the Hierarchies; the one serves as a model for much else through undergoing metamorphosis and appearing under various aspects on various evolutionary stages of world-being. The manifoldness of revelation is brought about through the activity of individual spirit-beings who are as original and concrete as the human beings living on the Earth; for the spirit-world is neither simpler nor poorer in content than the earthly world. But the latter has congealed into sharply outlined material forms, and can on no account be forced into a definitive series of easily surveyable abstract schemes.

In contrast to the spiritual world, the way in which phenomena are perceived in the physical world ensures the permanent correction of schematic and incorrect representations of it. The spiritual world is revealed to the human being only in conceptual form unless, as in the case of Rudolf Steiner, he has it before his inner eye as an immediately perceptible reality. In order to be able to grasp this in its full complexity the human being must, on the one hand, attain the faculty of inner beholding and, on the other – so as to be able to apprehend correctly what is beheld – carry through concentrated work in his thinking, achieving thereby a shifting of the boundaries of understanding and consciousness to the level of inspiration.* The thought-forms in which the picture of the spiritual world appears leaves one free, and thus there are also paths of minimal resistance, corresponding to the innate forces of understanding. In such a case the human being remains within his everyday associative thinking which only provides the basis for the attainment of this (picture of the spiritual world – Trans.). We will illustrate by means of the following example how this works out in practice.

In Rudolf Steiner's lectures there are indications regarding the Bodhisattvas, individualities who have a significant „head start" in advance of general human evolution, and incarnate on the Earth in accordance with certain laws, but not by stereotype. There are also communications of Rudolf Steiner concerning the Masters of Wisdom and Harmony of Sentiments (Meister der Weisheit und des Zusammenklangs der Empfindungen), who are united in the White Lodge of the leadership of mankind. In the description of these there is a certain similarity, a parallelism, but there are also important differences. In the present book we are not able to examine this more closely, and instead refer the interested reader to the relevant lectures of Rudolf Steiner.† Here we wish only to show how Prokofieff deals with this question.

---

* „The only thing that I can ascribe to myself is that I have gone through a rigorous training thanks to which I cannot succumb to the fantastic in any way. This was obligatory for me. For, what I experience in spiritual realms is thereby free from all illusion, from all deception, from all superstition … I know how to distinguish between truth and illusion" (Rudolf Steiner to Elisa von Moltke on 12.8.1904 – Ed.).

† Especially the lectures of: 31.8.1909 (GA 113); 25.10.1909 (GA 116); 17.9.1912 (GA 130); and GA 264, pp. 201-205.

In his first publication Prokofieff, citing Rudolf Steiner, comes to the over-hasty conclusion that in the Lodge of the Twelve whose teacher appears as the thirteenth, the Masters of Wisdom and The Harmony of Sentiments – a r e the Bodhisattvas (I, p. 73). To which it must be said that not everything that is analogous is identical – a truth apparently not grasped by Prokofieff. It can also be said of the disciples of Christ that, as the Twelve, they surrounded their Teacher as the thirteenth. Does this mean that they were the same persons (including Judas)?

In the attempt to justify his standpoint Prokofieff says: „Even the name 'Masters of Wisdom and Harmony of Sentiments' expresses this, for the true 'Harmony of Sentiments' – sentiment (feeling) is connected above all with the astral body – is only possible when the latter, as is the case with the Bodhi-sattva, has been transformed into Spirit-self" (ibid.). This „proof" does not stand up to criticism. For what does one prove by saying, firstly, „sentiment (feeling) is connected above all with the astral body"? One could infer from this that the plant does not, while the animal does, have feelings. And what would we gain from this play of associations? And, secondly, what is the meaning of the statement: „the true 'Harmony of Sentiments' is only possible when the as-tral body has been changed into the Spirit-self"? – Here we have the purest ab-stractions. Prokofieff would have to explain what he understands by the 'Har-mony of Sentiments' and how this is related to the Spirit-self; or what the dif-ference is between an u n t r u e harmony of sentiments and the true one. And thirdly, how does he know that in the case of the Bodhisattvas the transforma-tion of the astral body into the Spirit-self takes place? Prokofieff refers to p. 70 of his book (I), where he states that the Bodhisattva is only working with the angels at the transformation of his astral body into Spirit-self, and that he would only accomplish the full development of the Spirit-self in his final earthly in-carnation – i.e. when he ascends to the rank of Buddha. On the other hand, Pro-kofieff tells us that „the true 'Harmony of Sentiments'" is only possible when the astral body „has been transformed into the Spirit-self" (ibid., p. 73), at the Buddha and not the Bodhisattva stage, therefore! But in this case how could the Bodhisattvas be at the same time the „Masters of Wisdom and Harmony of Sentiments"? That such is indeed the case Prokofieff concludes from Rudolf Steiner's lecture of 20.5.1913 (GA 152), where it says that the angel attains freedom when the human being rises from Bodhisattva to Buddha. But this very argument ruins his „demonstration". Because this would mean that only the

3. The Spiritual World and its Beings in the View of S. Prokofieff

Buddha knows the „true Harmony of Sentiments", while the Bodhisattva, whose Spirit-self is not yet developed, is not endowed with this, and can therefore not be called „Master of Wisdom and the Harmony of Sentiments". Prokofieff refutes himself.

He seems to have noticed this himself, and tries now to extricate himself from this awkward position by concluding his „demonstration" in the following way: „It needs to be stressed in connection with what has been said, that in addition to the [highest and most fundamental] definition (thought up by himself) of the 'Masters of Wisdom and the Harmony of Sentiments' as the College of Bodhisattvas in the sphere of Providence, there are yet other great teachers of humanity (this is therefore the 'lower' and 'secondary' definition!) who can be called 'Masters of Wisdom and the Harmony of Sentiments' [in Christian esotericism]. For they too are inspired from this sphere and have a direct relation to it" (I, p. 74 [p. 86]. Here Prokofieff raises himself above the whole of Christian esotericism and shows what little regard he has for the reality of those he names 'Masters of Wisdom and the Harmony of Sentiments'. For if we have here to do with real individualities, then there can only be the definition of the reality, regardless of whether it is a „higher" or a „lower". Identifications of this (Prokofieff's) kind are normal in abstract algebra - they are what is known as „isomorphisms", where only the number of elements composing a quantity is taken into account, and the structure of their interrelationships, the „individuality" of the element being completely absent. In Anthroposophy we are concerned above all with individualities and not with relations, abstract structures and numbers. But for Prokofieff there appear to be no individualities. He treats the names of the spiritual beings as variable quantities which can, according to need, be made to mean all kinds of things through the attaching to them of the appropriate d e f i n i t i o n s . And, as he states in his „Autobiography", everything that Rudolf Steiner says about the Bodhisattvas was „already known" to him, only he „had not until then been able to express it in thoughts" ("My Path …", p. 85).

The situation appears still worse when he is speaking of the „Group-soul" of the Anthroposophical Society. This „variable" is assigned an endless variety of different meanings, which is particularly scandalous considering that the theme in question is the Christmas Conference, which he has chosen as the main emphasis of his life's work.

In his first book he says: „Just as [in evolution] the single 'I' of the individual human being is only ignited through contact with the physical plane, so also the esoteric essential being of Anthroposophy [the Being of Anthroposophy itself], its 'I', was only able to enter fully into earthly development when the Anthroposophical-Michaelic impulses had, at the Christmas Conference, united themselves completely with the earthly world, when the Anthroposophical movement and the Anthroposophical Society had become one. At that moment, in the 21st year of the life of the movement (from 1902-1923), the G r o u p - 'I' of the new community of Michaelites was truly [actually] b o r n . The birth of the new Group-'I' of the Michaelites as the spiritual foundation of their community is … [the profoundest mystery] of the Christmas Conference … If we ask ourselves: Which B e i n g can we bring into connection with what was here called the Group-'I'? Then the answer must be: This Group-'I' [is the leading Time-spirit of our age – Michael himself]" (I, p. 346, [p. 381-382]; emphasis S.O.P.). From this the following conclusion is to be drawn: Firstly, Michael would then be the esoteric essential Being, the 'I' of Anthroposophy, so that even the Being of Anthroposophy itself would be none other than Michael, which means that Anthroposophy is neither spiritual science nor anything else, but simply the l e a d i n g S p i r i t o f t h e A g e .

Secondly, it follows from what is said, that Michael was only able to enter fully into earthly development as the esoteric essential Being of Anthroposophy by virtue of the Christmas Conference. However, the present Michael epoch did not begin in 1924, but in 1879, nor is it the first. In addition we know from Rudolf Steiner's communications, of numerous cases of concrete Michael r e v e l a t i o n s in Earth development, which took place long before the Christmas Conference. But – did he perhaps not reveal himself c o m - p l e t e l y ? Unfortunately, Prokofieff does not let us know what he means by c o m p l e t e l y in this case.

If, thirdly, the esoteric essential core of Anthroposophy only came to full expression after the Christmas Conference, then what did Rudolf Steiner develop up to that point in time? Was it neither a h i g h e s t nor a f u n d a - m e n t a l Anthroposophy, but perhaps no Anthroposophy at all, since it had no esoteric central core, and true Anthroposophy only began with the Christmas Conference? We recall Prokofieff's words in his autobiographical essay: „After the Christmas Conference … everything becomes different … in the Anthroposophical movement" (cf. § 1.2.). If someone were to believe, in contrast to this, that the Anthroposophy developed by Rudolf Steiner before the Christmas Conference was the genuine thing, then he would have at the same time to acknowledge that at the Christmas Conference Anthroposophy had come to an end. For Rudolf Steiner did not say that Michael was the Group-'I' of the Anthroposophical Society, which in the passage quoted above is described by Prokofieff as the Michael community.

Let us now turn our attention to the question of the Group-soul of the Anthroposophical Society, and not be confused by the fact that, in the fragment quoted, Prokofieff calls it the Group-'I'. Both terms are familiar to us and are basically the same because, when occultism speaks of Group-soul, it is pointing to a concrete Spirit-being who has an individual 'I', and not an abstract s o u l. But with Prokofieff the whole thing drifts into the abstract again, as he asserts that Michael is this Group-soul; in other places he tries to assign this role to other Beings.

In „The Occult Significance of Forgiveness" (V) we read the following: „This 'Good Spirit of the Goetheanum' ought more and more to become a kind of (?) 'Group-soul' of the General Anthroposophical Society ... In the physically visible Goetheanum ... the visible expression of the Being of Anthroposophy itself", etc. (V, p. 165). As we have already explained, this „actual" Being of Anthroposophy is Michael himself. From this we infer that the Goetheanum is the visible expression of Michael. And if we take into account what has been said above, then it is he who at the Christmas Conference became the Group-soul of the Anthroposophical Society. In the eyes of Prokofieff, are Michael and the Spirit of the Goetheanum one and the same Being? Is the Goetheanum the visible expression of Michael? - But why should it become more and more a Group-soul? And if they are two different Beings, does this mean that the Anthroposophical Society will have two Group-souls, or that Michael's post will be taken over by the Spirit of the Goetheanum?

Let us try to state clearly what Prokofieff understands by the „Spirit of the Goetheanum". This will be no easy task. (It is always the first Goetheanum that is meant.)

In his book „The 12 Holy Nights and the Spiritual Hierarchies" (III) Prokofieff says: „This etheric development consisting of three successive steps, and the 'four soul qualities' which support this, were embodied in the forms, the painting, and the architecture of the first Goetheanum." He then goes on to speak of the Goetheanum as the „artistic revelation (objectification) – of initiation processes, which are connected to the ether-body of the human being." The Goetheanum appears, in this instance, not to be „the visible expression of the Being Anthroposophy", but „stages, qualities and processes". He continues: „This spiritual Goetheanum (which every human being can himself build up within his ether-body through developing the lotus-flowers) will bear him (the human being) into the worlds of the Cosmos, into the widths of etheric space, and up into that sphere where in the present time the 'macrocosmic Goetheanum' or the 'Spirit of the Goetheanum' is to be found, of which Rudolf Steiner spoke at the conclusion of the Christmas Conference" (p. 134-135).*

We will not linger to consider this remarkably abstract and arbitrary idea of Prokofieff's, which describes the three higher lotus-flowers of the etheric body as the „spiritual Goetheanum". Essential for us is the fact that, according to the statement in this book (III), the „spirit of the Goetheanum" is to be found in the widths of the Cosmos, did not therefore i n c a r n a t e at the Christmas Conference, and did not become the G r o u p - s o u l of the Anthroposophical Society; that conceivably it has no intention of doing so although, according to the passage in another book (cf. quote from given above: V, p. 165), it o u g h t to do so.

Let us now return to „… The Founding of the New Mysteries" (I), where Prokofieff says: „The Goetheanum shows us the picture of the human being in his eternal and divine aspect … The Goetheanum [is also] the true home of the 'Anthropos-Sophia', where the wisdom of man, born of the Holy Spirit, where this cosmic wisdom became for the first time visible also to earthly human eyes on the physical plane" (I, p. 156). Why „for the first time"? Were not all the temples and cultic centres of the past a visible expression of „cosmic wisdom"? Prokofieff tenaciously reiterates his (presumably h i g h e s t a n d m o s t f u n d a m e n t a l) definition of Anthroposophy as „the wisdom of man, born of the Holy Spirit". And what could be the meaning of: „the human being in his eternal and divine aspect"? On p. 163 (ibid.) he says that „the soul of the Nathan Jesus … the ideal, cosmic archetype of the human soul' is „the archetype of all mankind". Then who is actually the „Spirit of the Goetheanum" and the

---

* The chapter „The Building of the Inner Goetheanum as a Path to the Experiencing of the Etheric Christ", from which the quote is taken, is missing from the German translation available to us – Editor.

3. The Spiritual World and its Beings in the View of S. Prokofieff

„Group-soul of the Anthroposophical Society"? – The Nathan Soul? Or Michael? Or Anthroposophy (in the one or the other sense of this word)? On p. 157 (ibid.) we read: „Living, etheric divine Word, revealing itself in physical form, ... such was the first Goetheanum. It was the embodiment of Anthroposophy itself." – Now we will have to add to our list: „etheric divine Word".

Of the Goetheanum Prokofieff writes „that it was itself a living Being" (ibid., p. 158). What happened to it when it was burned down? - From Prokofieff we learn that „after it had, like a living Being, gone through the process of death and disembodiment [it] revealed itself during the Christmas Conference as a purely spiritual reality, as the S p i r i t   o f   t h e   G o e t h e a n u m" (ibid., p. 164; emphasis S.O.P.). Who was it who went through incarnation in the forms of the Goetheanum, through death, and resurrection at the Christmas Conference? – Michael? – the Nathan Soul? – or perhaps – the p r o c e s s e s o f   i n i t i a t i o n ?

Finally, Prokofieff himself grows tired of this chaos; he recognizes in it „a highly significant problem", and asks the question: „What is this 'resurrected Goetheanum' for us now? What is the meaning of the 'Spirit of the Goetheanum'? What will its significance be for the further development of the Anthroposophical movement and the Anthroposophical Society?" (ibid., p. 165). But his answer confuses the issue still further: „We have in the Goetheanum the f i r s t great Michael revelation, made visible to the physical eye of the human being ... The divine Word ... 'became flesh' in full reality in the forms of the Goetheanum ..." and „when within the fire-element it went through the solemn act 'of transsubstantiation in the great Temple of the Cosmos (?) [it became] pure spirit, the spirit of the Goetheanum ... it passed over, in agreement with world Karma, into the great Temple of the Cosmos, identifying itself with it, and thereby became the archetype of the s e c o n d great Michael revelation ... the archetype of the true communion, the 'beginning of the cosmic cultus which is appropriate for present-day humanity'" (ibid., p. 168; emphasis S.O.P.). Where do we stand now? Did it become the Group-soul of the Anthroposophical Society? – Or o u g h t this still to happen i n   t h e f u t u r e ? What about the first or second Michael revelation? – What about Michael himself, the Nathan Soul, and the Divine Word itself?

With this guided tour through the labyrinth of Prokofieff's demagogy we have tried to highlight the unintelligibility of his rhetoric. But there is still more to come, in the shape of the conclusive, depressing formulation of his theory of the S p i r i t   o f   t h e   G o e t h e a n u m   and of the emergent Group-soul of the Anthroposophical Society.

„Rudolf Steiner" – he states – „engages intensively in a profound study of the results of contemporary science. Then as an Initiate he bears them up to the gods in the Cosmos, and receives this knowledge of modern science – transformed into the language of the gods – back from them in the form of the world wisdom … He then endows this divine wisdom with a bodily sheath in the imaginative forms of the Goetheanum … ; during the fire these forms pass through the substance of the warmth-ether and return to the astral light, expanding then into remote regions of the Cosmos … From thence Rudolf Steiner receives them again, but now as the sublime divine Word, as the living Spirit of the Goetheanum as it returns transformed out of the depths of the Cosmos" (ibid., p. 211).

Thus the „knowledge of modern science", which has undergone transformation in the way described, ought   m o r e   a n d   m o r e   t o   b e c o m e   the Group-soul of the Anthroposophical Society … – Healthy common-sense has nothing more to say.

3.4. Occult Materialism Makes its Début in Anthroposophy

The epoch of the consciousness-soul had of necessity to become the epoch of materialism, as a right development of individual 'I'-consciousness needs the support of sense-experience and knowledge of the laws of the material world. In Prokofieff's view of things the epoch of materialism is already nearing its end, as we showed in 3.3. Since the end of Kali-Yuga and especially since the Christmas Conference a victory of universal spiritualization ought to have begun, many details of which he describes in Chap. 7 of his first book (I). And in our time, so he mentions in a later book (V), the whole of mankind stands on the   t h r e s h o l d   b e t w e e n   c o n s c i o u s n e s s - s o u l   a n d   S p i r i t - S e l f   (p. 124), so that the end of materialism is imminent.

But what is the reality of the situation? Rudolf Steiner warns us: The materialistic outlook is on the increase and will continue to grow for a further four or five centuries (18.11.1917, GA 178). The spirits who inspire materialism have altered neither their intentions nor their strategies, but only their tactics. They no longer deny the spirit, but attempt to present it to the world with concepts and pictures taken from physical reality. In this way a kind of world-view arises, which explains everything, including the spirit, with the technical terms „matter" and „energy". Among such pseudo-scientific occult-materialistic streams we may count parapsychology, Ufology, extra-sensory research etc., which speak of abstract, energetic processes, forces, fields, substances of the spiritual world, and represent these according to the model of the phenomena of the physical world.

That Prokofieff too is aware of this can be seen in his later writings. But, for him, even this knowledge remains an abstraction. He polemicizes against such occult streams and unmasks their occult materialism, but he succumbs, himself, to their influence. His materialistic conceptions of the spiritual world are hidden behind concepts which he borrows from spiritual science.

The first symptom of the infection can be seen in the way Prokofieff operates, as we have described, with the conceptions of spiritual beings, who appear in the role of nomenclature abstractions after the model of earthly „ministries and official bodies".

His altered concept of the Folk-soul, which now, instead of the archangels, comprises the numerical totality of angels, and his explanation of the manifoldness of such a soul by means of analogies with the processes and attributes of the human soul, call to mind the following words of Rudolf Steiner: „If, as a spiritual scientist today, you tell people that there is a Folk-soul which is an archangel, and so on, then they ridicule you. What in materialism is spoken of as the Folk-soul is only the abstract aggregate of the qualities possessed by the members of a Folk" (18.5.1915, GA 159). With his theory, Prokofieff builds a firmly-constructed bridge between spiritual science and materialism, which he is the first to cross.

In Prokofieff's books there is a progressive de-personalizing of the spiritual world; instead of concrete spiritual beings we find mostly nameless p o w e r s . Thus in the „Spiritual Origins of Eastern Europe ..."(IV) he speaks in the course of a very long chapter - repeatedly, not just in passing, but as an essential theme - of the „spiritual-divine powers, who guide earthly development" (p. 373); of „higher powers which direct the karmic relationships of human beings" (ibid., p. 379); of the „higher guiding powers of earthly development" (ibid., p. 383), etc. Nowhere does he tell us what he understands by these powers. In this way his argumentation is neither spiritual-scientific nor religious, for even theologians refer by name to the Beings of whom they speak.

The reference made by Prokofieff in the same connection, to „levels of metahistorical reality" - of which we will speak later (§ 6) – belongs in the same category. On these „levels" there are neither archangels nor Folk-spirits, nor is there a Time-spirit – there are no spiritual personalities at all; he describes only „powers", and „all-encompassing laws" (admittedly also „karmic undercurrents"), as in a well-designed mechanism. In Chap. 9 of the same book there suddenly appears an „inexhaustible source of the cosmic forces of child-hood and eternal youth, in whose lap are contained all the great possibilities of the future" (IV, p. 60). Is there concealed behind all this, perhaps, a star in the cosmos, which radiates these rejuvenating energies and a light-filled future?

In the book „The Occult Significance of Forgiveness" (V) Prokofieff exhibits his materialistic thinking even more plainly. There he attempts to describe the „occult mechanism of forgiveness" (p. 58), which works as follows: „By dint of the effort made by the moral will springing from the individual 'I' ... there are formed in the unbroken memory-stream permeating our 'I' and bearing our 'I'-consciousness (?), 'spaces which are free of memory', as it were, into which the substance [with the power to transform all evil], of the higher 'I' or Spirit-self, can pour itself. And this Spirit-self substance is borne further on the stream of memory, which carries it into the human 'I', transforming and spiritualizing it" (ibid. [p. 46-47]).

How such a theory can arise, it is difficult to say. Out of the free play of fantasy, perhaps, or out of the chimera of an atavistic clairvoyance? The description can easily remind one of a production-line. What could be meant by this „memory-stream"? At the beginning of the chapter in question Prokofieff makes reference to Chap. 2 of „Occult Science", where it says that the human 'I' has the faculty of memory. There is no mention of any kind of „memory-stream". Then Prokofieff goes on to say: „Having acquainted ourselves with this introductory thought, we can now consider the process of forgiveness from the standpoint of modern spiritual science" (ibid., p. 54). And here we now find this „memory-stream", of which the „old" spiritual science of Rudolf Steiner knew nothing, but which has only been revealed through today's „modernized" spiritual science of Prokofieff.

3. The Spiritual World and its Beings in the View of S. Prokofieff

With some effort we have succeeded all the same in finding the source from which Prokofieff probably drew, unconsciously, or without a clear understanding of what is being said. In the lecture of 4.11.1910 Rudolf Steiner describes the 'I'-development of the child, and says that when the 'I' starts to become aware of inner representations (Vorstellungen), „the 'I' must unite itself with the on-flowing stream, with that which we have called the ether-body ... At the moment when the child begins to develop its 'I'-consciousness, the stream of the soul-life has made an imprint of its own upon the ether-body. But the 'I'-representation (Vorstellung) also arises through this process ... The child, before it has the 'I'-representation [is] unable to sense its own ether-body; at the moment when it begins to develop 'I'-consciousness it senses its ether-body and mirrors back into the 'I' the being of its own ether-body ... This is the essential feature of 'I'-consciousness, that it is the ether-body reflecting itself inwards" (GA 115). In this way the memory of experienced events comes about.

Prokofieff makes no reference to this lecture. Although similar expressions are used in it, it is precisely this passage which shows the untenability of Prokofieff's constructions. – He asserts that the 'I' through an effort of the moral will arising from the individual 'I' has to make a small hole in the ether-body! For manipulations of this kind, at least a developed Life-spirit is necessary. And it will not succeed automatically in implanting the Spirit-self substance in this little opening: the Spirit-self has a substantial affinity with the astral body and not the ether-body.

The reader will have no difficulty recognizing the difference between these descriptions. Rudolf Steiner's is concrete, living, graspable as a whole, and the theme is the movement in the ether-body. In Prokofieff's we find nothing but abstractions. Whence and whither h i s stream flows, in what relation it stands to the supersensible members of man's being, whether it belongs at all to one of these members, or flows from e t e r n i t y t o e t e r n i t y – Prokofieff is silent on this; but his s t r e a m carries the 'I'-consciousness, and might carry it off completely. What is his stream composed of? Memory-substance, perhaps? And what might that be? From his description it grows clear, that it flows in and out through the 'I' (like the blood through the heart?). And then this 'I', through an effort of the will, makes a little opening somewhere in the stream, and lets the Spirit-self substance flow into the person concerned. All this happens w i t h o u t c o n t a c t w i t h t h e ' I ' , because, as we gather from the quote, the Spirit-self substance is c a r r i e d f u r t h e r by the memory-stream, and only afterwards does it pass over into the 'I'. We ask the following: Can the 'I'-consciousness, which b e a r s t h e s t r e a m, exist somewhere outside the 'I'? And who is that mysterious benefactor who watches on the bank of the stream and pours the healing substance into the opening just at the moment of its appearance? Prokofieff gives no precise indications. Presumably the whole thing proceeds with the movement of a well-functioning conveyor-belt – fully automated.

And as the process of forgiveness advances, the memory-stream receives „mending-patches" from the Spirit-self. This Spirit-self substance is borne by the stream into the 'I', which is thereby transformed. - Interesting! At the present stage of evolution the human being possesses only a germ of the Spirit-self, which begins to unfold as soon as the 'I' works upon the astral body. According to Rudolf Steiner the Spirit-self is the astral body transformed by the 'I'. In Prokofieff's theory the opposite occurs: the Spirit-self works upon the 'I'. But where does this Spirit-self come from? Is it the Spirit-self of the human guardian angel? If so, the guardian angel should let all the more Spirit-self substance flow into the human being, the more he forgives. This could become difficult for the angel, as his Spirit-self is involved in a process of development which will only culminate at the end of the Earth aeon. Rudolf Steiner says that for the creation of Saturn the spirits of will sacrificed of their substance; that on the Moon e.g. the spirits of movement let the astral body flow out of their being into the human being; and that on the Earth the spirits of form endowed him with the 'I'. It is not conceivable that Rudolf Steiner should have said that on the Earth the angels implanted the Spirit-self in man. In the 6th post-Atlantean period the angel will o v e r s h a d o w the human being with the Spirit-self, but even then it will not become his own possession. In connection with Prokofieff's view of evolution according to which the human beings on the Earth develop the Spirit-self, no further commentary is really necessary.

And yet the question still remains: when and how did Prokofieff see all this? In the electronic calculating machine such a thing is possible, when in the working process of a programme of any kind the content of the memory-cells is erased, and into the „spaces free of memory" new data are fed in, and all this is guided by a h i g h e r programme-system. Anyone who is familiar with these things is amazed at the similarity between Prokofieff's o c c u l t p r o c e s s e s and what is known from the world of technology.

3. The Spiritual World and its Beings in the View of S. Prokofieff

Prokofieff fabricates false pictures of the spiritual world. His listeners, having no supersensible experience of their own, rashly open their consciousness to materialistic imaginations of this kind, which are of the same nature as those with which Lucifer and Ahriman are building up the eighth sphere. To recognize such false teaching n o   s u p e r s e n s i b l e   e x p e r i e n c e   i s   r e - q u i r e d ; it is enough to study systematically, and understand, what Rudolf Steiner has given. The task of Anthroposophy can only be the attainment of objective knowledge of the spiritual world, and not some kind of   e x p e r i e n c e acquired by chance. Today a great deal can sound Anthroposophical, although it may come from a quite different source. The danger that threatens us from the camp of the occult materialists and their inspirers is great indeed. If we do not develop the capacity to counter these „viruses" from the   e i g h t h s p h e r e   – which can mutate to suit every taste – with clear insight into their true nature, an insight which stems not from atavistic experience but from a conscientious study of spiritual science, then Anthroposophy will before long become a tool of those spirits whose goal it is „to make the physical plane absolutely dominant. And a spiritual world will be spoken of only insofar as the revelations of the physical plane require it" (15.1.1917, GA 174).

4. Prokofieff as Propagandist and Teacher of Morals

Man is something
That must be overcome
F. Nietzsche: *Thus Spake Zarathustra*

4.1. A Few Instructive Generalizations

There is nothing accidental about Prokofieff's errors; only at first sight does it appear that we are dealing with a multiplicity of false assertions scattered in a chaotic way. In fact they all share in a single, deeply unified tendency. His „teaching" has a single „stem", from which the „shoots" of his conceptions reach out on all sides. The „stem" is more or less concealed behind these „shoots", but not so completely that it is quite unrecognisable. It becomes most clearly visible in his conception of the evolution of the human being; the „stem" has its „roots" in the „Autobiography" of Prokofieff, and whoever has not succumbed to intoxication by the phrases and the hymns to Prokofieff's own person will have no difficulty finding these „roots".

From this „Autobiography" we learn that Prokofieff began already in his youth to study Anthroposophy; at a time therefore, when he had gathered no life-experience. Already then he started to do esoteric exercises, without first awaiting the development of his own astral body. If at first it was his youthful age, then it was later his lack of interest that led him to ignore o n e element that has absolute priority for every human being of the 5th cultural epoch: the elaboration of an ordered thinking consciousness. Rudolf Steiner's writing on the theory of knowledge, which provides the foundation for an understanding of the individual 'I'-being and the individual freedom of the human being, remained outside the scope of his interests.

Among the works of Rudolf Steiner that made an „impression" on him the „Philosophy of Freedom" receives no mention. Moreover, in his later activity as lecturer and author (this we will return to in Ch. 7), he was at no little pains to show that these works of Rudolf Steiner were not at all necessary, that in writing them he was merely making a sacrifice in order to fulfil the task of others, and had therefore to postpone his own. And, finally, we can also conclude from Prokofieff's autobiographical essay, that he was able to come to supersensible experiences without a meeting with the Guardian of the Threshold. This meeting is, however, the precondition for a rightful entry of the human being into the spiritual worlds, and for his learning to distinguish what arises from his own being, from that which comes to meet him from without; in other words, for his being able to distinguish 'I' from not-'I' in the spiritual worlds.

The human being did not possess an individual 'I' from the very beginning; its genesis within the three-membered soul requires the entire Earth-aeon. In the present phase of development the human being must unfold his 'I' through active and purposeful effort, and develop the faculty of self-consciousness, the central point of the human 'I'. If this grows weak, the human being loses himself to retarded beings who strive to bring him under their influence. If the human being carries out exercises for the attainment of supersensible faculties without first strengthening his 'I'-consciousness, then he allows these beings entry into his soul.

The human being can attain individual, object-directed 'I'-consciousness only by virtue of his physical incarnation. Thus if a person has no interest in the facts and objects of the surrounding world – that which only life-experience can provide – he will in addition be unable to develop a healthy thinking, and will thereby neglect his own 'I'-development. From the spiritual world of pre-birth experience, of which he retained indistinct and half-consciousness memories, Prokofieff proceeded directly to supersensible occult experience. He started to practise at the age when the astral body is being developed, and soon after acquired a clairvoyance which opened up the spiritual world to him, not out of the 'I'-forces, but out of those of the astral body – which means that his clairvoyance is of an atavistic kind that is inappropriate in our time. (See Rudolf Steiner's lecture of 6.12.1920, GA 124). This fact found unique expression in his view of evolution, which is, at bottom, a reflection of his own biography.

In the Moon stage the human being – says Prokofieff – develops the astral body; in the Earth stage he has the task of fully developing the Spirit-Self. Within his view of evolution the development of the individual 'I' is lacking, just as in his own development this has had no special importance in the present incarnation.

Through pushing to one side the problem of the 'I', and failing to recognize its unique significance, he also remains blind to everything of a concrete, individual nature. He believes that, instead of the individual will, the will of the angel should work in the human being; the source of all wisdom he seeks exclusively in cosmic spheres, and disclaims the individual striving for knowledge; his spiritual world is schematic and de-personalized, the names of the spiritual beings appear as nominal concepts, and as such are built into his constructions. His fondness for schematizing, abstraction, generalization, avoidance of everything concrete (characteristic of Luciferic thinking – see Rudolf Steiner's lecture of 14.11.1919, GA 191) is visible even in his ethical views. He speaks, in many true and sublime words, of love, tolerance, forgiveness, self-sacrifice of the altar of humanity etc., but everywhere the essential is lacking: an understanding for the individual human being and his life of soul. He constantly uses the word „mankind"; but very rarely, and then only in a formal sense, the word „human being". In referring abstractly to „mankind as a whole" he loses sight of the single human being. All his statements are predicated of the „totality". They refer to everyone, and at the same time to no-one.

As a result of atavistic experiences he is inspired by the dream of founding an „Order of Grail Knights", and the Anthroposophical Society is to be the means whereby this dream is realized (see para. 1.2.). Tirelessly he preaches the idea of brotherhood and searches eagerly for the passages in Rudolf Steiner which he believes will support his intentions. But he has never, in any book, quoted the following words: „One might subscribe to the opinion that it is necessary to continually stress the universal love of mankind, or that one ought to found associations dedicated to the cause of the universal love of mankind. Occultism is never of this opinion. On the contrary! The more the human being speaks of universal brotherly love and of humanitarianism in such a way that he is intoxicated by it, the more egoistic will people become. For just as there is a sensual indulgence, there is also an indulgence of the soul, and it is a refined self-indulgence (Wollust) to say: 'I wish to ascend morally higher and higher'! Ultimately it is a thought that does not give rise to ordinary everyday egoism, but a refined egoism arising from this kind of self-indulgence" (5.6.1907, GA 99). And the following: „In the moral sphere Theosophy (Anthroposophy) will be an educator of humanity in the obligation to truthfulness" (30.5.1912, GA 155). The word „truthfulness" does not occur in Prokofieff's works, and this is symptomatic. He never speaks of the duty to defend the truth. But what would happen if people started earnestly to seek the truth and give expression to it, if what is hidden were to come to light? – Would the imaginary Order of Grail Knights stand the test of such a process? Better, therefore, not to reflect too

4. Prokofieff as Propagandist and Teacher of Morals

much upon the truth, and to content oneself with talking about the universal love of mankind …

For Prokofieff ethical individualism, which arises from an understanding of the human 'I'-nature, remains an abstraction. In his book „The Occult Significance of Forgiveness", which is devoted to the problem of morality, he touches upon ethical individualism, no doubt for reasons of expediency, only to go on to develop views that are far removed from it. Thus the human being finds himself caught up in the relentless struggle between the „lower" and the „higher", the lower earthly inclination of his own 'I', and the lofty moral duty to which the angel inspires him. A moral deed appears as the fruit of extreme self-denial, coupled with pain and sacrifice.

Whatever subject Prokofieff deals with, he always returns to his favourite theme: suffering, sacrifice, martyrdom. The leading thought in the „Philosophy of Freedom", according to which moral action arises from love for the deed, is incomprehensible to him. In everything he inclines towards the heroic tragedy, sacrifice, pathos-filled self-denial – all the things that stir up and oppress the soul. Next to his sentimentality the following words from the „Philosophy of Freedom" sound decidedly strange: „But the tasks that the human being has to fulfil he fulfils because, by virtue of his own nature, when he has truly recognized their nature, he wills to fulfil them … No ethical system can take from him the pleasure that he derives from this fulfilment of what he desires … Whoever strives towards ideals of lofty grandeur does so because they are the content of his own being and their realization will be a pleasure, compared to which the enjoyment won by poverty of soul from the satisfaction of everyday drives, is a very petty thing. Idealists luxuriate spiritually in the translating of their ideals into reality" (GA 4, Ch. 13).

Prokofieff p r e a c h e s . He wants to make human beings moral after his fashion, to teach them how they ought to be in order to be called genuine Anthroposophists. But there is not a trace of Anthroposophical spirit behind such an attitude. Anthroposophy can be neither religious doctrine nor an „evening sermon", as it is a path of knowledge. In it the laws of the life of spirit and soul are studied. Thanks to knowledge unredeemed human nature is moved to „voluntary surrender", and ethical ideas are developed.

In the following we will return from our general conclusions to analysis, and to the presentation of the facts which make the first necessary.

4.2. The Theory of Occult Non-Forgiveness

Prokofieff's theory of forgiveness has been touched upon in connection with other matters. We now wish to examine it more closely. Quintessentially it consists in the following:

The human 'I' has the ability to remember, and on this is founded waking 'I'-consciousness. Interruptions of the memory, says Prokofieff, cause harm to the 'I'-consciousness. But how can one forgive, he asks in astonishment, without thereby losing consciousness? One has to forget the bad, if one is to forgive! For this reason, the human being cannot forgive of his own free will ... And Prokofieff sets out in search of a factor that works on the 'I' in such a way that forgiveness may take place without the extinction of consciousness. He proceeds from the assumption that one must of necessity work upon the lower 'I', as this by reason of its egoism refuses in every possible way to forgive (V, p. 89).

At this point Rudolf Steiner's pedagogical law from the Curative Education Course saves the situation. There it says that the members of man's being work actively from the higher to the lower (cf. 26.6.1924, GA 317). Eureka! That is the Spirit-Self! „In the process of forgiving" – he goes on to explain – „the working of one's higher 'I' (the Spirit-Self) or, what is the same, one's Guardian angel [upon the everyday human 'I' takes place]" (V, Ch. 6, para. 4; [p. 87]). The hiatus that has arisen in the memory is closed through the fact that the angel pours into it the substance of the Spirit-Self, and consciousness is thus maintained.

On the surface everything looks in perfect order: 'I'-consciousness has been taken account of and the laws observed. What he fails to realize, however, is that the whole theory is utter nonsense; and in order to see this one does not need to be an occultist. It is enough to forgive somebody and to observe the process. In order to forgive it is not necessary to forget the incident; one must keep it firmly in one's memory and find within oneself the strength to alter one's relation to it. No hiatus in the memory is needed for this. If one f o r -g e t s what is past (i.e. when the hiatus occurs, of which Prokofieff speaks), then that is not forgiveness. How could one forgive what one has forgotten? This reminds us of the saying: „Memory must disappear, only then can you forgive"! In our opinion one should not make a mockery of the standpoints of spiritual science.

Thinking and feeling are not the same thing. Memory, in which 'I'-consciousness is founded, has is roots in thinking and is connected with the building up of mental pictures. Not being able to forgive is connected with f e e l i n g . To forgive, one must alter one's feeling and in no way create a hiatus in the stream of memory. Forgiveness requires understanding. Only understanding for the motive of an action allows us to alter our attitude towards it in the sphere of feeling. And understanding is only possible if one remembers.

4.3. From the Experiencing to the „Overcoming" of the Consciousness-soul

Although Prokofieff's construction is artificial, it can awaken our interest, as he reveals in it with particular candour both his relation to the human 'I' and his ethical views. In para. 2.2. we showed that the terms „individual I", „lower I", „everyday I" are, for Prokofieff, synonymous. He defines the „lower I" as the fully-developed individual 'I', which unfolds in the consciousness-soul (V, p. 17 [p. 13]). This premise should be recalled in the course of the following considerations.

In para. 2 we showed how Prokofieff excludes the development of the individual 'I' and of 'I'-consciousness from general human evolution and replaces them with the Spirit-Self. In „The Occult Significance of Forgiveness" he displays openly his deep antipathy for the 'I'-principle. We will bring a few examples of this from the book.

On p. 66 [p. 53] he speaks of the „lying thinking", of vengefulness and envy of the earthly 'I' (which he calls 'I', the „lower I", etc.); on p. 89 [p. 71] we read the following „... [the lower 'I'] because of its egoism shies away from forgiveness in every possible manner, clutching at any pretext or any excuse that will allow it not to take this inner step. For in its very nature the lower 'I' is always inclined to hold grudges, and not to forget 'of its own free will', as it sees in forgetting a jeopardizing of its own purely egoistic wholeness"; on p. 90 we hear again of the „hard struggle of the higher with the lower 'I'"; and on p. 92-93 he speaks of the „negative inclinations of the lower 'I', particularly all kinds of vengefulness and envy", and on the „egoistic drives" of the lower 'I'; on p. 107 he speaks again of the „active refusal to forgive, which occurs in the form of vengefulness and envy", etc.

The „inability to forgive", and „envy" are mentioned five times in succession over several pages and yet again on p. 58 [p. 46]. Is it possible that someone is here engaged in the spiritual investigation of his own problems? On p. 66 [p. 53] Prokofieff declares: „From the spiritual point of view envy is a form of vengefulness [of the inability to forgive]" – whereby two negative qualities are transformed into one!

Prokofieff has not made one discovery only, in the field of this „renewed" Psychosophy. Although the remark to follow is not related to the question of forgiveness it has a direct bearing on the subject, as it once again illustrates his intention to make the human being into a medium and a moral automaton of the spiritual world. In „Spiritual Origins of Eastern Europe" he maintains that doubt „always arises from a certain 'dullness' of the soul" (IV, p. 117). He refers to a lecture of Rudolf Steiner which, however, contains the following statement: „Actually there cannot be a modern soul of any depth who does not go through nagging doubt. The modern soul needs to have experienced at first hand this nagging doubt! Only then will it win through, with the necessary strength, to the spiritual knowledge that is appropriate for the consciousness-soul, and which must be poured from the consciousness-soul into the rational or mind-soul, in order to attain mastery there. Thus we must try to penetrate with the reasoning faculty all that is offered out of occult knowledge to our consciousness-soul" (6.2.1913, GA 144). Here Prokofieff is mobilizing his „psychosophical" speculations and catchwords, for open battle with the consciousness-soul; at the same time he has no qualms about using the statements of Rudolf Steiner and turning their meaning and content into their opposite.

In Prokofieff's work, the more the black and ominous clouds gather around the lower, fallen, earthly, egoistic, very envious and vengeful 'I' (which is manifested in the consciousness-soul), the more alluring is the radiance emanating from the halo surrounding the heavenly, angelic, spotless, all-forgiving (even the shortcomings of the lower 'I' – V, p. 55) Spirit-Self. The human being is seen to be caught up in the relentless and tragic conflict between the lower and the higher, the earthly and the heavenly, but also – if Prokofieff's definition is taken into account – between the consciousness-soul and the Spirit-Self. In the case of the last two, a man has to make a clear choice. But what this human being must really be like, who is tossed back and forth between two extremes, of two 'I's – of this Prokofieff says nothing. But he ought to tell us, because in his conception there is no provision, beside the l o w e r and the h i g h e r 'I', for any third element. Thus there is no middle, no mediating factor ... Must an explanation be sought from those with experience in split-personality disorders?

If Prokofieff had studied the laws of the human life of soul, the Psychosophy of Rudolf Steiner, he would not have constructed such a dualistic system for the abasement and levelling of the human 'I'. But then he would have realized that so agonizing a conflict between good and evil as he describes is experienced by the human being in the intellectual soul – not between the Spirit-Self and the consciousness-soul. This fact is indicated in the Grail Legend by the figure of the mortally-wounded Amfortas. Prokofieff continually brings up the Grail theme, and ought therefore to be informed in these matters.

The human being constructed by Prokofieff does not step beyond the confines of the rational soul, and experiences within it the contradiction between the inclinations of his desire-nature and the purely external conception (Vorstellungen) of the Good – but ethical norms of this kind have not become the content of his intuition and he has no inner need, in the sense of the Philosophy of Freedom, to follow them. Hence the agony of having to choose (die Qual der Wahl). But what use is the Spirit-Self in this case?

We know from Anthroposophy that the bearer of all dichotomy and inner conflict in the human soul is its middle member, the rational soul. It is that part of the human being which can justifiably be spoken of as the „lower I", who chooses between good and evil. And this choice takes place within the soul and is not inspired by the Spirit-Self (or the angel); precisely this is the guarantee of the fact that man can become a free being. The „lower I" chooses between good and evil, not some abstract human being who, according to Prokofieff, makes a choice between Spirit-Self and consciousness-soul. The relation between lower and higher 'I' is not determined by the contradiction between good and evil, but by the difference between levels of consciousness.

In the consciousness-soul the opposites within the rational soul come to their rightful synthesis. There understanding and knowledge take the place of choice, of conflict, in the rational soul. But for Prokofieff the principle of synthesis is just as foreign an element as is knowledge. If one cannot raise oneself from the conflict in the rational soul to knowledge and insight in the consciousness-soul, one will slide downwards inevitably into the instinctive religiosity of the Sentient-soul. The way out of this dichotomy is then sought in one-sidedness, in the complete and final victory of the higher 'I' (the Spirit-Self), over the lower 'I' (in the consciousness-soul). This thought is developed by Prokofieff step by step (just as he lets the negative qualities of the lower 'I' steadily rise to a climax), and in such a way that he gradually wins the confidence of the reader, who in the end is willing to accept the author's recommendation – that he renounce the earthly 'I' and the individual will, and place it in the hands of the higher, hierarchical beings.

According to Prokofieff the higher 'I' at first influences the lower only insofar as it shows toward it compassion and forgiveness. But after this the conflict grows in intensity. On p. 89 (V) he already speaks of the necessity for „an at least partial overcoming of the lower by the higher 'I'", and on p. 90 of how difficult it is „to achieve a victory in the hard struggle of the higher with the lower 'I'"; also how an act of forgiveness is only possible „a f t e r the victory, that is, out of the h i g h e r 'I' itself" (ibid.; emphasis S.O.P.). Here we should recall that in this book Prokofieff claims that the higher 'I' of the human being is identical with his guardian angel (ibid., p. 56, 108). This means that only the angel can forgive, not the human being! Again and again, with no sense of moderation, Prokofieff repeats: „... the 'difficulty' or 'ease' with which true ... forgiveness can be attained ... depends ... upon the degree of its (the Spirit-Self's) victory over the lower I"; and further on he speaks again of „the overcoming of the lower by the higher I"; and, towards the end of the chapter, of „the necessity in life on Earth to overcome oneself again and again (to overcome one's lower 'I')" of the „power ... on Earth to gain within one's soul the victory of the higher over the lower 'I' ... The power to o v e r c o m e o n e s e l f, which leads to the [eternal] victory of the higher over the lower 'I'" (ibid., p. 91-95 [p. 75]. – A tautology as a war-cry!

On p. 149 (ibid.) he speaks of „that polarization and dichotomy between the higher and lower I" etc., and on p. 156 of „the problem arising from life itself, of the contrast and polarization of higher and lower I", etc. So it goes on almost without end ...

Now Prokofieff arrives at the incredible formula which we discussed in part in para. 2.2.: „T h e h u m a n b e i n g i s f r e e o n l y w h e n h i s w i l l p r o c e e d s e n t i r e l y f r o m h i s h i g h e r 'I' (i.e. his angel – see above) a n d i s l e d b y t h i s" (ibid., p. 122; emphasis I.G.). In other words, the human being is free only when he has no individual will, but the angel wills through him – otherwise, „even in the most trivial stirring of evil in the soul the will straight away loses its freedom and becomes a blind instrument of egoistic drives of the lower I" (ibid.). – But we still insist: The human being treads the path to freedom when he is able, out of his lower 'I', to choose independently between good and evil.

No regularly-developed angel has the intention to control in this fashion the will of the human being under his guidance; it is his task to lead him to independence. But there are many retarded spirits who would wish to act towards the human being in precisely this way. It is without question the Luciferic beings who – says Rudolf Steiner – „obstruct the free will of man. They try to bring about in the human being a lack of clarity regarding the exercise of his free will, in that they make him into a good being – Lucifer actually wants, from the standpoint I am touching upon here, the good, the spiritual, for the human being, but he wants to make it automatic, without free will; the human being is to be led to clairvoyance according to good principles, as it were automatically, but the Luciferic beings wish to rob the human being of his free will, of the possibility of evil. They want to fashion him in such a way that he acts out of the spirit, but like a spiritual reflected image, namely without free will ... These Luciferic beings have a strong interest in taking hold of man so that he does not come to freedom of the will, because they themselves have not attained free will. Free will can only be acquired on the Earth. But they want to have nothing to do with the Earth, they want only the Saturn, Sun and Moon development, and would stop there, have nothing to do with the Earth-development. They hate, as it were, the free will of man. They act in an exalted spiritual fashion, but they act automatically – this is extremely significant – and they wish to raise the human being to their own spiritual heights" (9.8.1918, GA 182).

Are these, perhaps, the spirits who guide the hand of Prokofieff as he writes, in order to distort the ideas of Rudolf Steiner so grossly in his books? But even if we demonstrate this in a quite factual way, we will be accused of prejudice. We urge readers, therefore, to compare exactly the assertions of Prokofieff with the corresponding statements of Rudolf Steiner. Even on the question of forgiveness and freedom we ask you to read attentively what Rudolf Steiner says, e.g. on 30.7.1922. We quote an extract only: „If the Christians had been conscious in themselves, then, every time they wished to be good, they would have had to extinguish their 'I'-consciousness in order, through extinguishing this

'I'-consciousness, to awaken the Christ within themselves. They would not have been able to be good themselves, but only the Christ in them would have been able to be good. Human beings would have had to wander about here on the Earth, the Christ would have had to dwell in them, and through Christ using the human bodies, the healing of these human bodies would have taken place. But the good deeds performed by human beings would have been Christ-deeds, not human deeds.

This was not the task, the mission, of the divine Son, who had united Himself with the Earth-development through the Mystery of Golgotha. He wanted to indwell humanity, but He did not wish to cloud the emerging 'I'-consciousness of human beings. This He had once done in Jesus, in whom, from the Baptism onwards, there lived in the place of the 'I'-consciousness the Son-consciousness. But this was not to happen with the human beings of future times. In the human being of the future the 'I' was to elevate itself in full consciousness, and the Christ would nevertheless be able to indwell these human beings" (GA 214).

Does anything further need to be added? This one extract from the lecture of Rudolf Steiner is sufficient to completely undermine Prokofieff's theory of forgiveness and his understanding of freedom. But Prokofieff even dares to question the mission of the divine Son. Behind this is concealed the wish to cast off as quickly as possible this detested earthly 'I' in its oppressive egoistic wholeness, with its ability to succumb to evil, with its agonizing doubts arising from dullness of the soul! Far better to combine the Luciferic principle at once with the Sentient soul, and with Lucifer's help dissolve into nothingness in the highest moral cosmic spheres! That would be freedom in the sense of: the freedom from all the toil of further individual development, free flight into the abyss of the unconscious ...

Such an attitude in the question of human freedom is foreign to Anthroposophy and has nothing in common with it. In the „Philosophy of Freedom" Rudolf Steiner has clearly shown that human freedom has its ground in the ability to create motives for action out of the pure thinking element; this ability he called „moral fantasy". This has nothing in common with moral arbitrariness, and in practical life employs a complex moral technique. When the human being possesses moral fantasy he sets himself moral goals in full consciousness and acts accordingly; then his deed is a free one. The human being is free, says

Rudolf Steiner, only insofar as he is able within his own consciousness to create conceptual motives for his action (GA 5, Ch. 2, para. 29). It is sufficient to compare this statement of Rudolf Steiner with the above-quoted maxim of Prokofieff in order to recognize without further commentary that we have before us (we cannot find a suitable expression for it) an unbelievable falsification of the concept of human freedom.

Equally far removed from Anthroposophy is Prokofieff's impassioned sermon against egoism. It may sound romantic, but it is rooted in his failure to comprehend, in chaos of the soul, and in the ever-present contempt for the 'I'-principle. The human being is, after all, an 'I'-being and thus cannot act non-egoistically; the question is merely what his 'I' wants: to serve only the interests of his own personal life, or also those of other people, of the world, as though they were his own. The human being is not asked to free himself from egoism, but to transform it: „Widen your self" – says Rudolf Steiner – „to the Self of the world, and then act egoistically" (GA 30, p. 431).

Where the personal interest, the subjectivity, the selfishness of man are so ennobled that he is concerned not only with his own person, but with the whole world, there alone is truth; where the human being is so limited in soul that he is only able to engage in the wider concerns of the world through denial of his personal interest and his subjectivity, then he lives in the worst possible lie of existence (GA 30, p. 429). To destroy the egoistic wholeness of the human 'I', to make the human being into an automaton of a higher will, is the aim of Lucifer and not of Anthroposophy.

To the category of the „worst possible lie of existence" belongs Prokofieff's ideal: „to exclude everything 'personal' from my work", which he proclaims on the first page of his „Autobiography". The ceaseless talk of selflessness and sacrifice is a form of refined egoism, involving not merely the impossibility of widening one's own interests to embrace the interests of the world, but actually placing universal human and world interests in the service of the glorification of one's own personality; for genuine self-sacrifice does not advertise itself.

In his book Prokofieff outlines a hymn of praise to forgiveness. He claims that one who has overcome and denied himself and has become an instrument of the will of another spiritual being can now begin to „overcome" others. On p. 106 (V) he speaks honestly and with deep conviction, of the „possibility that the higher 'I' (Spirit-Self) of one human being could work upon the lower 'I' of the other, right down to the karmic foundations of the latter" – in other words, of the possibility (held to be desirable) of exercising magical influence upon the will of another human being (as the karmic foundations are connected with the will-sphere)! – We decline to comment.

4.4. Occult-ideological echoes of the Categorical Imperative

> *Something supremely evil and wicked is on the way*
> *The parody begins: no doubt about it ...*
> F. Nietzsche: *Prologue to „The Joyful Science"*

Prokofieff tirelessly and unceasingly assigns tasks to the Anthroposophical Society. This is taken so far, that he publishes programmatic articles in brochure form, in whose title the phrase „Tasks of the Anthroposophical Society" appear, but hiding coyly behind the words: „From Rudolf Steiner's Karma Research" (VI). He imposes upon the Society his own personal programmes, combining together a selection of statements by Rudolf Steiner and re-interpreting them in his own fashion.

In his books he explains who are the true Anthroposophists, and wherein the real and deeper meaning lies of this or that statement of Rudolf Steiner; he decides who has rightly understood the significance of the Christmas Foundation, but also who does not understand it – and hence the central core of Anthroposophy – at all [I, p. 454]; he tells us how we ought, as true Anthroposophists, to act in this or that regard; how we ought to think; what we should feel and do, and even what we need „in order to fulfil our karma" (VI, p. 30). He overwhelms us with different calls to action and slogans, speaking now in the name of Rudolf Steiner, now in that of the Time-Spirit, now in that of Michael himself.

Here we would like to bring just one of these grandiose appeals from his first book: „Let us activate within ourselves the 'Michael Thought', so that it may become in us resounding world-word, which pours forth from Michael's garment of light in which he appears before us as the great [sublime] leader of the new Mysteries, and, in our wish to lay the dodecahedral Stone of love in our hearts, calls to us with his 'wise pointing' [wisdom-filled sign], his gesture, admonishing us: again to experience the Whitsun Festival as the World-message of Anthroposophy; to take up the 'word of love' into our souls, so that

4. Prokofieff as Propagandist and Teacher of Morals

the 'sacred will of worlds', in which there lives t h e W i l l o f t h e
E t h e r i c C h r i s t, may be realized on Earth.

[This fact (i.e. this summons)] is that C u l m i n a t i o n of Anthroposophy
which is to occur at the end of this century as a World-Day of Pentecost, as the
true Festival of the Holy Spirit … We are called upon to participate consciously
in this Culmination" (I, p. 381 [p. 419-420]; emphasis S.O.P.). We will not pur-
sue the above quotation any further, although it would be worth while doing so.
The reader is invited to open the book himself some time and draw „edification" from this passage alone. If in so doing he neither falls asleep nor applauds
enthusiastically, we would recommend a few more examples, taken from the
booklet „The Tasks of the Anthroposophical Society" (VI).

On p. 32 [p. 38] we read: „[And only through the fulfilment of this task will
it be possible for the Anthroposophists to see themselves as the] true Michaelites, [the successors and servants of Michael. But this can only be achieved if
the following is taken into account]…" Prokofieff goes on to prescribe how one
becomes a „true Michaelite": „Michael strives today to carry into the General
Anthroposophical Society the forces of karmic fulfilment" (did he tell him
about this „yesterday"?). On p. 33 [p. 39]: „And if we experience today that the
forces of brotherhood in the [Anthroposophical] Society are not sufficiently
strong, then we are obliged (all of us together, under the pressure of 'our' collective categorical imperative) honestly to admit that we have not yet permeated ourselves (all of us together, as group-beings) to a sufficient degree with
Michael-Will … For if we succeed [as Anthroposophists] during the phase of
our life from 28 to 49 years [in working with the required intensity at the fulfilment of our karma – and this above all in the realization of the] impulse of
brotherhood which unites us all (a new definition of the concept of karma), then
in the following period from the 42nd [49th] to the 63rd year we will be able,
with the help of the second Hierarchy, to unfold an immense creative force in
all fields of life, above all in the social realm." Thus writes a person who has
barely attained his 40th year.[*]

---

[*] Here we would remark that, while reading the „works" of Prokofieff, one always has
the feeling, when he is speaking out of himself, that one has read all this somewhere
in Rudolf Steiner (which is why superficial readers are so willing to take on trust everything Prokofieff teaches), although in a different connection and with another meaning. If one now asks oneself what memories of things he has read in Rudolf Steiner
might account for the passage quoted above, then one recalls that Rudolf Steiner said

107

So, if karma is the impulse towards brotherhood which will soon draw us all into unity, and the impulse towards brotherhood which is soon to unite us all is – Karma, then all those of us who are younger than 49 would like, as Anthroposophists, to add our bit to the slogan calling for the fulfilment of karma in the name of a flowering of brotherhood: „Long live Liberty, Equality – and Karma!"

P. 36 [p. 42] „[From what has been said here (by Prokofieff) there emerges for us] the most important task placed before [all] his pupils through the karma research of Rudolf Steiner, and which (to a certain degree) must be fulfilled before the end of the century ... This is what Michael expects today of the Anthroposophical Society." – Thus the conclusion drawn by Prokofieff in h i s brochure.

The reader will have no difficulty finding dozens more examples in the books and lectures of Prokofieff. Already his first book reminds one in certain places of the programme proclaimed by a top politician before the elections. Through his impassioned speeches there glimmer unmistakably the features of an ideologized consciousness; a phenomenon that is perhaps not so well-known in the West, but which is easily recognized by former Soviet citizens – those, of course, who are not yet befuddled by the new ideology. Because Prokofieff's slogans are lacking in cognitive content, they attain their goal all the better. For the aim of every slogan is the paralyzing of individual 'I'-consciousness.

Who are the „we" who „must" do something or other? In what cosmic spheres is to be found this inexhaustible source of the categorical imperative which, through Prokofieff, assigns us our tasks? The Anthroposophical Society is not meant to be a sect that draws up group opinions and in which one submits to a collective duty, but a community in which the principle of ethical individualism is realized. Here the human being attains, by way of spiritual-scientific knowledge, to moral intuitions of his own which determine his actions, the responsibility for which he carries personally.

---

that the human being lives in childhood in the element of equality, in mid-life in that of fraternity, and at the end of life in the element of freedom; that Christ is the Lord of Karma and brings the impulse of brotherhood into social relationships; that different karmic streams have come together in the Anthroposophical Society, etc.

The impression might arise, that someone has fed chips of humanitarian information into a computer and has applied to it a programme intended for mathematical calculations.

Rudolf Steiner: „When this 'we' disappears, then we do not have everyone in the Society sitting as it were in a pond in which everyone is supported and to whose authority he can appeal where necessary. But if within the Society he has to represent his own opinion and, above all, himself, then he also feels full responsibility for what he speaks as a separate individual, as an individuality" (16.6.1923, GA 258). This is what Rudolf Steiner expected of the Anthroposophical Society. But this Society let itself be turned into a flock of sheep. And today we must inquire: Why in all these years did no-one ask Prokofieff: „Who gave you the authority to assign tasks to us?"

Rudolf Steiner did it in his time with regard to the Anthroposophical Society as a whole. And besides, Rudolf Steiner is the Master (quod licet Jovi non licet bovi – what is permissible to Jove is not permissible to the ox). If someone wishes to assign tasks to people, his right to do so must be clearly demonstrable. Assertions such as „this is what Michael wills today", are in this case not sufficient. An Anthroposophist should also give evidence of his competence in basic questions of Spiritual Science before he is allowed to speak of the fulfilling of duty by others. „One who inclines to make personal propaganda cannot be, at the same time, an occultist!" – says Rudolf Steiner (31.8.1912, GA 138). In the case of Prokofieff this was resolved long ago. It does not affect him in any way.

4.5. The End Justifies the Means

Prokofieff ought first to have put his ethical conceptions to the test on imaginary figures, before setting out to illustrate them with examples from the life of Rudolf Steiner. It can be claimed that the condition of moral blindness must have befallen simple Members of the Anthroposophical Society, if they pass by, as though it were the norm, the phenomenon of which we are about to speak.

In his book „The Occult Significance of Forgiveness" Prokofieff describes the founding of the General Anthroposophical Society by Rudolf Steiner, citing this as the highest example of forgiveness and self-sacrifice. He says that Rudolf Steiner accomplished a deed whose consequences were not known to him in advance, and that he thereby r i s k e d h i s e n t i r e s p i r i t u a l m i s - s i o n , for the beings who guide the Anthroposophical movement could also n o t have accepted his decision, and thus the sources of revelation would have

109

been closed to him. We now ask the reader to follow Prokofieff's train of thought with special attentiveness. He says: „Through the fact that Rudolf Steiner had united himself with the earthly institution of the Society, he had entered directly into the sphere of the densest death-forces, which are active in every earthly institution. And no human being could escape from this sphere by dint of his own forces, unless he is led out of it by the only divine Being who conquered death" [V, p. 132]. From the fact that the source of revelation did not dry up Prokofieff concludes: „And this means that the Christ was that highest power, whom Rudolf Steiner [followed when he resolved to enter] consciously [the realm of the institution that had become most earthly], the realm of powerlessness and death, out of which he was led – in response to the sacrifice he brought, whose depth we can barely conceive – by t h e C h r i s t H i m s e l f – who led him as the pupil who sacrificed everything on the path of his 'imitatio' (Nachahmung)" (ibid., p. 168 [p. 133-134]).

What does this signify? According to Prokofieff the purpose of the founding of the General Anthroposophical Society was the setting up of a new Mystery centre on Earth. A lofty aim, undoubtedly. And in order to realize this Rudolf Steiner undertakes a bold venture. What does he do? – He founds an earthly institution, of which he must know at least as well as Prokofieff that it is a sphere pervaded by the densest death forces.

Now this institution is not an abstract machine, but consists of several hundred living human beings. Thus every member of this Society founded by Rudolf Steiner enters into t h e r e a l m o f p o w e r l e s s n e s s a n d d e a t h. At the same time, he too (Rudolf Steiner) must have been aware that no-one was able to escape from this realm by dint of his own forces. Thus he was not only putting at risk his own spiritual mission, but also the destiny of several hundred human beings. But as Rudolf Steiner is a pupil of the Christ, he will be led by the Christ, in answer to the sacrifice he has made, out of the realm of death. How then? Through his tragic death? And what happens to all the rest? – They all remain behind in the realm of death! So in the final analysis what sacrifice was made for the sake of this lofty goal? – The sacrifice of hundreds of human beings who were not in a position to free themselves and had therefore to remain in the realm of death, and also those who had no idea of the fate that awaited them, and continued to enter this realm. In this way the Anthroposophical Society is based – according to Prokofieff, of course – on a mass human sacrifice performed by its Founder! You and I, esteemed readers, are among those unwitting victims, if you are a Member of the Anthroposophical Society. What are we to do in such a case? Our only hope is to make ourselves worthy, so that the Christ can lead us out of there. But how can we be saved, if the General Anthroposophical Society, this realm of powerlessness and death, continues to exist? Only through death, or … expulsion from the Society! (For to withdraw from it ourselves does not lie within our power …)

How could any person think up a scenario of this kind? But Prokofieff goes still further. He even draws analogies between his monstrous fantasy-picture and the Mystery of Golgotha. But did not the Christ, we ask, take the death on the Cross upon Himself alone, and descend into Hell? And did He sacrifice a single human being beyond Himself, so that the Mystery could be accomplished?

Thus a mockery is made of the spiritual mission of our Teacher, and of the highest ideals of Christianity. Are human beings nothing more than anonymous cogs from which a kind of diabolical machine was made in order to make possible the Mystery of Golgotha? Anyone who questions our interpretation is recommended to read again attentively those one-and-a-half pages from Prokofieff's book.

But this is not Prokofieff's only sinister fairy-tale. Out of the „materials" of Anthroposophy he continually spins strange, dark, profoundly untrue myths (further examples in paras. 6 & 7). They come about mainly through small, inconspicuous distortions which are scattered everywhere; he describes everything a l m o s t correctly, and at the same time the truth is always a hair's breath removed from what is said; he „corrects" it with a few „strokes of the brush" – now here, now there – and finally he distorts it beyond recognition; where and when this occurs is very difficult to establish, and requires thorough and meticulous research.

The Anthroposophical Society founded by Rudolf Steiner is by no means a realm of powerlessness and death; it is the form created by him for the incarnation of Anthroposophy on Earth, a form in which the impulse of esoteric Christianity is to live, and which can at the same time bring about a renewal and rejuvenation in all spheres of modern culture and in every human being who is connected with this impulse. In the lecture of 25.10.1918 Rudolf Steiner says that through the objective conditions inherent in the 5th epoch, death everywhere permeates what is created on the physical plane, „that on the physical plane one cannot but create in the awareness of the fact that – what one creates will pass away" (GA 185). But this is not what Prokofieff is saying!

Prokofieff's hostility towards everything earthly prompts him to use such inappropriate expressions. It is similar to the aversion felt by Lucifer towards Ahriman, and shows Prokofieff's inability to find the balance. While he doubtlessly recognizes in the earthly form of the Society something evil, namely the realm of powerlessness and death, he strives at the same time to conserve this realm by every means, and to draw into it as many people as possible.

„Our perception of outer life", says Rudolf Steiner, „must become such that we gaze out into the surrounding world boldly and without cowardice, and say to ourselves: Growth and fading away, this is something that must be consciously brought about in every sphere of life. Nothing social can be built in an absolute sense and for all eternity. Whoever works for the building up of social life must have the courage ever and again to build something new, not to stand still; because what has been built grows old, fades, must die away; because the new must be built" (ibid.).

The form is not in itself evil; it is that which is absolutely necessary for the realization of the content. It becomes something evil, a realm of death, only when its development is hindered.

5. Christology in an Entirely New Light

We would like now very briefly to point to a further branch cultivated by Prokofieff on his tree of Anthroposophy, on which skilfully camouflaged „anor-
ganic" fruits are attempting to grow in the sphere of Anthroposophical Christology. The author's basic tendency is here the familiar one, of radically dimin-
ishing the value of the human 'I' and underestimating its significance; of blur-
ring the true picture of earthly 'I'-development, and persuading human beings
to return to the primal, „paradisal" condition – that of group spirituality – to a
morality that is dictated from above, and a non-autonomous thinking.

In evolution there is no „way back". What was once the „paradisal condition" is therefore only possible now in the sphere of the retarding beings – in
Lucifer's realm, to which many people are trying to flee in our time. The understanding of the Christ, as is given in Anthroposophy, stands counter to this.
No evasion is possible, unless one were, so to speak, to insinuate oneself into
this Christology in order to distort and weaken it from within. Using spiritual-
scientific terminology and with the help of selectively gathered statements of
Rudolf Steiner, one would be able to place oneself in the service of other, quite
alien, purposes, in order thereby to lead human beings away from the meaning
of earthly development. To qualify as an instrument for the realization of such
aims pursued by retarded beings, it is by no means necessary to be an evildoer
who is ready to lie and falsify consciously – such people would be easily recognized – but a pure idealist who is lacking, however, in a capacity for objective self-knowledge and in the ability to distinguish between his/her higher 'I'
and Luciferic possession.

Abstract reference to the Christ, and enthusiastic repetition of well-tried
phrases are of no avail here. Nor the fact that the person in question basically
admits the development of the consciousness-soul in the 5th epoch, and also the
necessity of the human striving for freedom. Prokofieff, for example, uses his
correct words only as a camouflage for completely un-Anthroposophical conceptions which systematically pollute the consciousness of those who consume,
as Anthroposophists, the fruits cultivated by him.

Through his one-sided interpretations he destroys the core of esoteric Christianity, which he transforms into a kind of Church dogmatism. Prokofieff inclines not only formally, but essentially, to share in the views of the latter insti-

113

tution; for the Church, man's earthly development is a veritable vale of tears filled with sin and error, in which the human being has become embroiled as a consequence of the Fall, but for which he must repent through renunciation of his own free will and through surrender to the will of God, in order to be saved (in Prokofieff's version this happens through the overcoming of the lower by the higher 'I'). In order somehow to co-ordinate the different aspects of his religious world-view, Prokofieff has to subject to a thorough revision the communications of Rudolf Steiner concerning the Christ-being and the conditions of His incarnation. The indications regarding the Nathan Soul are especially helpful to him here. Through over-emphasis of the principle of the heavenly Man – the Nathan Soul – he pushes the Christ-principle into the background; the Jesuits arrive at the same result in a similar way, by over-emphasizing the principle of the Earthly man Jesus.

As we know from Anthroposophical Christology, two Jesus boys were incarnated at the beginning of the events in Palestine. In the one, the Nathan Jesus, of whom the St. Luke Gospel tells, there was incarnated that soul-part of the old Adam which had been preserved from the „Fall into sin", and remained without the experience of earthly incarnations. This pure, heavenly being bore within it the wholly unsullied forces of primal humanity, but had not undergone an individualizing development in the material world, and thus did not possess an 'I'-principle of the kind developed by human beings since the Lemurian epoch. This being was trans-personal, and had no affinity to the physical plane, whose forces he lacked the ability to use.

In the second child, the Solomon Jesus, of whom we read in the St. Matthew Gospel, was incarnated the individuality of Zarathustra, the Initiate of antiquity who, after numerous incarnations and a many-sided activity on the material Earth, had evolved the capacity to prepare the bodily sheaths which could be used by the Christ-being. Zarathustra had – so far as this was at all possible for a human being – complete mastery of the physical plane.

In the twelfth year of his earthly life the individuality of Zarathustra, his 'I', passed over into the Nathan Jesus child, whereby the latter received a mature, individual human 'I' (that of Zarathustra). Through the course of eighteen years this 'I', aided by the experiences of his earthly incarnations, worked upon the Jesus body and prepared to receive into himself, at the age of thirty years at the Baptism in the Jordan, the Macrocosmic Christ-'I'.

114

5. Christology in an Entirely New Light

Thus we find working together in Jesus of Nazareth two ancient spiritual streams which are in their essential nature opposed to one another; streams which are spoken of in the Temple Legend: those of Cain and Abel. At this point the two antipodes finally meet: the one that works downwards from above, descending from spiritual heights, that is entirely grounded in the Divine and is untouched by anything earthly – the being of the Nathan Soul; and the being of Zarathustra which works, creatively active, from below upwards, using and transforming the material forces out of its own individual 'I'. The meeting of these two can be represented by the intersection of the descending and the ascending triangles of the Star of Solomon, to which Rudolf Steiner referred as the symbol of the Holy Grail. Into it is poured as into a chalice the Macrocosmic 'I' of Christ.

A knowledge of esoteric Christianity affirms that only in a being who finds the balance between the „Earthly" and the „Heavenly", the masculine and the feminine, and combines within himself the creative-active Cain principle with the Abel principle of heavenly revelation, can the principle of the individual 'I' light up in its true nature; this grows ever more closely related to the unitary Macrocosmic Christ-'I'. In the triad: Zarathustra – Nathan Soul – Christ two opposite principles are brought to a synthesis through a third, higher, principle that embraces both and unites them within itself.

These general considerations should suffice to make visible the essential nature of the distorted view of Prokofieff. Let us see what he proposes. Through his antipathy for the earthly-human 'I' he can understandably – as is the case with the Church – not evince any sympathy for that event which laid the primal foundation for the development of the 'I'-principle: what we know as the „Fall". His consciousness enshrouds itself entirely in that part of the soul of Adam that did not partake in „sin" – the Nathan Soul – which appears in a romantic halo beckoning to us from cosmic distances. The passage in the Bible, where God the Father breathed into the human being the breath of life, Prokofieff quotes with the commentary: „Since that time the Nathan Soul has also lived as such a 'living soul' in the cosmos, while the rest of mankind, which succumbed to the Luciferic temptation and sank ever deeper into matter, into the realms of darkness and death, ceased to be a l i v i n g soul" (II, p. 38; emphasis S.O.P.). In a single sentence of this kind, which negates the principle of the three-membered soul within which the individual 'I' evolves, Prokofieff obliterates not only the meaning of evolution, but also the significance of the

115

Mystery of Golgotha. In the „fallen" part of the world he sees only darkness and death, and remains blind to the God Who has poured Himself out into the „world" and united Himself with it. Prokofieff fights doggedly for his favourite conception – that of dualism.

In the course of evolution the dichotomy of God and world, spirit and matter, is resolved through the human being who raises his 'I'-consciousness from the earthly to the divine; for this development Christ is the Way, the Truth and the Life. The evolutionary standpoint is foreign to Prokofieff, and in view of his antipathy towards the earthly 'I', his dualism is in danger of remaining unresolved. The way out is always sought by him in a connection with the one extreme and exclusion of the other.

Prokofieff's 'I'-aversion and his bias in favour of the Spirit-Self are especially noticeable when he is dealing with the central object of his religious veneration – the Nathan Soul. But even that part of the fourth principle which has not succumbed to sin alarms him, so that he writes: „In this connection one can also speak of the 'I' of the Nathan Soul, but with the qualification, that it has more the original nature (?) of the Spirit-Self ..., because ... it was held back from earthly incarnations" (ibid.). Then he quotes from a lecture where Rudolf Steiner says that the 'I' of the Nathan Soul was „that which was poured down by the Spirits of Form, and now flows on; except that something was, as it were, held back from entering into bodily incarnations – an 'I' that did not continually reappear as a human being, but which retained that form, that substantiality, which the human being had before he had advanced to his first earthly incarnation" (Ibid.; 12.10.1911, GA 131). On the strength of this quotation Prokofieff asserts no less than that the Spirit-Self had been given to man by the Spirits of Form during the Earth aeon, and is none other than the 'I' that has not undergone incarnation. What remains for us to say?! – The statement of Rudolf Steiner to the effect that the Spirit-Self was laid as a seed into the astral body of man on the Old Moon, is surely one of the elementary truths of Anthroposophy; also the fact that the Spirits of Form endowed the human being in the Earth aeon with the autonomous f o u r t h   p r i n c i p l e , which is distinct from both the three-membered body and the threefold spirit (Atma – Buddhi – Manas, which were impressed into the three bodies in the three preceding aeons).

Now this is only a minor prelude to what Prokofieff goes on to tell us about Christ-incarnation. In his account the Nathan Soul appears as the most important and almost the sole active entity; the Christ Being is assigned a secondary, passive role, and the individuality of Zarathustra has no part to play, save for two fleeting and unimportant references, once in brackets on p. 180, where it says that Jesus of Nazareth is (to the exclusion of all else) the Nathan Soul, while the Zarathustra individuality during the eighteen years of its indwelling presence merely s t r e n g t h e n e d the Nathan Soul! Prokofieff asserts the essential identity of Jesus and the Nathan Soul, and demonstrates yet again that for him the 'I'-principle is without significance. – But the Zarathustra-'I' l i v e d in Jesus, and it was precisely this circumstance that Rudolf Steiner was at pains to emphasize. Thus he says, for example: „In the historical personality of Jesus of Nazareth we have in the first place to do with a highly-developed human being (i.e. with Zarathustra), who has passed through many incarnations" (31.5.1908, GA 103).

Prokofieff mentions Zarathustra again in a Note on p. 440 (Russian edition), where he states that Jesus of Nazareth preserved within himself the ancient ideal of initiation. But even this he regards as something that has been acquired by it (the Nathan Soul) through cosmic activity in ages past. Yet he is talking about Jesus before his thirtieth year – i.e. Zarathustra, who was incarnated in him and whose individuality had retained the memory of the earlier initiations, also as a Hierophant. – So Prokofieff has mentioned Zarathustra all the same! And yet the fact that this reference occurs at the end of the book, amongst the Notes in small print, and thus far removed from the actual text, will appear to him adequate and quite justified.

But this modest gesture does not prevent Prokofieff from completely playing down the role of Zarathustra in the events of Palestine. Thus he says that the Nathan Soul „...in the thirtieth year became, not an 'external' b e a r e r of the Christ in the Macrocosm, but the 'C h r i s t - R e c e i v e r ', the first human being to receive the Christ into the innermost core of its own being (what „core" is meant here? – The innermost core of the soul is the 'I' – but this had just left the body), so that at the Baptism in the Jordan he could unite himself with [the innermost being of the Nathan Soul] (?) and, in the course of the following three years, could permeate its astral, etheric and physical bodies" (II, p. 186 [p. 193-194]; emphasis S.O.P.).

Thus the Nathan Soul had received the Christ into its innermost core, thereby enabling Him to unite with its innermost being. Is any further commentary necessary? Prokofieff himself seems to have noticed that something is wrong here. So he takes a new breath and, on the next page, repeats almost the same thing. He speaks of the Nathan Soul as „the h u m a n being of the primal beginning, who [had received into himself] the Sun of Christ in [such] fullness, [that the possibility was thereby given to him to permeate] his sheaths with the substance of the 'Divine Light'" (ibid., p. 187 [p. 194-195]; emphasis S.O.P.). But this leads us to conclude that in the first quotation Christ Himself permeates the sheaths, while in the second the Nathan Soul is already doing this unaided. If Prokofieff were to repeat his „opus" two or three time with modifications, then in the end even Christ would go unmentioned. The Nathan Soul would manage everything alone.

According to Prokofieff the incarnation of the Christ was able to take place thanks only to the „fourth sacrifice of the Nathan Soul". This it was, that „... made possible His entry into the human 'I', so that in it He can become the source of human intellectual and moral forces" (ibid., p. 188). Thus Prokofieff stands everything on its head. It is not the Nathan Soul – here it is the Christ who made the sacrifice. He, who did not need the sacrifice for the sake of his own development, sacrificed himself when he, the God, took upon himself earthly incarnation and passed as man through suffering and death. The second being willing to make a sacrifice here was Zarathustra. Not the Nathan Soul sacrificed its 'I', but the 'I' of Zarathustra sacrificed to the Christ the sheaths that had been prepared through eighteen years. Rudolf Steiner says: „If the individuality of Zarathustra had not permeated this bodily instrument up to the thirtieth year, its eyes would not have been able to endure the substance of Christ from the thirtieth year to the Mystery of Golgotha; the hands could not have been permeated with the substance of Christ in the thirtieth year. In order to be able to receive the Christ, this bodily instrument had to be prepared, to be extended, through the individuality of Zarathustra" (12.10.1911, GA 131). Because the Nathan Soul was lacking in the experience of dealing with the lower principles, it could only accompany as a beholder the working of Zarathustra.

Sacrifice is a free, conscious act, which springs from the forces of the individual 'I'; the Nathan Soul did not possess such an 'I', as it had not yet undergone any incarnation. It merely possessed its primal substance. Prokofieff cannot grasp this fact, he demonstrates again his disregard for the 'I'-principle. In those sacrificial processes the Nathan Soul was no more than a m e d i a t o r.

5. Christology in an Entirely New Light

We say this with no intent whatever to belittle its significance, but only to counter the misrepresentation of events of that time.

As little as the sacrifice of Zarathustra exists for Prokofieff, just as little does he take account of the influence exercised by the Buddha on the astral body of Jesus of Nazareth. He hold firm to the Nathan Soul. Although it is a being „without sin", it is nevertheless a human entity which, in Prokofieff's conception, even eclipses the Christ Himself. For him it is „... the heavenly archetype of the higher goals [of all pre-Christian] Mysteries" (II, p. 185 [p. 193]), etc. – This he repeats several times: monotonously, insistently, impressing it upon the reader's mind, so that he/she will never again recall that the highest goal, the content of the highest strivings of all pre-Christian Mysteries (not of all, but only the light Mysteries) – according to Rudolf Steiner – was not the Nathan Soul, but the Christ who dwelt in the Sun-sphere.

But Prokofieff does not confine himself to the ancient Mysteries. The Nathan Soul is – „... the true Anthropos" (II, p. 180) – „... the great archetype of Man, who realized within himself [completely] the first supersensible Christ revelation ... the Archetype of the human being ... [permeated by the Christ], the [archetype of the future development of all mankind]" (ibid., p. 187-188 [p. 195]); „the Nathan Soul is the h u m a n bearer of the [three Rosicrucian mottos]" (?! – ibid., p. 190 [p. 197]); „... [for all future times the archetype of the ultimate purpose (!) and of the highest strivings of all true Christian Mysteries, and above all] ... of the [new Michael-Christ-Mysteries whose foundation is] the Christmas Conference of the year 1923", and it is also: „... the highest ideal of the new Mysteries, a pointer to the human being of the primal beginning, who received into himself the Sun of Christ" (ibid., p. 189 [p. 195-196]; and finally, „the Nathan Soul proves to be not only the archetype of the highest goal of the new Mysteries, but also directly that which leads towards its realization" (ibid., p. 190).

After such eulogies the one question remains: What, then, is this Nathan Soul n o t for us? Is there in the spiritual world anything essential besides the Nathan Soul?

When Prokofieff presents his ideal of all past, present, and future Mysteries, and of the entire future development of humanity, he speaks neither of Jesus of Nazareth nor of Jesus Christ, but of the Nathan Soul. An identification of Jesus with the Nathan Soul is indeed correct in two cases: firstly, where one is speak-

119

ing of the Jesus child of the Luke Gospel, up to the moment where the Zarathustra individuality incarnated in him; and secondly, where we are considering Jesus of Nazareth, when the Zarathustra-'I' parted from him – i.e. during the Baptism in the Jordan. Thereafter we must already speak of Jesus Christ. As to the first situation Rudolf Steiner says the following: „a developed 'I' such as had evolved through the Atlantean and post-Atlantean periods, is not present in the St. Luke Jesus boy … in the St. Matthew Jesus boy we have to do with a fully-developed human being; in the Jesus boy of the Luke Gospel we have to do with a physical body, ether body, and astral body, ordered in such a way that they harmoniously represent the human being as he emerged as a result of the Saturn, Sun and Moon development." But what do we have before us in Jesus of Nazareth at the moment when Zarathustra departed from him? Rudolf Steiner says: „… neither an adept nor anything else in the nature of a higher human being … For an adept is an adept by virtue of the fact that he has a highly development individuality; but this has just departed from the threefold bodily instrument of Jesus of Nazareth. We have only the threefold bodily organization, which has been so prepared through the presence of Zarathustra, that it can receive the Christ-individuality" (12.10.1911, GA 131).

We believe that these characterizations are sufficient to clarify Prokofieff's „highest goals": to exclude absolutely the individuality, to banish it from the Mysteries, and from development altogether. (Here we would recall the communication of Rudolf Steiner already quoted on p. 103 concerning the Luciferic beings: „They want only Saturn, Sun and Moon development, and to stop there; they want to have nothing to do with the Earth development.")

This intention of Prokofieff has nothing in common with the true aims of the Christian Mysteries, but quite directly with something different. We have often spoken of the Luciferic element which pervades such works and determines their direction. We have not yet referred explicitly to Ahriman, but he too is involved here. In such a case Lucifer dictates the overall tendency, the strategy adopted, while Ahriman – this being his „forte" – is responsible for the „technology" employed for its realization. The „technique" applied here consists in the dissolution of thinking, the distortion of logic, the undermining of healthy common sense, and the general corruption of the power of judgment. „Thus for Ahriman the situation is such that he is never concerned about the correspondence of an idea (Vorstellung) with objective fact, but rather with its effect, with what can be achieved" (28.8.1916, GA 170) – Rudolf Steiner explains. When the human being follows Ahriman he sins against logic and healthy common sense (19.5.1910, GA 120). We have been dealing with a „sin" of this kind from the beginning of the present study.

When Lucifer and Ahriman do not mutually extinguish one another, but, on the contrary, give each other assistance, then this has a mighty outcome whose final goal is the synthesis of the two. This syntheses is characterized by Rudolf Steiner as the worst of all temptations awaiting humanity; it is the temptation by the Asuric spirits. The evil with which the human being is afflicted through Lucifer and Ahriman can be completely compensated for in the remaining cycles of Earth development. „… but the evil brought by the Asuric powers cannot be atoned for in this way" – Rudolf Steiner warns. The Asuras will try to attack the innermost being of man, the consciousness-soul and the 'I', and to destroy them. „All that falls a prey to the Asuric powers will be irretrievable lost … One could say: Today it is still somewhat theoretical to assert that the Asuric powers tempt the human being. Today they conjure before him the illusion that his 'I' is merely a by-product of the physical world" (22.3.1909, GA 107). It is the aim of the Asuras to alter the course of evolution, to separate the creation from the creator and rule over it themselves. The means used for the attainment of this goal is the paralyzing of 'I'-development.

Only esoteric Christianity can oppose these intentions of the Asuras, the mightiest of the adversary powers. Its strength flows from the union of two principles in Jesus of Nazareth: „On the one hand the old Chela (Zarathustra), who was deeply connected to the physical plane, who was also able to work on the physical plane and hold it in equilibrium through the use of his forces; and, on the other hand, the Christ Himself, a pure spiritual being. This is the cosmic problem lying at the foundations of Christianity" (10.6.1904, GA 93). Thanks only to this particular constellation of forces – so Rudolf Steiner explains in the lecture quoted – did Christ succeed in taming the Asuric powers. „They were, so to speak, held in check, so that they became immobile. This was only possible through the fact that they were worked upon from two sides" (ibid.).

The Asuras were „bridled" through the event known to us as „Christ's Descent into Hell". But their lethargy does not last forever. Rudolf Steiner says that the Antichrist was „fettered", but that he will rise up again if he is not confronted by the Christian principle in all its strength (ibid.). In our present day the Asuric temptation has moved very close to humanity, its influence show itself now here, now there, in all that unfolds in modern civilization. For this reason Anthroposophy must make accessible to human beings those truths of esoteric Christianity which enable them to recognize the evil that is approaching them by stealth, and to resist it. Any falsification of such truths can only serve to weaken its original power. The Zarathustra principle is one of those two principles that live in Jesus of Nazareth, but which only in their combined working can resist the Asuras; it is the principle of the human being as such, who commands the forces of the physical plane. If this is excluded, however, then only the Nathan Soul remains – a being who has no experience on the physical plane. Esoteric Christianity contains within it the forces that can paralyze the Asuras. – But it must not be taken hold of by viruses that are inclined to paralyze these forces.

6. Prokofieff as Meta-Historian and Researcher into World-Karma

In the previous chapters we have tried to view from various angles the new Tree of Anthroposophy cultivated by Prokofieff, and to determine the laws of its growth and fruit-formation. We have seen how, out of a trunk into which he has woven a false conception of evolution, branches shoot forth, which extend into various realms of spiritual knowledge. Now we are about to make acquaintance with one of these branches. In para. 2.3. we showed how his false interpretation of the developmental task of the Earth aeon leads him to view the fundamental tasks of the 5th epoch incorrectly. At this point the path begins which leads him further to a distortion of the historical facts.

Just as in real Anthroposophy everything stands in interconnection and in reciprocal determination with other elements, so also in Prokofieff's Anthroposophy something similar happens, but here in a deceptive, even a caricatured manner. One error follows from the other, in a chain of false conclusions..

When Prokofieff in his early youth had „experienced", as if by chance, something of the esoteric nature of the renewed Mysteries, he heard the call of the Spirit of the Age – who had approached him personally – and felt himself to be this Spirit's faithful servant and helper (cf. § 1.2.). As a consequence of this it is his aim to intervene in the destinies of the peoples through determining their mutual harmony (IV); then he becomes the representative of Russia in Europe, where he explains the true nature of his people and the spiritual tasks which have been assigned to it by the „Guidance of the World" (IV). Finally he steps forward in the role of an interpreter of meta-history and as a mouthpiece of the law of World-karma. In the book „The Spiritual Origins of Eastern Europe ..." he answers the question: „What is the meaning of the history of the Eastern European peoples" (in the period) „from the Bolshevik uprising until today, seen from the [highest] and at the same time [most spiritual] standpoint – namely, from the standpoint of the all-encompassing forces of Karma?" (IV, p. 372 [348]). We will now attempt to describe how this can be viewed from that absolute, „most spiritual" – and for us inaccessible – standpoint.

6.1. The Rescue-Mission of Bolshevism in Russia

We have already pointed out on many occasions that Prokofieff sees in the [complete] spiritualization of the consciousness-soul the „principal task" of the fifth post-Atlantean epoch, but that he is not interested in its actual development. He avoids everything that cannot lead to the fulfilment of „his" primary task (which on closer examination is striving for no less than a premature realization of the Spirit-self principle), as this would spring from an external, superficial standpoint.

Prokofieff is forced to acknowledge the necessity of the development of materialism in the 5th cultural epoch. But from this high level of objective cognition he immediately slips down to the level of emotional, one-sided judgments. When he characterizes materialism as „the [most deeply-rooted] mass – l i e " (IV, p. 378 [p. 353]; emphasis S.O.P.), he fails to realize that in the philosophical sense materialism is not a lie, but an „error", and that the natural science which has unfolded within the framework of the materialistic world-view has also contributed much that is valid and significant, towards a knowledge of the material world.

It is upon the basis of such a one-sided attitude – not at all upon the knowledge of the all-encompassing laws of World-karma – that Prokofieff builds his interpretation of Russian history, with which he deals in the chapter entitled „The Spiritual Destiny of Eastern Europe in the Light of the Karma of Mankind" (from „The Spiritual Origins of Eastern Europe"). We will be following Prokofieff's thoughts with the help of a direct reading of this chapter, and will be astounded at many of the detailed statements contained in it.

The population of Eastern Europe, and particularly that of Russia, says Prokofieff, has – in contrast to the peoples of Western Europe and North America – not been permeated with the impulse of materialism. If this is so, in what category one is to place Herzen, Chernyshevsky, Pisarev, Belinsky, Tkachov[*] – and even Peter the Great – Prokofieff does not explain. „If the facts do not support the theory, then too bad for the facts!" – one would like to add. As Marxism – so he continues – is a fruit of Western European materialistic development, and thereby foreign to the Russian folk, it had been imported into Russia and had thus led to the successful realization of the „socialistic experiment". –

---

[*] Russian Socialists, publicists and atheists of the 19th century (Ed.).

6. Prokofieff as Meta-Historian and Researcher into World-Karma

Statements like this do not fully correspond to the truth, to put it mildly. Marxism was accepted as a teaching by the Russian Socialists through no outer compulsion. But what was imported was the Bolshevik conspiracy – including its leaders Lenin and Trotsky. However, these are details which cannot be recognized from the „very highest standpoint".

„But what is the deeper, k a r m i c meaning of this fateful 'import'?" (IV, p. 378, emphasis S.O.P.) - Prokofieff asks. Here he recalls that materialism is a lie, and must therefore bring about bad karma. As an occasional ally Prokofieff calls upon Rudolf Steiner, according to whose research there is indeed the „Karma of untruthfulness", which in some measure lived itself out in the First World War. For our part we would recall what Rudolf Steiner said about this war: „… it is a fact that through this catastrophe mankind was protected from a terrible decline into materialism and utilitarianism. Even if this cannot be seen today, it will become apparent …" (21.12.1918, GA 186)). Prokofieff does not reflect upon this statement of Rudolf Steiner, does not look for a connection between this and his own view. He uses Rudolf Steiner's research only as a pointer to the existence of the Karma of untruthfulness and, with scarcely any mention of the First World War, he sweeps this research to one side with an imperious gesture, thus making room for theories of his own. (In this he reminds us of the Russian Socialist and Nihilist Bazarov in Turgeniev's novel „Fathers and Sons", who incessantly repeats: „I share nobody's opinion; I have my own".) And so Prokofieff continues: „The spiritual situation in Europe and (North) America in the last third of the 19th century was such that, from the standpoint of the higher, guiding spiritual powers (this standpoint is known to Prokofieff), humanity was faced increasingly with a quite specific danger. The danger that the negative karma of materialism would gradually become so [oppressive], that humanity at the end of the dark age of Kali-Yuga in 1899 … might not be in a position to fulfil the [main tasks] of the 5th post-Atlantean cultural epoch to the degree that was necessary (from Prokofieff we know that humanity in the course of 500 years has not yet begun to take hold of its „main tasks") … and at the same time to carry the full burden of the consequences" (IV, p. 378 [p. 354]; emphasis S.O.P.).

Here, as so often before, we find ourselves obliged to interrupt the author's lofty flight of thought, and remind him that Goetheanism, which attempts to fulfil the most important tasks of the 5th cultural epoch in a very direct way, had appeared in the world long before; in addition, through intensive work done

125

in the course of the last quarter of the 19th century, Rudolf Steiner elaborated the epistemological foundation of Goetheanism and, from 1902 onwards, Anthroposophy. Thus Middle Europe and, with it, the rest of humanity had begun to fulfil its spiritual mission in the 5th cultural epoch long before the start of the „socialistic experiment" in Russia, for which Prokofieff would like to provide a „karmic foundation". But such a fact escapes his memory completely, because it would again stand in the way of his theory. And so he continues: „Thus [one is justified in assuming that] the powers (what powers?) which guide the [entire] Earth development, for the sake of the p o s s i b i l i t y that this [humanity] should be able one day (why one day? cf. 2.2.) to reach the goal it has been set, [had to] weaken in some way the effect of the … karma of materialism" (ibid., p. 379 [p. 353-354]; emphasis S.O.P.; How can one, in such decisive questions, just arbitrarily assume something?).

In consequence of this – we are still keeping to the author's line of thought – something remarkable happens: Prokofieff takes us into his confidence and reveals to us a „[great] secret of the historical development of earthly humanity", which is the following: „In harmony with the [higher karmic laws in our cosmos] the consequences of the deeds we have performed can never, in any circumstances, stand alone for themselves, but must a l w a y s b e c a r r i e d by a concrete Being or a group of Beings in this or in other worlds" (ibid., p. 379 [p. 354]; emphasis S.O.P.). This assumption can hardly prove to be a great „mystery", as it clearly shows itself to be a tautology. – What are, in actual fact, the consequences of our deeds? In the physical world they are further deeds of human beings, or of nature processes, which inevitably include elementary beings, and beings of the natural kingdoms. In the spiritual world there is, without exception, nothing but Beings. So how could one imagine that the consequences of a deed could stand „alone for themselves", and not be carried by Beings? What is the secret or mystery here?

Even if our comparison may seem far-fetched, we would say that all this reminds one of the famous question in Alice in Wonderland: „Can the smile of the Cheshire Cat exist without the cat?" – But the adventures of Alice in Wonderland are characterized by a fine and unforced wit and ingenuity, and differ in this radically from Prokofieff's „Land of Anthroposophy", which is heavy with a darkly portentous earnestness. Thus the amusing and light-hearted problems of Alice are transformed by Prokofieff into great mysteries and lofty laws of the working of Karma in our cosmos. But these laws are only necessary for h i m – for his further inventions, in fact.

„Therefore" - he continues – „the higher powers which guide the karmic relationships of human beings, in order to free it (i.e. humanity) at least to some extent from the consequences of the negative karma it had itself created, had to find another bearer for it ..." And with unerring logic the next discovery follows: Those higher powers had to find such a bearer „outside humanity", and they found it ... in Russia! Whoever this non-human, „other" bearer might have been, who had grown up in „enigmatic" Russia (is it perhaps that superhuman being (Übermensch) whose five main members are enumerated by Prokofieff on p. 53 of the same book?), he at any rate possessed two corresponding qualities. Firstly, he could „wait for the fulfilment of his own mission" and, secondly, he had „a number of soul characteristics which enable him to take upon himself the karma of another ... without protest or resistance" (ibid., p. 379).

If this were the case, then one would have to upbraid those „higher powers" for their lack of historical foresight. From history we know what resistance was put up by the Russian people against every conqueror and despot – for example, in the Battle of Kulikovo-Polye;[*] in the war of 1812; and the civil war, the uprising of the peasantry against the Red terror?! In order to make subservience more appetising to this people one ought to have told them that it was a sacrifice for another's karma. But no-one did this. No doubt this was why the civil war – has Prokofieff ever heard of it? – broke out ...

And now Prokofieff suddenly loses sight of the theme and talks about the Christmas Conference (his favourite subject!) for three pages. But he picks up the thread again and repeats: „At the beginning of this chapter we spoke of how, at the end of the 19th century, in Middle and Western Europe (with its North American continuation), a spiritual situation had arisen in which, for the higher guiding powers of earthly development, it became necessary to 'transfer' to another or to other peoples a part of the karma of materialism which was threatening the further spiritual development of mankind" (ibid., p. 383). – At this juncture we must correct the author and point out that it was not „spoken of", but was simply assumed with no reason given! Or after a few pages of reflection on the Christmas Conference have his assumptions already become fact, entitling him now to inform us that the Eastern European peoples have

---

[*] „Field of the Snipe" – against the Mongolians and Tatars (Editor).

taken on the consequences of the karma caused by the peoples of Western and Middle Europe?

It would be appropriate here to ask the author a question, as he has undertaken to unveil the secrets of meta-history from the standpoint of spiritual science: What does he mean by saying that a people has taken upon itself the consequences of the karma? Is this a deed of the archangel, of the Folk-spirit, or has the Folk-soul (which in his opinion consists of the collective of guardian angels) consulted with itself and then made the decision, or did the people gather at the „veche",[*] „rack their brains", and decide to take on that karma, whether it was their own or not?! – But Prokofieff does not unveil this mystery, and leaves us with the bare facts!

As Prokofieff's initial assumption has gradually been transformed into a fact, he decides to descend to a deeper layer of meta-historical reality (we will be speaking of these layers at a later stage), in order to invent yet another assumption. May we permit ourselves here the simple statement of fact: Scientific, including spiritual-scientific, work cannot be based on assumptions; and still less can conclusions be drawn from them. What sort of logical conclusions are made here, we will see later. But if Prokofieff would like to write literary works, then he should try the historical novel. This would allow him room for fantasy, he could unlock many mysteries, and no-one would need to contradict him. And instead of writing and reading this tedious critical work, you and I, dear Reader, would perhaps find it interesting to draw edification from Prokofieff's novels. But no; he wants to be a spiritual researcher! This being so, we are obliged, willy-nilly, to become his opponents - for the sake of the quest for truth.

But let us return to Prokofieff's breathtaking assumptions. „[It may be assumed that] on the deepest level of meta-historical reality it was so, that the leading initiates in certain secret lodges of the West who, to a certain extent (the author is of course totally informed) had become acquainted mediumistically with the karmic consequences of the centuries-long development of materialism in their midst, which were especially threatening to the Western peoples, decided to make the attempt to find another place – in the form of the peoples of Eastern Europe – where the consequences could be unloaded" (i.e.

---

[*] Popular assembly in medieval, more or less free, Russian towns such as Novgorod (Editor).

to take hold of this karma and displace it geographically, as these initiates can do whatever they want with this spiritual „object"!). „[They chose for this purpose the Eastern European peoples.* The same occult circles then worked out the plan of the] 'socialistic experiment', which was designed to cause, in an artificial way, the 'living out' of the] karma of materialism in Eastern Europe, [and thereby protect] the Western peoples, in the opinion of the Western lodges, from [its destructive consequences. When Rudolf Steiner spoke of this ...]" (IV, p. 384 [p. 359]). But Rudolf Steiner did not speak of this. He said that one had not been willing to tolerate a „socialistic experiment" in the West of Europe. Prokofieff brings this same quotation. And by means of this, and another from a different lecture – where again nothing is said to support his claim – he tries to awaken the impression that his line of thought is based on Rudolf Steiner. No doubt he is confident of his success in this, for he concludes by drawing both quotes together thus: „And so, that which in the West, in the secret lodges of the English-speaking lands, one d i d   n o t   w a n t in any shape or guise to have for oneself, but which had of necessity to be unloaded on humanity as karma of materialism, was displaced to Eastern Europe in the form of the socialistic experiment" (ibid., emphasis S.O.P.). And with this one stroke he succeeds in uniting the intentions of the higher guiding powers with those of the lodges and the Bolsheviks.

After this digression Prokofieff returns to his lofty heights and says: „[At this deep level of meta-historical reality this situation could take on a different aspect (but what is it   r e a l l y   like?): through the highest] leadership of Earth development [as a whole] (it is as unclear to us as ever, what he means by this „leadership"), the Eastern Slavic peoples [had been called upon (by whom? - the archangels? - the angels?) to be the bearer of this [most onerous and] completely foreign karma, in order through this sacrifice to make it possible for the Western and Middle European peoples to fulfil their [central mission] in the 5th post-Atlantean epoch on the one hand, and, on the other, to attain [themselves] those inner soul-forces which in spiritual development can only flow from a [most pure] and [most selfless] sacrifice" (ibid. [p. 360]). Could there be hidden

---

* Here too, Prokofieff is building on assumptions and constructing an absurd fable. If one were to think in this way about an everyday situation and try to describe it, one might come up with the following: Looked at externally, this passerby appears to have been served with a burned pancake by his wife this morning, because her shoes were pinching.

behind this whole „sacrificial litany" an unwillingness to see or understand how destructive, how lethal, the „socialistic experiment" was for those peoples who were subjected to it, especially the Russian people? The effects can still be felt today. Whoever is ignorant of them – whether he lives in Russia or abroad – shows that he has no interest in all these problems!

On the next page Prokofieff repeats without variation what he has already told us: „[But at the same time this whole process shows itself from] a higher level of meta-historical reality ... to be a sacrificial taking upon themselves of the karma of materialism originating in the West by] the Eastern Slavic people." And then once again, but with the additional remark that the Eastern European peoples took hold of the karma and, at the same time, of „the p o s - s i b i l i t y of [one day] (here it is again – one day) ... becoming a living witness of the return of Christ in the Etheric, and thus attaining what Rudolf Steiner describes with the words ..." (ibid., p. 385 [p. 362]).

Rudolf Steiner spoke of the experiencing of the etheric Christ, which should become possible from the thirties of the 20th century, for all human beings regardless of nationality and involvement in revolutions; but we will not find a statement saying that this experience would one day become possible for the Eastern Slavs, if they should take upon themselves the karma of materialism. These are fairy-tales for adults who cannot outgrow their childhood; it has nothing whatever to do with the spiritual science of Rudolf Steiner, which does address this theme, but differently from Prokofieff. In spite of this he tries to „confirm" his ideas by referring to Rudolf Steiner, and concludes that „this clairvoyant beholding of the Christ, ['the true spiritual end result'] of the Russian tragedy, m u s t [become] ... a fruit of the sacrificial taking upon themselves and the humble enduring of truly unspeakable suffering, which arose out of the realization of the 'socialistic experiment' in the shape of the unrestricted domination of Bolshevism and its ideology" (ibid., p 388 [p. 362-363]; emphasis S.O.P.).

History is thus falsified by Prokofieff twice at one stroke. We have already pointed out that there was no sacrificial taking-upon-themselves, no shouldering of the burden „without protest or counter-struggle". On this point Prokofieff's „heavenly history" diverges noticeably from earthly history. The latter confirms that the Russian people resisted Bolshevism with all their might and for a very long period. But in doing so it was, according to Prokofieff, rebelling against the will of the „leading powers of Earth evolution as a whole". In pathos-filled words he speaks of the sacrifices and sufferings of the Russian people, but at the same time he implicitly shifts the responsibility on to them for the triumph of Bolshevism in the world, and for all the misery it brought in its train. We therefore take the liberty to ask the question: What is his attitude to the Russian people? Does he wish the destiny of this people to be understood by the West? ... But it is not the humble subservience of the Russians to which the world „owes" the triumph of Bolshevism. It is rather the fact that behind it occult circles are working, against which the Russians could not prevail; in addition to this there was the activity of those circles who knew how to take advantage of the „submissiveness" of the Russians, calling this cynically – though of course not openly – an inclination to „servitude".

But this is only one side of the coin. In the history of Russia there came the moment after the Bolshevik uprising, when the resistance of the people was broken. And what happened then? Still a „silent enduring of all sufferings"? Who caused all the suffering? – Can it conceivably have been an abstract „Bolshevism"? What sort of abstractions are we being served up? Who, then, carried out the „socialistic experiment" in Russia? Who were the standard-bearers of the ideology of Bolshevism? Who brought it to power? Whose hands perpetrated the „Red terror"? Who was responsible for the Stalinist repressions? Who persecuted and denounced? Who were the people who formed the Party and State organs, the nomenclature and the security services? Who, in the countless meetings, demonstrations and assemblies supported the regime and branded the dissidents „madmen"? – Was it e x c l u s i v e l y the powers of heaven? And those who had recognized the nature of the Soviet regime and had summoned up the courage to offer at least passive resistance to its measures – after the 2nd World War it was only a minority – it was they who became the voices of the national conscience, not the ones who patiently supported and consolidated the Soviet regime „without protesting or putting up a struggle against it". The facts show, however, that the Russians were not only victims of the „socialistic experiment", but were also those who actively, nay creatively, supported and perpetrated it! If the ones had not participated in the „socialistic experiment" quite readily and without protesting, then the others would have been spared the „incalculable sufferings". But here Prokofieff's thinking remains caught up in the same question: „Can the smile of the Cheshire Cat exist separately from the cat?" For whatever reason, he dispenses with his „higher law", and resolves the problem thus: Bolshevism came to power, but there were no bearers of Bolshevism, Bolshevists – only their victims.

And he has no scruples about suggesting an analogy between the way the Russian people behaved during the socialistic experiment, and the sacrifice made by the Christ. Then he brings forward twice what he has already said repeatedly about the humble shouldering of the cross of a materialistic karma. With his endless repetitions he thereby churns up ever more strongly the feelings of the patient and humble reader, in order finally to lead him, drained of all his forces, to the sensational conclusion: „Thus in an astounding and paradoxical way, the past 70 years of Bolshevik rule in Eastern Europe was, at the same time, a most incisive testimony to the fact that still today a 'Christ-Folk' lives, which in our time is treading, on the plane of outer history, the path of repetition of the supersensible destiny of Christ in the higher worlds!" (IV, p. 391).

Thus facts are distorted, healthy common sense wiped out, although the highest objectivity and clarity of thought was supposed to be achieved, as the book was intended as an impulse for the „awakening of individual and national self-knowledge" (ibid., p. 10). And with this we have before us the „highest objectivity and clarity" in Prokofieff's thought-world.

Nevertheless we will take another look at the innermost core of Prokofieff's theory. According to this, the karma of the lie created by Western materialism lived itself out in Russia through the „socialistic experiment". But it was as a result of the Bolshevik seizure of power in Russia that for the first time in history materialism became a state ideology – a state religion in fact. In the course of Bolshevik rule almost the entire population of Russia was drawn into this religion, and materialism was forced by Bolshevik regimes also on other lands such as China, Cuba, Germany etc. ... There this „lie" was propagated in schools and institutes; people talked with their own children in the language of this lie. Here this lie was created, realized and put into everyday practice; here became reality what had never existed before, and could never have existed if the Bolsheviks had not come to power. How could one maintain, therefore, that here the consequences of the old Western materialism had lived themselves out? On the contrary, with great effort and intensity an entirely new and terrible karma was created here. Rudolf Steiner says: „And if today under the banner of the realization of socialism in the East of Europe a fearful destructive force is being unleashed, then all that is experienced there will be carried as a terrible outcome into the worlds beyond the Threshold" (26.3.1922, GA 211).

If the Russian people took this karma upon themselves in such a spirit of sacrifice, then one would have to admit that it went on with the utmost generosity to share it with the peoples of Asia, Europe and Latin America. It is no secret that the installing of Communist regimes throughout the world was orchestrated from Moscow, and that it was from here that financial and military support was provided.* One statement of Rudolf Steiner could apply to Prokofieff personally in his zeal as a researcher: „This Russian Bolshevism – I have said this often before – does not correspond to the original, essential qualities of the Russian people. It was imported from outside. But this is not of crucial importance if one wishes to face the facts; for it is present on a large scale within the region that was once the empire of the Tsar, and it must be observed like a nature-phenomenon, like a nature-phenomenon that has within itself the urge to extend itself ever further and further" (30.11.1918, GA 186).

A fleeting review of the development of events in Europe over the last 70-80 years is enough to show the absurdity of Prokofieff's claims, according to which what he calls the living out of the karma of materialism in the shape of the „socialistic experiment" in Russia „created the possibility for the peoples of Western and Middle Europe to fulfil their central task". Right at the outset of these events Rudolf Steiner pointed out that Europe could expect no good to come from it: „Trotskyism and Leninism" – he said – „mean sickness for the entire cultural development of Europe. The East, if Marxism is realized, if it succeeds in penetrating right into the schools, will bring about by artificial means the sickness of European culture" (11.5.1920, GA 301). Or: „Out of the materialistic teachings from the university lecture-hall there arises, in the next generation but one, Bolshevism. That is the objective connection. And anyone who wants to continue the cultivation of materialism in the search for knowledge, should take note of the fact foretold by spiritual science, that he is conjuring up conditions - after two generations it will be far worse - that are far worse than what we now see ... in Russia" (9.7.1920, GA 198). And with regard to the world as a whole, he warns: „If those things which are now beginning in Russia were to be realized in practice, then this would mean that the Earth

---

* Here Prokofieff ought to have explained the rôle played in his Karmic scheme, by those peoples who took on Bolshevism from Russia.

would lose her task, would forfeit her mission, be taken out of the Cosmos and ahrimanized" (22.8.1919, GA 294).

But Prokofieff contradicts not only the historical facts and the indications of Rudolf Steiner; he also contradicts himself. On p. 242 of the same book he says e.g. that the subsequent total isolation of Russia made it possible for the Western states to play a leading role in Europe unchallenged, and to force Germany to accept the Versailles Peace Treaty ... which gave to the later political and socio-economic development in Middle Europe a direction which would of necessity lead sooner or later to the catastrophe of 1933 and the next World War (IV).

We know from history that Hitler was supported by the Germans because he had declared himself an enemy of Bolshevism. The first Fascist organizations were founded as resistance groups against the Communists. The further course of events, including the 2nd World War, the partition of Germany, and the subsequent Americanization of Middle Europe made it extremely difficult for the latter to fulfil its spiritual tasks – thus occurred precisely the opposite of what is claimed in Prokofieff's theory. The 'I'-development itself was imperilled in the 5th cultural epoch. But this kind of development is – as we have learned in the meantime – not Prokofieff's concern. This, therefore, is Prokofieff's meta-historical concept. But let us return to his Anthroposophy-Tree, and to the misinterpreted sense of evolution, which forms its trunk.

Prokofieff's theory is based on what he calls „layers" of meta-historical reality. The belief that they exist independently of one another and of the historical facts, is a pure abstraction. They are only possible in a thinking that builds schemes and has lost connection with reality; in living reality nothing of this kind is to be found.

But let us look more closely at these „layers".

6.2. The „Karmic Biography" of Karl Marx and Friedrich Engels, the Creators of „Meta-History"

If a reader who knows Anthroposophy – i.e. a person who is addressed by Prokofieff in his book „The Spiritual Origins of Eastern Europe" – picks up a work of his, then he has the right to expect meta-history to be dealt with from the standpoint of Anthroposophy. The reader will assume that behind the historical destinies of peoples there stands the activity of their archangel, the Folk-spirit, through whom is determined the first layer of the meta-historical process. One stage higher stands the leading Time-spirit who is responsible for the tasks of the cultural epoch. Thus the classification of the meta-historical levels which is usual in Anthroposophy is very concrete. It is founded in the activity of the hierarchical Beings who in varying degrees exert their influence in the course of the cultural-historical development of humanity.

Such a way of viewing things the reader also expects to find in Prokofieff's approach to the theme of meta-history. But his expectations will be disappointed. As we have already seen, Prokofieff speaks now of abstract „forces", now of the Folk in general, and finally also about the „higher laws of the Cosmos" behind which – so we must conclude – nothing stands of a concrete nature. His meta-history is lacking in the individual element, and can therefore not be described as Anthroposophical. He introduces the concept of meta-historical layers, but in so doing employs a vague principle of classification, whose central idea (if there is one) he at no point clarifies.

To the first (starting from below upwards) Layer of Reality belongs, according to Prokofieff, external or purely earthly history, i.e. all that one can know from extant documents. The next layer he calls „occult-historical reality", without, however, characterizing it in any way. In the introduction to his classification he also speaks of the „deeper foundations of Russian history" (IV, p. 240); then his horizon narrows itself progressively and finally focusses on the theme of the Russian Revolution. Through the simultaneous shifting of the focus to the West, this entire occult-historical layer proves to be carried exclusively by the activity of the English-speaking occult-political Lodges. Within the third layer – it is the first meta-historical one – his construction suffers a collapse. It, likewise, is not characterized in more detail, and as its only content there stands before us the „karmic background of the Founders of B o l s h e v i s m " (ibid., p. 250). Then it emerges that there are only two who merit consideration: K. Marx and F. Engels. Previously they had been looked upon as the founders of M a r x i s m , which is not quite the same thing.

One could of course object that this is quite obvious, so long as the problem is confined to the meta-history of the Russian Revolution and is not applied to general meta-history. But what is to be said of the fourth layer which, in his system of layers, lies immediately above the third – i.e. above the „karmic background of the Founders of Bolshevism", and shows itself to be at the same time the most sublime, the most spiritual, and inhabited by the all-encompassing karma-forces, the highest leaders of humanity, who determine the destinies of the world? – In this layer meta-history ends, one can reach no higher. On p. 249 Prokofieff calls this final layer the fourth and the deepest in the meta-history of the „Russian Revolution"! (We may recall here that the interests of the Bolsheviks are in harmony with those of the „highest guiding powers" – cf. § 6.1.).

We are unable to create order here, nor to work out a single element of law in this meta-historical confusion. Let us therefore confine ourselves to the third layer, and focus on the karmic biography of Marx and Engels which Prokofieff has c o n s t r u c t e d. He begins with an inaccurate summary of what Rudolf Steiner told us in his Karma Lectures about the incarnation of these two individualities in Northern France in the 8th-9th century, and describes it to us in the following way: In this incarnation the future individuality of Marx had, through a special working of various circumstances, suddenly lost all he had - parental inheritance, castle and possessions, and felt a bottomless hatred „for those who had deprived him of everything he possessed. It was this burning hatred which appeared in the 19th century in the founder of Marxism as a relentless hostility towards the so-called (?) 'class of exploiters'" [ibid., p. 236]. Two pages further on he adds: „hatred of the 'ruling class' and denial of the spirit was characteristic of both of them (the future Marx and Engels) from the very beginning" [ibid., p. 238][*] – and upon this he builds up his argument. But what does he mean to imply with the phrase „from the very beginning"?

Let us now turn to Rudolf Steiner's karma research, which Prokofieff has only referred to in a careless and tendentious way. Firstly, in Rudolf Steiner we find nothing about a denial of the spirit by the individualities of Marx and Engels in their incarnation at that time. Secondly, he points out that individualities then belonged to the ruling class. They could therefore hardly have been able to hate it as such. And in any case, who hated whom? This is glossed over by Prokofieff, otherwise his theory would not be tenable. At that time the following happened: The „Marx" of that time (we will call him this, as his earlier name is not known) lost his possessions, not through an unknown „special working of circumstances", but in a quite concrete way. In his absence

---

[*] These passages are only found in the latest Russian edition; possibly they are more recent results of Prokofieff's research (Editor).

working of circumstances", but in a quite concrete way. In his absence the „Engels" of that time seized his property with the help of an armed troop of s e r f s . And „Marx" h a t e d t h e o n e („Engels", and not t h e o n e s , as Prokofieff would have it) who had seized his property (6.4.1924, GA 236). The „Engels" of that time had no need to hate anyone! Thus there had not been a „class hatred" „from the very beginning", but a conflict between two personalities which had, understandably, to go through a certain metamorphosis after their death in order to find its specific expression in the new incarnation: they became known to the world as Marx and Engels. Rudolf Steiner speaks of this in his Karma Lectures.

So what does Prokofieff mean by „from the very beginning"? This is no idle question, because upon it rests the entire structure of Prokofieff's theory. Have the individualities of Marx and Engels denied the spirit and hated the ruling classes since the creation of the world? This would be a fact of world-shaking significance!

Instead of giving answers, Prokofieff begins to wonder whether these individualities were incarnated in the time of the Ecumenical Council of 869 or not. As there is no authority to consult on this matter, one will have, willy-nilly, to decide for oneself. Finally he concludes that it is of no consequence whether they were incarnated or not, as „it is of no decisive importance for the following considerations" (?) [IV, p. 237]. The main thing is, that they should at all events participate in the Council. But how?

In this case too one cannot follow Prokofieff's discussion without being deeply shaken. If they were incarnated - so he reflects - then the period spent in the spiritual world after the previous incarnation must have been short. But „life in the supersensible worlds between two incarnations (except in the case of high initiates) is shortened only for those human individualities who carry in themselves too much (?) of a demonic nature. After their death they are obliged to return to the Earth more frequently than is normal, as they are repulsed from the spiritual world itself" [ibid., p. 237]. From the supposition that the individualities were p o s s i b l y incarnated at the time of the Council, he arrives at the c o n c l u s i o n that there was in them „too much of a demonic nature", for which reason they were repulsed from the spiritual world. This cannot be called an antinomy or a sophism. Here Prokofieff shows himself to be, as a thinker, quite unique.

As he now considers the demonic character of these two individualities to be proven, he passes over to the alternative possibility, namely that the two were n o t incarnated at the time of the Council. However, as they were re-pulsed by the spiritual world as „demonized beings" there was only one option open to them: „they became servants of the Ahrimanic powers in the spiritual realm bordering on the Earthly, and were able with the help of these spirits to intervene directly in the events on Earth". – A truly casuistic logic!* „In the lat-ter case" – he continues – „the above-named individualities would have been able to inspire that group (been able? – or did they really inspire them?) which was working most actively for the 'abolition of the spirit', and was doing this with such intensity that a temporary incorporation into one of the most zealous participants cannot be ruled out as a possibility" [ibid.].

So, to sum up: A person can be somewhere, or maybe not, and through working with exceptional force can exert a decisive influence on the course of world history. In order to corroborate this, Prokofieff brings an indication which appears to, but does not in reality, stem from Rudolf Steiner. He says: „Rudolf Steiner points to the possibility of such a (?) temporary incorporation, in the lecture of 18.7.1924 (GA 240), where an example (but in a positive sense) is given from the 19th century!" – Now in that lecture Rudolf Steiner did not speak of s u c h a n incorporation, but of a different one, and of quite dif-ferent matters altogether. But this suffices for Prokofieff. If incorporations are in principle possible, then they are also possible in the case of Marx and Engels – especially considering that, in the 9th century when the Council was held, it could – so he conjectures – happen much more easily than in the 19th century; for at that time there was as yet no materialism [ibid., Footnote 166, p. 485]. And spirit-denial was a feature of them „from the very beginning".

Now Prokofieff returns unexpectedly to his initial conjecture and says: „In the case of their new incarnation and their physical presence at the Council (t w o arbitrary assumptions: a new incarnation a n d their presence at the Council), they were w i t h o u t d o u b t (without doubt, indeed!) the young-est and the most fanatical representatives of the group who were fighting for the complete abolition of the spirit, and who then finally won the victory" [ibid.,

---

* Again one cannot help thinking of the picture of the burned pancake and the pinching shoes.

p. 237].* And now, moving on to the 19th century, he says: „And b e c a u s e they had borne hatred towards the 'ruling classes' and had denied the spirit from t h e v e r y b e g i n n i n g, they were also obliged, in order to carry out the intentions of those powers under whose sway they had stood a l r e a d y in the spiritual world ... (so Prokofieff asserts), to abolish the soul" [ibid., p. 238]. – That there was no original hatred and no denial we have already shown.

Where does all this dark fantasy come from? Is it not unseemly to vent one's antipathy towards historical personalities in this way? – To create for them such appalling karmic biographies, combining all this with spiritual-scientific speculations? It also seems to us misguided to blame the „higher guiding powers" for having inflicted the burden of Marxism upon the Russian people ...

But let us follow Prokofieff's further exposition. After summarizing what he knows from Rudolf Steiner about the Academy of Gondishapur, he again draws conclusions of evil omen, which are nothing more than conjecture: „There participated at the Council - present physically or supersensibly – two individualities who on the Earth (?!) and also in the spirit-realm bordering upon it, were especially willing (?) servants and submissive mediators of all the will-impulses of that - in the highest degree – Ahrimanic being of superhuman nature who from the supersensible worlds stood behind the activity of the Academy of Gondishapur in the year 666 ..." (ibid.; the Sun-demon is meant here). – But in that case, we should have to conclude, „Engels" on the Earth in the 8th-9th century incarnation would have seized „Marx's" property under the direct guidance of the Sun-demon!

And now from page to page Prokofieff „elevates" the darkly occult rank of Marx and Engels, to inform us finally that these individualities were none other than the c h i e f i n s p i r e r s behind the 8th Ecumenical Council [ibid., p. 243].

If our will to resist is not completely extinguished by now, we will recall that Rudolf Steiner conducted thorough research into the spiritual, historical and karmic background of Marxism and into the abolition of the spirit at the 8th

---

* Let us extend our analogy: The pancake was burned; the woman's shoes were pinching, doubtlessly because the International Monetary Fund was hesitating to grant a loan to Russia. And this could all be seen through a glance at the passerby.

Ecumenical Council, and he revealed the connection and the continuity between the two phenomena. He described in detail the earlier incarnations of Marx and Engels, and pointed out the connection between these and the character of the world-view and the activity of both men in the 19th century. How is it that he failed to disclose to us so crucially important a fact as the role of the individualities of Marx and Engels as the „chief inspirers" of the 8th Council? Why, after the description of this incarnation in the 8th-9th century, did he pass on directly to that in the 19th century, with no mention of this tremendously important and decisive intervening incarnation – or incorporation – at the time of the 8th Council?

Let us follow Rudolf Steiner's words attentively: „Now ... these two personalities of that time went in their individualities through the portal of death, took part, in the spiritual world between death and a new birth, in all that could be participated in from that time onwards, and appeared again in the 19th century. The one who had lost his entire estate and had become a kind of serf appeared as Karl Marx, the founder of modern socialism. And the other, who previously had stolen from him his estate, appeared as his friend Engels. What they had to do together at that time, was transformed during the long journey between death and a new birth into the impulse to balance out what they had done to each other" (6.4.1924, GA 236).

Is there here the remotest suggestion that these souls had been repulsed by the spiritual world, that they had been quickly incarnated or incorporated again, had taken part in the 8th Ecumenical Council, and faithfully served the Ahrimanic spirits? We must again ask: How does Prokofieff arrive at such conceptions? Is he a new spiritual researcher? Is he creating a „new" spiritual science, which even outranks that of Rudolf Steiner? Already in his first book he was taking a „bird's eye view" of the life-path of Rudolf Steiner. He seems to know things of which Rudolf Steiner had no idea! For only if we take account of his – Prokofieff's – theory can the deeper meaning of Rudolf Steiner's words be understood [IV, p. 244]. But what is the deeper meaning of the words of Rudolf Steiner? It is, of course, that which is added to them by Prokofieff.

Rudolf Steiner undertook a precise socio-historical spiritual-scientific analysis of the theories of Marx and Engels, and revealed the origin of these theories and the factors which have contributed to their widespread adoption in the 19th/20th century (cf. e.g. 16., 17., 22.11.1918, GA 185a). Prokofieff, however, who calls himself a pupil of Rudolf Steiner, did not wish to tread this difficult path of knowledge. For in order to make a contribution to a real understanding of the spiritual-historical foundations of Marxism and Bolshevism, which could have helped to provide a so urgently-needed understanding of the critical phase of Russian history we are going through now, he would have had to follow the work of Rudolf Steiner. Instead of this he thought up a terrible, dark fairy-tale lacking in all that would qualify it as knowledge; a fairy-tale which nevertheless works powerfully on the subconscious and the emotions of those who uncritically follow Prokofieff. But this contradicts fundamentally the indications of Rudolf Steiner, for in the epoch of the consciousness-soul we have to learn to judge on the basis of u n d e r s t a n d i n g , not out of feeling, instincts and prejudice.

In their fundamental tendency – we must emphasize this again and again – his writings shift the central task of Earth-development, viz. the unfolding of the 'I'-consciousness, into the background. They make no reference to it. Not only theoretically, but also practically, Prokofieff aims in this direction; now leading the reader into dreams about the „Cosmic" heights of the Spirit-self, now trying to „correct" his will, or „exert pressure" on his feelings.

7. Prokofieff as Renewer of the Mysteries

Prokofieff is of the opinion that the Mysteries of the 5th post-Atlantean cultural epoch were founded by Rudolf Steiner at the Christmas Conference of 1923-24. In accordance with his view he regards this Conference as the culmination of Rudolf Steiner's life-path and of the development of Anthroposophy.

If we look at Prokofieff's production as a whole, we discover a culmination in his treatment of the theme of the Christmas Conference which should neither gratify nor surprise us, as we are here in a kind of „mirroring zone". The culmination of the „path" corresponds to its beginning, with all the consequences that this brings ...

This truly original procedure, which involves „winding everything backwards" from the end (possibly in order to imprint upon life on the physical plane the law of the astral time-stream), was already applied by Prokofieff in his booklet „Rudolf Steiner's Karma Research and the Tasks of the Anthroposophical Society". In it he recommends to Anthroposophists that they tread the path of Rudolf Steiner in the reverse direction [VI, p. 31-32].

In our discussion of this we will restore the natural sequence and place the culmination theme at the end, but it will oblige us to return to the beginning, to Prokofieff's first book, albeit on a new level, since we have sampled the fruit of his new Anthroposophy-tree, the seeds of which we encounter in all his writings. Admittedly we are, in so doing, flouting the procedure recommended by him, according to which one interprets the „culmination" before one has gained knowledge of it. – So we began patiently to study his Anthroposophy-tree and, starting at the roots, have climbed up the trunk, making our way between the scratchy branches, and have risked being infected by the sweetly poisonous aroma of its pale blossoms. But we have „descended" unscathed to the „summit" of the tree, and have thus arrived in the magic garden. Soon it will be time to leave it again. Lucky the one who does not yield to its temptation!

For the founding of the new Mysteries Rudolf Steiner made – according to Prokofieff – four great „life-sacrifices". But Prokofieff too tries to come forward as a Founder (and risks thereby turning everything upside-down in his „mirrored world"). We already have a foreboding of the central core, as he tries to administer to our individual 'I'-consciousness the „draught of forgetfulness". We believe we have discovered four sacrifices of Prokofieff also: the surrender of a true understanding for: 1. the course of Rudolf Steiner's life, 2. the true meaning of the Christmas Conference, 3. the central spiritual impulse of our time, and 4. spiritual science as such.

The first two sacrifices we will examine, not exhaustively, but in greater detail from the standpoint of the tendency we have already indicated. The last two we have already discussed; it remains for us only to illumine one particular aspect more closely.

7.1. The First Sacrifice on the Altar of the „New" Mysteries: the Biography of Rudolf Steiner

Already in his first book Prokofieff began to introduce a new ideal of initiation. On his path to this ideal the human being must surrender more and more of his individual consciousness, in order to become a highly moral automaton, a kind of medium for spiritual beings, through which they can translate their will into deeds. Thus Prokofieff interprets Rudolf Steiner's biography in such a way that it corresponds to the archetype of this ideal. In order to forestall any element of surprise or protest that may come from his reader he draws attention to the unusual nature of his approach and declares that he has seen „through the veil of outer events" and takes as his starting-point „those cosmic forces" which „worked continually" in Rudolf Steiner's life [I, p. 20]. From there, from out of the cosmos, Prokofieff describes „the archetype of the new, modern path of initiation … which today's civilization as a whole must tread" [ibid., p. 99]. From this unfathomable height Prokofieff looks down upon the biography of Rudolf Steiner, just as though it were lying in the palm of his hand and appeared in the form of a simplified scheme consisting of a succession of seven-year periods. In connection with periods four to seven in this scheme Prokofieff develops the view of the four life-sacrifices of Rudolf Steiner, or the four stages of his path of sacrifice. Let us now examine this – from the „cosmic" standpoint.

In Chap. 2 of his book Prokofieff says that in 1899 Rudolf Steiner had a personal meeting with Christ in the sphere of intuition, and he concludes from this: „At the moment when Rudolf Steiner, at the end of his great Sun-epoch, lived consciously through the Pauline Damascus experience and thus realized the word 'Not I, but the Christ in me', he made a truly spiritual sacrifice: h e s a c r i f i c e d a s a n I n i t i a t e h i s e a r t h l y 'I' t o t h e B e i n g o f t h e C h r i s t. I n t h i s d e e d w e h a v e t h e f i r s t s t a g e o f t h e g r e a t path of sacrifice of Rudolf Steiner ... From now onwards the Christ himself is working through the 'I' of Rudolf Steiner" (ibid., p. 61; emphasis S.O.P.). And straight away he explains: „If we ... ask ourselves what these words of St Paul mean in the occult sense, then we must say: – the human being who realizes it within himself has thereby offered up his earthly 'I' in sacrifice to the Christ" [ibid., p. 72].

Succinctly and with a single imperious gesture Prokofieff here misrepresents the innermost nature of the Christian Mysteries. If we call to mind what has been described already, it is not difficult to recognize this distinction. – And we ask: Did not Christ Himself, for the sake of the salvation, the development and the strengthening of the e a r t h l y human 'I' – this free 'I', which stands on its own ground, and acts out of itself – make the unique, the greatest, sacrifice in the history of humanity through his enactment of the Mystery of Golgotha? From then on the human being was endowed with the possibility of uniting his 'I' with the Christ and thereby realizing the true nature of his 'I'. „Through the receiving of the Christ-impulse into human nature ... this nature will be deepened ever further; this human nature will receive ever more light and love into his own being, so that human nature will have to experience light and love as something that is its very own. The inwardizing of the human soul into infinite depths, this will be the gift of the Christ impulse" (9.1.1912, GA 130). So speaks Rudolf Steiner, and so we too ask: Who sacrifices to whom? Does Christ demand back what He has once given to the human being? Never does the Christ work through the human 'I' as though it were an instrument, but He lives within it as its very own, innermost essence. Did the Apostle Paul say: „Not, I, but the Christ t h r o u g h me"?! As He was in ancient, pre-Christian times, the Christ remains for Prokofieff a purely external, c o s m i c Being, to whom sacrifices can be brought, a Being who approaches Man from above and works through him. The impression arises that the essential nature of the Mystery of Golgotha, as a result of which the Christ united Himself with the Earth, does not exist at all for Prokofieff. For the human being the experiencing of the Christ had to become something ever more inward. Rudolf Steiner pointed this out on many occasions.

As Prokofieff assures us in his „Autobiography", he understood already in his childhood when he read the book „Knowledge of Higher Worlds" ... that the meeting described in it, of the pupil with the Greater Guardian of the Threshold, is the meeting with the Christ Himself. He says: „For me personally, however, it was a fact of great significance that I had discovered, not from 'Occult Science' but from an intensive experience of the contents of 'Knowledge of Higher Worlds', w h o is revealed in the picture of the Greater Guardian of the Threshold" („My Path ...", p. 83). – It is quite clear that Prokofieff had an intensive experience of something different, and a meeting of quite another kind. If one turns to the corresponding passage in Rudolf Steiner's book one will recognize this without difficulty. The Greater Guardian does not ask the pupil to sacrifice his earthly 'I'; on the contrary, he challenges the pupil to sacrifice his egoistic striving, in order to enter the higher regions of the spirit-world (– that „spiritual cosmos", those „most sublime, most spiritual" cosmic spheres, towards which Prokofieff is ceaselessly striving), that he should make a sacrifice for the sake of the freeing of his fellow human beings who are still fettered to the sense-world, and of all living beings in the entire world! It is not to the Christ that the pupil makes his sacrifice, but to all suffering creatures on the Earth, and he does not sacrifice his 'I', but only his egoistic wish to accomplish the ascent alone.

Christ sacrifices Himself for human beings. He says: „The Son of Man came not to be served, but to serve, and to give up his soul for the redemption of many" (Matth. 20; 28). And further: „Yea, I say unto you, what you have done to the least of my brethren, that you have done to me" (ibid., 25; 40). A sacrifice of this kind on behalf of our fellow-men, which represents a true „imitatio Christi", is what ought to have been spoken of in regard to Rudolf Steiner's life. But let us not forget: Prokofieff's intentions are not connected with the quest for truth, but in them is concealed the passionate wish to proclaim the denial of the individual 'I'.

If the human being surrenders his own 'I' he becomes a medium. And if we are to believe Prokofieff, this is precisely what happened to Rudolf Steiner; through his „sheaths" countless other beings had begun to work. One can be persuaded of the baselessness of Prokofieff's theory even if one knows nothing of Rudolf Steiner himself; one only has to examine the theory as such in order to discover that it lacks all consistency and logic; the case is similar with the misleading „arguments" which he brings forward in its support.

As Prokofieff goes on to describe the next sacrificial deeds, he forgets the preceding ones ... For just supposing Rudolf Steiner sacrificed his 'I' to the Christ who from that time onward worked through him, then the consequence of this would be that Rudolf Steiner did not himself make the subsequent sacrifice of the sheaths, but the Christ t h r o u g h him!

Could there be anything more absurd? In spite of this, Prokofieff solemnly reveals to us „one of the most important mysteries on Rudolf Steiner's life-path", which consists in the fact that „from a certain moment of his life … gradually the Being of the new Bodhisattva begins to work though him" [I, p. 82]. Thus was made the second sacrifice – that of the astral body. Here Prokofieff's enthusiasm is heightened to such a degree that he presumes to confirm Rudolf Steiner's communication, with the help of his (Prokofieff's) conjectures: „Thus we may suppose that the permeation of the astral body of Rudolf Steiner by the new Bodhisattva began in the period around 1902-1903 … This is at the same time a further confirmation of Rudolf Steiner's words to the effect that the Bodhisattva was a l r e a d y incarnated, and that he was born at the beginning of the 20th century" (ibid., p. 71; emphasis S.O.P.). If it is a truism that conjectures cannot give confirmation, but are in need of confirmation themselves, how can one here equate the „permeation of the astral body" with „being born" or „incarnation"? – Who, then, is the person who is describing all this in Prokofieff's book? Is it Prokofieff himself, who was born, or somebody else, who has permeated his astral body and writes through him? Are these all the same thing?

And now Prokofieff unabashedly asks the reader to realize in full consciousness „that this connection (made by himself) between Rudolf Steiner and the new Bodhisattva (which was formerly a conjecture) is a real occult fact". From the heights which have now been scaled he now begins „to cast an entirely new (?) light on certain parts of Rudolf Steiner's biography". A feeling of the author's superiority in relation to the man he refers to elsewhere as „my teacher", cannot be overlooked (let us not forget that this is his first book). The intention is, therefore, to cast „an entirely new light" on the following passage in Rudolf Steiner's Autobiography: „… a time in which with all my s o u l - f o r c e s I stood under the impression of the facts and B e i n g s of the spirit-world which were a p p r o a c h i n g me" (I, p. 72; emphasis S.O.P.). At this point he begins to fabricate proofs by means of verbal manipulation: „If we become aware of the fact that the 'soul-forces' must be brought into connection with, above all, the astral body(?), and if we take quite literally the statement 'the Beings of the spirit-world which were approaching me' (i.e. we come closer to them in the way Rudolf Steiner approached them, for example in his lectures on the Gospels – what parallels!), then the total picture grows much clearer for us" (ibid., p. 72).

„Clearer", but still not entirely clear. Why did Rudolf Steiner use the word Beings in the plural if, as Prokofieff wishes to persuade us, he was pointing to the Bodhisattva? - Prokofieff has no difficulty coming to terms with this. He resorts to the well-tried procedure: ascribe no independent value to the individual and treat him as an instrument t h r o u g h which (the word „through" is usually given affectionate emphasis by Prokofieff) other beings are working, t h r o u g h whom yet others ... Thus we have the continuous stream of a faceless spirituality which strives towards the infinitude of a „Cosmos of desire" – where everything finally loses its „egoistic wholeness" ... The Bodhisattva would also be regarded as no more than a medium – t h r o u g h whom the college of Bodhisattvas works; and for us it grows much clearer that he ought to be referred to in the plural – after all, we are, without exception, group beings (cf. § 5.4.)

One might now object that with the method applied here by Prokofieff, anything can be proved. This is undoubtedly true. Therein lies the secret of its „power". By means of it Prokofieff has „fortunately" to „prove" only Rudolf Steiner's communications plus a dozen of his own absurd theories; and now and then he „proves" that there exists a connection between them. Here he „proves" that the Masters of Wisdom and the Harmony of Sentiments are the Bodhisattvas (we have discussed his „proof" in § 2.3.), and then he brings, as final confirmation of Rudolf Steiner's mediumism, the following words from an esoteric Lesson: „The great Masters of Wisdom and the Harmony of Sentiments guide us in our inner striving for knowledge" (14.11.1906, GA 245).

Rudolf Steiner says „guide", and not „influence" or „permeate the astral body", but this does not disturb Prokofieff. How, though, are we to view the „us", the plural, when Rudolf Steiner speaks of himself? Here Prokofieff commits the next travesty, but this time in reverse: by casually mixing up the plural and the singular. He instructs the reader as follows: „One ought to realize quite clearly (not suppose or assume, but – realize quite clearly!) that in these words the regal plural, the [rhetorical] 'us' can in the case in question refer above all to Rudolf Steiner (i.e. he actually wanted to say „me", but could not, as the l e c t u r e r , bring himself to do it!), and their meaning will become clearly apparent (no question of that!). This utterance is a further proof (where are the

147

rest?) of the fact that through the future Maitreya Buddha the e n t i r e Bodhisattva circle, the great Lodge of the 'Masters of Wisdom and the Harmony of Sentiments' worked in upon Rudolf Steiner" (I, p. 74 [p. 87]; emphasis S.O.P.).

And as if that were not enough Prokofieff adds to the twelve yet another five teachers, only to proclaim solemnly in conclusion: „And all these exalted Teachers of humanity worked from then onwards upon Rudolf Steiner, and made possible through their inspiration the birth of Anthroposophy on the Earth" (ibid., p. 87).

Mighty efforts indeed were required to motivate Rudolf Steiner to bring Anthroposophy into the world! Up till then he had worked doggedly at Theory of Knowledge, Goetheanism and the Philosophy of Freedom – subjects that were of no use to anyone apart from Schröer and Hartmann, and he refused to understand what the exalted leaders wanted of him!

Finally Prokofieff promises to show the reader the passage in a lecture „where Rudolf Steiner says, in a form which admits of no other explanation, that through him the new Bodhisattva [together with other great teachers] works inspiratively." How interesting! - But what comes now? – Well, the same as before: „One must only put in the place of the [usual] 'we' (the regal plural), a (normal human) 'I' (he should rather have said „fabricate"), [and the true sense becomes clear]" (ibid., p. 75 [p. 87]. – It remains only for us to thank Prokofieff for revealing the t r u e s e n s e of Rudolf Steiner's words, which the speaker has concealed from us with his orator's tricks!

And now, printed with extra emphasis, so that it is impressed more easily upon the reader's memory, we read the following: „R u d o l f S t e i n e r s a c - r i f i c e d … h i s e a r t h l y a s t r a l b o d y , p l a c i n g i t a t t h e d i s - p o s a l o f t h e e x a l t e d s p i r i t u a l B e i n g o f t h e B o d h i s a t t v a a n d , b y e x t e n s i o n , t o t h e e n t i r e c i r c l e o f t h e a b o v e - n a m e d M a s t e r i n d i v i d u a l i t i e s , w h o s p o k e t h r o u g h h i m f r o m t h e n o n w a r d s . … the word 'my' (from the title of the book „The Path of My Life") can be applied henceforth not only to himself as an earthly human being, but also to the Cosmic beings working through him. From this time onwards (1907) the Being of the Bodhisattva begins to [take possession of] the astral body of Rudolf Steiner ever more strongly" (ibid., p. 76/77 [p. 89]).

7. Prokofieff as Renewer of the Mysteries

Even the „pious" Anthroposophical reader, who knows the basic truths concerning the nature of the modern Mysteries, which can only be founded upon the individual human 'I', and who knows also what Rudolf Steiner says about mediumism – the illegitimate entry into the spiritual world o u t o f t h e f o r c e s o f t h e a s t r a l b o d y – and is familiar with the nature of human freedom, individual creative power etc., this reader's „hair should stand on end" in face of the above statements. But why does nothing of the kind happen? Has no-one read Prokofieff's book? – But we have made yet another amazing discovery, namely that Prokofieff now places the entry of Beings of cosmic rank – especially the Bodhisattva – into the astral body of Rudolf Steiner, in the year 1907 instead of the years 1902-1903 as he had done before. With this, everything that arose before 1907 was not Anthroposophy. Highly interesting! What was it then?

Finally Prokofieff concludes that Rudolf Steiner completely sacrificed all the fruits of his individual development (including the fulfilment of the words „Not I, but Christ in me") to the spiritual stream which had poured itself through him. – Thus Rudolf Steiner's individuality was dissolved into countless streams of cosmic spirituality (including the „Christ in him").

At this point Prokofieff brings a remarkable Footnote which begins as follows: „These words must not be taken to mean that the e n t i r e content of Anthroposophy flows [from the inspiration of these Teachers of humanity]" (ibid., p. 396, Footnote 39; [p. 442, Footnote 46]). A seed of hope springs up in the reader, that Rudolf Steiner might yet be allowed to play a certain part in the coming into being of Anthroposophy, but this proves to be without foundation! „[Those Beings] work from now onwards" - Prokofieff continues - „primarily through the astral body of Rudolf Steiner ... Through his other bodies work other W o r l d - F o r c e s (!) ... in the different periods of Rudolf Steiner's life these different Beings work upon him with varying intensity ... The alternating influences can be seen in their differentiation if one familiarizes oneself with the development of the basic themes which pass through the entire lecturing activity of Rudolf Steiner" (ibid.).

It is really no pleasure for us to trace the content of this sacrilegious and cynical „Biography". The principle underlying it should by now be quite clear: Rudolf Steiner simply did not exist; there were only „Cosmic streams" which were working through him. Is there perhaps no „Prokofieff" either, only „streams" working through him?

On the third stage of his path of sacrifice, Rudolf Steiner offers up his etherbody. The Nathan Soul is claimed to have made use of this sacrifice. „Thus it can be said categorically:" – so we are assured - „just as on Earth we have four Gospels, the Gospel of John, Luke, Mark and Matthew, so do we have in the Fifth Gospel the Gospel of that Being whom Rudolf Steiner calls the heavenly soul of the Nathan Jesus [it] is that Being thanks to whom the Fifth Gospel was able to come to the Earth through Rudolf Steiner" (ibid., p. 86-87 [p. 99-100]). And again Rudolf Steiner is only the mediator, the medium. In contrast to John, Luke, Mark and Matthew, who are acknowledged as the writers of the Gospels, Prokofieff does not raise the question of Rudolf Steiner's authorship – but only that of the Nathan Soul, and answers it - as we might have guessed – in the negative: „In this sense the Nathan Soul does not appear as the author of the Fifth Gospel, but ... [through the Nathan Soul there also worked] ..." (ibid.). – But why the endless discussion? Why don't we adopt the „very highest", the „most spiritual", the „most a b s o l u t e standpoint" of Prokofieff „himself", and come to full realization of the fact that the source of everything is the Creator of the Universe, and everything else is only creatures, mediums and plagiarists!

We recall that Rudolf Steiner, on the previous, the second, stage of his path of sacrifice had – according to Prokofieff – already surrendered a l l the fruits of his individual development, so that he had nothing left. How great is our astonishment, therefore, when we now read: „That is the third stage of the [sublime] path of sacrifice of Rudolf Steiner, which consisted in the surrender to the [true leaders of World evolution]" (does this mean that the leaders of the previous stage proved not to be genuine and could not receive the sacrifice?) „of the spiritual forces which he had been able to acquire in his ether-body on the path of his individual development, and the renunciation of all personal advantage that might have been gained through these forces" (ibid., p. 104 [p. 118]).

In the transition to the third sacrifice Prokofieff forgot not only the second, but also the first. Can one at all speak of „personal advantage from one's own achievements" with regard to a person who has already sacrificed his 'I'? In what state of mind does Prokofieff write down revelations of this kind? Could h e conceivably have sacrificed „all the fruits of his individual development", including rational thinking, logic and, finally, his conscience? Which of the „ever-changing influences" cause him continually to forget what he has just written?

It is obvious that Rudolf Steiner, as we learn from Prokofieff, did not live through the next phase in his life independently either, for now Michael worked t h r o u g h him. As a consequence of this, Anthroposophy completely altered its „signature" once again. Initially it was inspired by the seventeen Teachers of humanity, then they were joined by the Nathan Soul and the rest of the World-forces, who finally withdrew again. In his later booklet „The Cycle of the Year and the Seven Liberal Arts" (VII), Prokofieff defines Anthroposo-phy as follows: „Anthroposophy is a gift of Michael to humanity through the mediation of Rudolf Steiner" (p. 9). This would mean that those Teachers and the rest of the World-forces had „given notice". If Michael were also to go, then no-one would be left but our author, who through Rudolf Steiner's media-tion has made the gift of Anthroposophy to mankind. He leads us to this bitter conclusion.

In the final stage of his path of sacrifice Rudolf Steiner brings about the Christmas Conference and thereby unites his karma with that of the Anthropo-sophical Society. In a later book Prokofieff manages, as we have seen in § 5, to make a caricature of the nature of this sacrifice also. But he had already in his work drawn an entirely false picture of the Christmas Conference, and in so do-ing misrepresented completely the true principle of modern initiation. No doubt this was from the beginning the aim of those cosmic beings who have spoken and worked t h r o u g h P r o k o f i e f f.

At the close of this section we would like to assure those who continue (in the spirit of Prokofieff's favourite expression – „in spite of all this") to seek the actual grain (like the hen in the proverb) in his incorporation „theory", that we do not question the possibility of the incorporation of spiritual beings, and their working through human beings incarnated on the Earth. But our task here is a different one: it is to show that the way in which Prokofieff deals with this enormously difficult theme, where one can, more easily than anywhere else, confuse the gift of God with a pancake, is inadmissible. A deepened under-standing of the phenomena of the individual 'I' (we repeat: this understanding is entirely lacking in Prokofieff) is the first and overriding prerequisite for any-one who wishes to recognize the difference between a medium and - an initiate, or even an ordinary, but self-assured personality; and the difference between an unconscious incorporation and one that is entered into consciously by the individual. And in many other questions too, there is the need to bring clarity. Otherwise one risks coming into a situation where one is oneself „incorporated" – who knows by whom?

7.2. The Christmas Conference – A View Taken from the Land Behind the Looking-Glass

In Chap. 5 of his first book Prokofieff says: „Now, nearly 60 years after [that decisive] event (the Christmas Conference), we can experience inwardly that this event is truly imperishable; that a real act of initiation [of modern times took place. In this act of initiation not only the deepest mysteries of the new Christian path of initiation became manifest, but they took place i n t h e souls of those 700-800 members of the Anthroposophical Society who were present]. For what happened on that occasion is a real mystical fact, the fact that since that time there has been a modern path of initiation for human beings" (which till then had not existed – Rudolf Steiner is not modern enough), „which leads directly to the Temple of the new Christian Mysteries" (I, p. 215-217 [p. 242-243]).

Thus, according to Prokofieff, at the Christmas Conference a new collective Christian initiation was performed ... (Even under the Soviet regime a person was received i n d i v i d u a l l y into the Party.) But Prokofieff always works as one who brings renewal. And he is right, because previously there had been no Christian c o l l e c t i v e - initiates. In 1912 Rudolf Steiner said: „No soul is in the same position as another. Therefore ... the path up into the supersensible worlds is, for every soul, an individual one" (30.8.1912, GA 138). He did not yet know what our author knows today.

In Chap. 7 Prokofieff gives us some essential details. We learn what was the state of consciousness of the 700-800 human beings, the Conference participants, when above their heads this mystical act was performed; we also learn about their state of consciousness before and after the Conference. Prokofieff characterizes this as follows: „Since the burning down of the first Goetheanum the [general] consciousness of the Society Members was dimmed to a considerable degree ... But when the Anthroposophical Society had failed to save the 'House of the Word' through wakefulness and inner activity, it was unable, after the fire, to recover from this [terrible] blow ... The actual inner cause of the decline was the fact that the members sank into an ever deeper sleep ... up to the moment ... when he (Rudolf Steiner) took the decision [to carry through the Christmas Conference] ... in complete isolation ... But even the Christmas Conference [which then followed] was not able in sufficient measure to arrest the process of falling asleep ... For the awakening that was necessary did not take place, despite the grandiose activity of Rudolf Steiner after the Christmas Conference" (I, p. 353-354 [p. 389-390]).

So it appears that before, during and after the Christmas Conference the Anthroposophists s l e p t . And that they are sleeping to this very day – Prokofieff speaks of this on p. 355 [p. 391]. And – is he likely to be wrong in this? He can allow himself to write such things, and nobody notices; many are even enthusiastic when they read them, as his popularity amply demonstrates. The Anthroposophists are sunk in a profound sleep and are not even in a position to notice how he ridicules them – but perhaps he is sleeping too, and writes his books „in his sleep".

Healthy common sense cannot directly grasp the staggering nature of what is being perpetrated here. Let us just imagine: In a respected Anthroposophical publishing house a basic work appears, written not by a slanderer or opponent of Rudolf Steiner, but by someone who is to become one of the leading figures of the Anthroposophical movement. In this work, which contains countless references to Rudolf Steiner, innumerable quotations which are supposed to endorse the standpoint of the author, the world at large is being told of Rudolf Steiner's spiritual mission, of the Anthroposophical movement and Society. The fulfilment of this mission – so the author writes – reached its climax at the Christmas Conference where the founding of the new Mysteries took place. Their central core is the modern Christian Rosicrucian initiation, which belongs according to the words of Rudolf Steiner to the basic principles of civilization. It is in this direction that the newly-founded General Anthroposophical Society should be working. This new initiation, which was performed as „a real mystical act" by Rudolf Steiner at the Christmas Conference, was brought about through a powerful influence exerted (with the help of the seven initiation rhythms of the Foundation Stone meditation) simultaneously upon all those present, without the participation of their own consciousness. – Thus they do not know what is happening to them, as they are in a sleeping state! In this way they all together – in sleep – pass by the Greater Guardian and cross the Threshold to the spiritual world!

Let us now compare this with the words of Rudolf Steiner: „The science of initiation addresses itself exclusively and in every case to the individual human being. Even when it speaks to a group of people it is still actually addressing the individual human being. One cannot represent the true science of initiation in the way one worked upon human beings in earlier times. The Catholic Church, for example, carried over this approach into the present day; not only the Catholic Church, but certain Party directions use the same method still to-day. One worked in such a way that, if I may use the expression, one made use of the mass-psyche; one appeals to that which instils something into a community of human beings in a certain, I might say, hypnotic way. You know that, as a rule, if you only apply the right means, it is easier to convey things to a gathering of people than to each individual to whom one would wish to speak ... Such means, which are highly effective, cannot be used by a true wisdom of initiation ... It must speak in such a way that it addresses each individual human being and appeals to the power of conviction of every single human being" (17.1.1920, GA 196). Rudolf Steiner says the exact opposite of what this author maintains.

Already in Prokofieff's first work the method of massive suggestive influence is falsely ascribed to Rudolf Steiner (whereby no mention is made of the true method of spiritual science), and the essential character of the Christmas Conference is represented as a séance of a collective „initiation". In this way the author (or the spirit working through him) has attempted to legitimize such a procedure in Anthroposophical circles in order to be able to apply it himself with impunity at a later date. We will speak of this in § 8.

Meanwhile this book is becoming a kind of Anthroposophical classic, and plays an essential role in the shaping of the world-view of the members of the Society. The author develops further with unerring consistency the theses put forward in it. And the majority of Anthroposophists agree with what he writes and says, accept it without reservation. He thereby becomes the messenger and prophet of an eternally „living Christmas Conference", which he has h i m - s e l f thought up. The books are sold and anyone can form a judgment about Anthroposophy on the basis of the distorted picture contained in them, which transforms the innermost nature of the modern path of initiation into heaven knows what.

Why is this noticed only by very few people? And why do even they keep silent – with hardly any exceptions? It is not a matter of hair-splitting, but of the crudest distortions of the basic truths of spiritual science. – The answer could be very straightforward: the distortion is so outrageous that one can scarcely believe it to be really there. It dulls the consciousness and rushes past it in wild tumult. And the intellectual, sensible and rationally-thinking people of the West „knock" with their ears,* instead of acquiring more thorough knowledge of Anthroposophy.

In the phenomenon described we can see in addition one of the dishonest methods of this author Sergei O. Prokofieff or, rather, of his inspirer (nothing will prevent us from believing that, in spite of everything, he is asleep). He contradicts himself openly, in a crude manner, without showing any embarrassment. Thus in Chap. 5 of the book in question he tells of a shared, but nevertheless c o n s c i o u s, crossing of the Threshold (I, p. 255). Then in Chap. 7 he describes in detail the „sleep" of the Anthroposophists, but says nothing about initiation. Between Chaps. 5 and 7 there is Chap. 6, which deals with quite other things. After the reader has perhaps „dozed off" in the course of Chap. 6, he moves on to Chap. 7 and has totally forgotten what was in Chap. 5. It is thus all the easier for this content to sink as a residue into the subconscious. If someone were now to draw Prokofieff's attention to all the incorrect things he has written, he would immediately cite a passage where everything is described correctly - with regard to the same questions.

In this way certain spirits are working to confuse the author. This does not mean that he has no weak points. The „incorrect" things he says form, as we have tried to show, a unified and essentially clear world-view with an un-Christian tendency. This is sufficient to cancel out the legitimate force of the correct views which are also contained within it.

---

* Untranslatable Russian expression meaning that someone is talking nonsense although at bottom he is not stupid (Ed.).

7.3. The Race of the Future – „The Coming Race"

We would now like to discuss a further aspect of Prokofieff's conception of the Christmas Conference. It is his at first sight foolish theory of the formation of a new, Michaelic, race out of the membership of the Anthroposophical Society. But here too we are dealing with an attempt, far-reaching in its consequences, to distort what we know as the Michaelic impulse for our time and place it in the service of an elitist group-egoism.

We know that the impulses of the Time-spirit have universal human qualities. They are valid for everyone who lives in the historical period concerned, whether or not he/she belongs to this or that group of human beings. It is in this universal human sense that Rudolf Steiner speaks of the „race-forming impulses" of Michael; and anyone who has an inner relation to the impulses of the Time-spirit can participate in the „community of Michaelites".

This communication of Rudolf Steiner regarding the deeds of the Time-spirit is used by Prokofieff in a restrictive sense when he says: „The race-forming impulses of Michael, which had worked hitherto solely out of the supersensible into the Anthroposophical movement, were able from then on to stream into the Anthroposophical Society, down into the physical bodies of its members. With this the foundation was laid, of a true Michael community on Earth. To speak of this in an earthly sense was not possible before the Christmas Conference (although the new Time-spirit has been active since 1879). ... Thus we have since the Christmas Conference a Michael community on the physical plane, which is different from all other communities of the present and past. It is a community which forms not only a spiritual, but a spiritual-physical unity, and which will develop more and more in the future ... to the point where 'race'-characteristics will become outwardly visible. In this sense the Christmas Conference is the true portal to the emergence of a Michael-race in the world" [I, p. 378-379] (cf. p. 343-344).

In another passage Prokofieff proclaims enthusiastically: „[therein is] hidden the secret of the new Michaelic mysteries, the secret that is connected with the emergence of the new race of Michaelites!" And further: „[For we should become fully aware of] the occult reality which stands behind the words: 'On Earth a new race will come into being!'" (ibid., p. 346, 347 [p. 381]).

7. Prokofieff as Renewer of the Mysteries

Let us try to „become aware" of the „occult reality" behind Prokofieff's mythological picture. We are struck by one fact above all: only those can belong to this „new race", this „Michael community", who are members of the General Anthroposophical Society. And on p. 346 [p. 381] Prokofieff says that at the Christmas Conference, for the first time in Earth development, the Being of Anthroposophy itself, its central esoteric core, its 'I', came to manifestation; that this was born in reality at the Conference, as „the Group-'I' of the new community of Michaelites". This Group-'I' formed the spiritual foundation which united all (members), and was able to work as a completely „new race-forming principle right down into the physical body of every single Anthroposophist". And then comes the definition stating that this Group-'I' is the Time-spirit Michael himself. (Here we will not concern ourselves any further with the absurdity of the theory according to which, during the Christmas Conference, Michael came to manifestation „for the first time in human development" and before this Conference Anthroposophy had no central esoteric core. In § 3.3. we discussed this already; what concerns us now is the f u t u r e r a c e .) In the Footnote to Chap. 7 [p. 522] he adds that the impulse of the Christmas Conference – as he has characterized it – is „the fundamental Christian impulse of our time".

And on page [454] we read the following: „In this sense, stemming as it does from a profound misunderstanding with regard to the Christmas Conference, and hence to the c e n t r a l c o r e o f A n t h r o p o s o p h y a s a w h o l e (Emphasis I.G.; he said before, that this 'central core' is the Time-spirit Michael), the attitude of those people is characteristic, who engage more or less intensively with Anthroposophy, but in the end still do not join the General Anthroposophical Society." From this we conclude: Anyone who does not join the General Anthroposophical Society has no connection at all (because the deeper understanding is lacking) to the central core of Anthroposophy as a whole, and thus not either to the leading Time-spirit and his community; this relation is also lacking to the „fundamental Christian impulse of our time", as this proceeds from the Christmas Conference. Such people have also no relation to their t i m e , as the Time-spirit confines his activity exclusively to the Anthroposophical Society. But what are they living for then? The only use they can possibly have is to pollute the heavens!

But whoever joins the Anthroposophical Society belongs directly to the „chosen people", the „race of the future", and to its Manu who is gathering in

157

„his own" from around the whole globe. In so doing, however, he risks laying claim for himself to the Michaelic impulse, through use of the age-old, spurious means – the play on human vanity and the belonging to an elitist group.

Indeed, the idea is popular, but not new. Long ago there was, as we know, the chosen people of Israel (which was not a „race"). Their task of preparing the body of Christ had been accomplished. But when Christ, the God of the in-dividual 'I', appeared, this people was unable to receive him, because the Group-'I' predominated. The people of Israel was the last legitimate „chosen people". Since the Mystery of Golgotha only the individu-alities are legitimately chosen ones.

The impulses which have grown obsolete are taken hold of by retarded spir-its and work in the creation of „chosen" peoples, sects and communities. Thus arose, for example, the People of the Church. The same underlying idea is at work, only applied to the Church. Here: outside the Church, no Christian. There: outside the General Anthroposophical Society – no understanding for the Christmas Conference impulse, which is the fundamental Christian impulse of our time. Where is the difference? The Jesuits want to create a chosen people by means of collective suggestion. The principles are: Group-consciousness and unconditional obedience to the supreme authority – in this case the Pope.

Another example is especially familiar to the citizens of the former Soviet Union: „The Soviet People – a new historical community that has never existed previously". Here the same techniques were used – suggestion, group-consciousness, unconditional submission to the ideology.

And finally our ideologue also appears. Living as he did for a short time in the Soviet Union, he was able to absorb enough of the emanations of the crea-tors of a new Soviet „race",[*] that historic community which is welded together by a uniform ideology that is valid for all. Is this where his similar-sounding, new and previously non-existent „Michael community" comes from? But in what sense is it „Michaelic"?

Anyone conversant with Anthroposophy knows that, according to Rudolf Steiner, in this Michael Age it is not groups of human beings, but human indi-vidualities which are of decisive importance (25.12.1919, GA 195), as Michael watches, in the strictest sense, over the individual freedom of the human being.

---

[*] „Homo sovieticus" (Josef Novak - Ed.)

How could he be the Group-'I' of a community of the kind described by Proko-fieff, a community which, with a dimmed 'I'-consciousness, crosses the Threshold to the spiritual world in a sleeping state and as a group? The birth of the Group-'I' in such a community is a catastrophic event. It can only fall a prey to the power of a retarded spirit. From this there springs the realm of pow-erlessness and death, of which Prokofieff speaks as though „en passant" in his book „The Occult Significance of Forgiveness". And it is quite misguided to wish to find an analogy between his „community" and that of the Apostle of Christ. For „Christ is that Being who never takes possession of groups, who never becomes involved with groups of any kind," says Rudolf Steiner. „Christ is the Being who knows no groups, who knows only single individuals; and anyone who believes that a connection of any kind can arise within a group with the help of the Christ, misunderstands the Christ-Being. For the spirit can resurrect only in the single human individuality. The spirit can only resurrect if the possibility of development is granted to single human individualities" (28.3.1921, GA 203). For this reason the humanity of the future will, according to Rudolf Steiner, be built upon the nature of the individual 'I' (and not upon a community with a group-consciousness).

Prokofieff has revised the history of the Christmas Conference (the Soviet ideologues were also continually engaged in the revision of history in accor-dance with the „tasks in hand"), and while he ostensibly represents its impulses, he creates a race-group. Its features are not striking in their originality, and are easily recognizable to the attentive observer. They are: a sinking into sleep on a mass scale, a lapse into group-consciousness, and blind servility towards cer-tain „impulses of renewal".

7.4. Prokofieff's „Metamorphoses": Anthroposophy – The-osophy – Theology – Ideology

Initially Prokofieff gave the year 1902 as the time when Anthroposophy first came into being. Then, as we saw in § 7.1., he changes it to 1907. Finally even this was too early, and so he declared that the „central esoteric core of Anthro-posophy" in its earthly development manifested for the first time at the Christ-mas Conference (cf. § 7.3.), and „after the Christmas Conference ... e v e r y-t h i n g became different in the Anthroposophical movement and Society" (cf. § 1.2.). Hence Anthroposophy began with the Christmas Conference, and the

„Prophet" of its „true nature" reports on it from beyond the Threshold (cf. § 1.2.) ... etc. Once he has found in this way a historical basis for his intentions and has proclaimed his „new type" of Christmas Conference impulse, he finally begins, with enormous energy, to serve up to his unsuspecting, sleeping audience a new „Anthroposophy", which we can only describe as pseudo-Anthroposophy.

Now one cannot falsify an entire science easily and completely unnoticed. The truth can also stand on its own ground. But in every science the object and the method are connected to one another in mutual dependence. Respect for the method protects science from false claims and distortion. For this reason abolition of the method lies at the focal point of all falsification; however, it must be abolished, not in a partial, but in an absolute sense: no-one should be allowed to pay a single thought to it again; even the memory of it must be eradicated from the consciousness of all those living now. Merely to remain silent about the method is not adequate for this purpose, nor is it enough to separate Anthroposophy ever further from the time when the method was worked out by Rudolf Steiner. These were only half-measures. One must make it fundamentally clear that the method is unusable, nay, worthless. But in order that no-one should notice any „foul play" or protest against it, one must work upon people's feelings, so that everything is accepted without question.

This was ultimately the purpose of Prokofieff in his book „The Occult Significance of Forgiveness" and also in at least the two lectures held in Moscow on Feb. 19th 1995 and at Michaelmas of that year. In order to work upon the feelings of the „masses" he used the well-tried method: speculation about Rudolf Steiner's biography and sentimental, pathos-filled talk about his sacrifice. Prokofieff had on this occasion to extend Rudolf Steiner's „path" of sacrifice somewhat, reaching back in time to his philosophical and Goetheanistic work which forms the basis for his elaboration of the spiritual-scientific method; and he had to declare these to be, as it were, a „zero-sacrifice", as previously he had described the meeting of Rudolf Steiner with Christ in the sphere of intuition as the „first" sacrifice.

In the book „The Occult Significance of Forgiveness" Prokofieff tells us nothing at all about what Rudolf Steiner had said concerning Goetheanism and its fundamental importance for the fulfilment of the cultural tasks of our epoch, nor about the development of the spiritual-scientific method and the innermost nature of human cognition etc. Regarding the latter question he directs his attention only to an aspect of secondary importance: a kind of complaint of Rudolf Steiner about K. J. Schröer, who had not studied Goethe's natural scientific writings, with the result that the task of editing these works had fallen to Rudolf Steiner, who then took it on. And from this he concludes that Rudolf Steiner had been obliged for this reason to postpone for many years the fulfilment of his own mission (V, p. 151 [p. 122]).

How many years, or seven-year periods, this lasted – of this Prokofieff says nothing; the question should be of no interest to us. What we do know is that Rudolf Steiner was occupied with the works of Goethe between 1884 and 1887, and that his work with the Goethean world-view became the starting-point for the development of his theory of knowledge. In this period he wrote the following works: „Outline of a Theory of Knowledge from the Goethean World-View" (1886), „Truth and Science" (1892), „Philosophy of Freedom" (1894), a series of important articles in defence of Haeckel, on individualism in philosophy etc. – writings which truly lay the foundations of the spiritual-scientific method. But Prokofieff insists stubbornly on his standpoint that they bore no direct relation to Rudolf Steiner's „actual mission". And if this is so, one doesn't need to mention them! – Thus Prokofieff removes the main obstacle in the way of his „renewed" Anthroposophy, and sacrifices for its sake the „central core" of Rudolf Steiner's path of knowledge.

In a lecture Rudolf Steiner uses the following picture to characterize the difference between Anthroposophy and Theosophy on the one hand, and conventional science on the other. Theosophy, he says, stands as it were on a high mountain peak and, as it beholds the divine heights, is unable from there to gain knowledge of the concrete human reality down below. Science, by contrast, stands at the foot of the mountain, is able to see many concrete particulars, but cannot raise itself to the spiritual, as it remains stuck in the depths. Anthroposophy, on the other hand, stands in the middle of the slope and maintains the balance between the two, as it can lift its gaze to the spiritual heights and also direct it to the concrete practical life of human beings. In this way Anthroposophy comes to a knowledge of its true nature. Rudolf Steiner characterizes Anthroposophy in other ways too. He says, for example: „By Anthroposophy I understand an activity of scientific research into the spiritual world" (GA 35, p. 66), or: „Anthroposophy, that is; Wisdom which arises when the human being finds himself in his higher self" (11.7.1910, GA 198).

Prokofieff always defines Anthroposophy in one way only: as „the wisdom of the Holy Spirit concerning man (Mensch)" or as the „divine wisdom of Man (Mensch)"; never as a wisdom which can be attained by the human being himself. But his standpoint, as we have seen, is always the most sublime and the most spiritual, while at the same time he remains blind towards everything human and earthly. One is inclined to believe that he is working with Theosophy. But this is not the case; still less does he have any knowledge of what is happening „down below".

A disparagement of present-day concerns, as demonstrated by Prokofieff, is entirely foreign to Anthroposophy. In the General Anthroposophical Society he is trying to consolidate his mythical picture of the „Christmas Conference", a picture that, as to its basic content, bears no relation to present or future reality, or to that of the past. Historically the sixth cultural epoch stands for him right at the centre, though if it depended upon him it would perhaps never materialize. It is symptomatic that the content of his book on Russia is divided into a distant past and – above all – a still more distant future. A few trivial remarks on the present-day situation is to be found in the Postscript. He comments on this as follows: „With regard to the general contents of this book it may surprise the reader that nothing is said about the recent events in Eastern Europe which arouse great interest throughout the world. But this relates to the actual aim pursued in this work: to consider before the eye of the reader, and with Anthroposophy as our point of departure, the most important perspectives arising from the … development of Eastern Europe and … its higher tasks and spiritual goals" (IV, p. 10-11).

How could one possibly succeed in such an enterprise: to present the „higher tasks and spiritual goals" without taking into account the present-day problems in real development? What an unnatural attitude to things is necessary to lead someone to say that, for the sake of an Anthroposophical view of the situation, questions of the present time must be completely set to one side!

Rudolf Steiner said: „Yes, that is what pulsated through our spiritual-scientific movement from the very beginning: it was not to be just another sectarian movement, but our striving was that it should really take account of the impulses of our time, and of all that, in every possible direction, is important and essential to humanity in the present day. This was our aim, increasingly. And yet this is the most difficult thing to get people today to understand, for the simple reason that, again and again – not in everyone's case, but [only] in the case of many – the attitude prevails that in what they call Anthroposophy they want to have nothing more than a slightly better Sunday afternoon sermon to satisfy what one needs for one's own private-personal edification, but which one keeps far removed from all serious matters" (25.10.1918, GA 185).

The reducing of Anthroposophy to a Sunday sermon forms one of the tendencies of Prokofieff's activity as a teacher, which can at the same time appear harmless in the light of its other „ingredients".

In this connection the imagination of the Michael Festival which Prokofieff brings in his booklet „The Cycle of the Year and the 7 Liberal Arts" is symptomatic. Here he recommends that one should imagine Michael standing at the „Cosmic altar" celebrating the „World liturgy". Then he continues: „The outcome of this sacrificial ritual is that the Cosmic intelligence descends to the Earth in order to be received by individual human beings. Anthroposophy is, on the Earth, an image of this process" (VII, p. 8). An invented imagination of Prokofieff's containing nothing more than the ambition of the author. But it represents a destructive potential for spiritual-scientific cognition.

In his autobiography „My Path to the Book" Prokofieff describes what a deeply moving impression he received from Rudolf Steiner's Arnheim lectures. He felt himself at once as one of those who had stood at the side of Michael in his supersensible School, and from thence had followed the descent of the Cosmic intelligence to the Earth. That was in the 15th century. Apparently, by the time he was writing his booklet on the Cycle of the Year he had forgotten that event, for how otherwise could he declare with the utmost assurance that this event had taken place not long ago - i.e. when Anthroposophy came into being, which was, therefore the transformed intelligence, „bestowed as a gift" by Michael? Now the precise opposite of this is the case. Anthroposophy teaches that the intelligence which has become earthly raises itself, by dint of the effort of individual cognition, to the supersensible – i.e. returns to Michael. With this imagination alone, Prokofieff succeeds in throwing a false light upon the essential feature of the development of the 5th post-Atlantean epoch. (Does he do this unconsciously?) Or is he o b l i g e d to represent Anthroposophy as a gift inspired from above, and therefore calls upon us to experience it as a „gift of Michael to humanity through the mediation of Rudolf Steiner", as „a projection of the Cosmic laws into human souls", as „an image (Abbild) of the spiritual architectonics of the entire Cosmos", as „the all-encompassing thought-cosmos" appearing before us „since the primal beginnings", etc. ? He proclaims insistently that the Cosmic intelligence has been administered by Michael to this very day: „If we grasp the full significance of this intelligence administered by Michael, we can experience the Cosmos which surrounds us as a majestic Temple ..." And Anthroposophy is the image of this Temple, etc. Let us compare this with the following words of Rudolf Steiner: At the time of Alexander the administering of the final phase of heavenly Cosmic intellectuality belonged to the regency of Michael. Starting in the „... eighth century A.D. ... Michael and his followers [saw] ... how in the earthly realm ... the rays of intelligent life reached their destination; they knew: down below intelligence will develop further!" (19.7.1924, GA 240).

Prokofieff's main tendency consists in the elimination of all individual creativity and of individual cognitive activity from Anthroposophy, and the transformation of this into a House of God attended by church-goers. – „The Temple has been built out of the creative world thoughts of the nine divine Hierarchies" (VII, p.8). It is completed, immovable, perfect. This is no longer Theosophy, here we have to do with theology, and its temple is no longer that Temple of Humanity of which Theosophy spoke.

Ever again Prokofieff circles around that chapel which he has erected in honour of the spiritual science he has „discarded", and sings the praises of its „architecture". Unable to maintain himself within the sphere of Sophia, he confines himself to the „logy", but here too we meet nothing but empty phrases.

So far we have only concerned ourselves with Prokofieff's weak points. Is there, in addition, anything right in his works? Certainly there is. One would have to sift out what is not incorrect and at the same time not a quotation. Not much would be left; only a few extremely well-known things expressed in superficial terms; and slogans like: „Only Anthroposophy is in a position to give an answer to the burning questions of the present time", or: The Christmas Conference „is a radiant and imperishable archetype of spiritual development" [V, p. 7-8].

Prokofieff likes to speak in solemn and elevated terms about what is lofty, spiritual, divine; but he does not permeate this with cognitive activity. He takes over quotations of Rudolf Steiner as though they were dogmas, or a „Ding an sich" (Kantian thing-in-itself – Trans.), and constructs out of them, as out of building-bricks which he joins together with the help of single corresponding words, the abstract edifice of his remarkable „Temple". One can manipulate with words „ad infinitum" – until all combinations are exhausted – and there is no scarcity of these. But the worst thing is when Prokofieff begins to e x - p e r i e n c e his constructions. For then the catch phrases appear. – No doubt the followers and admirers of Prokofieff will dispute all we have said here. One would like to recommend that they spend ten minutes each day communicating together without the use of catch phrases. Maybe this would help.

8. Anthroposophy or Jesuitism?

In recent years Prokofieff has been specialising in criticism of Valentin Tomberg (1901-1973). Tomberg was at first an enthusiastic follower of Rudolf Steiner, but he soon came forward himself as an independent spiritual researcher. It was his intention to „enliven" the Anthroposophical movement through the forces of a certain esoteric stream, whose representative he felt himself to be; he claimed to stand in direct connection with its original source. However, in the 1940's he distanced himself from Anthroposophy and was from then on a member of the Roman Catholic Church, having previously declared on several occasions that he was a pupil of the founder of the Jesuit Order, Ignatius de Loyola.

In his activity Tomberg was more open and thus more exposed than Prokofieff: he criticized Dornach instead of praising it, and he also claimed that his esoteric impulse had a source of its own; it was therefore not the impulse of the Christmas Conference. But despite seemingly incompatible features they are very similar in one respect, namely in the wish, under the pretext of bringing new life, to insinuate new contents into it.

The essential quality of the Jesuitical strivings in our time is characterized by Rudolf Steiner as the battle against the consciousness-soul; and it is on precisely these grounds that Prokofieff criticizes Tomberg. In Chap. 2 of his book „The Case of Tomberg" (IX), which bears the heading „The Battle against the Consciousness-Soul" he quotes the following statement of Tomberg: „As the consciousness-soul development has failed, the human 'I' must be supported on the one side by the rational or the sentient-soul, and on the other by the Spirit-Self. In other words, a 'dictatorship of the spiritual world' will guide humanity" (IV, p. 52). This is, of course, a misjudgement (Tomberg was overhasty in his conclusions; although the reality at the time, including that in the Anthroposophical Society, gave sufficient cause for pessimism). But what, then, does Prokofieff do? Does he not say the same thing? – No, not directly. To all appearances he champions the „rights" of the consciousness-soul. But what is his real attitude towards it? Let us recall what he says in „The Occult Significance of Forgiveness" (see para. 4.3.) about the complete overcoming of the lower 'I' (for him this is a fully-developed individual 'I', revealing itself in the consciousness-soul) by the Spirit-Self, and how the human being upon whom the

166

8. Anthroposophy or Jesuitism

Spirit-Self wishes to impose its will, is in his consciousness – we follow Proko-fieff – unable to transcend the boundaries of experience within the rational soul. Or his view of evolution, whereby he aims to reach across from the rational soul epoch directly to the threshold of the 6th epoch, without waiting for the completion of the development of the consciousness-soul (cf. para 2.3.). – In fact our entire study has brought to light a collection of different manifestations of the struggle against the consciousness-soul, which is practised through Pro-kofieff today, but this time in the guise of Anthroposophy.

In his Tomberg book Prokofieff quotes a passage from the foreword to his „Anthroposophical Reflections on the Old Testament", where Tomberg con-fesses that he „... owes to Rudolf Steiner e v e r y t h i n g that he has been able to acquire as knowledge", that „... as the air which one has breathed in is difficult to separate from the outer world, so it is difficult for the author to draw a line between the results of his own work and the communications of Rudolf Steiner". Prokofieff counters this confession of Tomberg with a trite and, in this case, inappropriate remark: „... in [real life] every human being can [distin-guish very quickly between the air he breathes in and the air he breathes out]" (IX, p. 106 [p. 101]).

And how is it with Prokofieff in this regard? Does he not honour Rudolf Steiner outwardly in loud and enthusiastic speeches, so that one inclines to the belief that he too, like Tomberg, owes all his knowledge to Rudolf Steiner? And at the same time he develops in his works, as we have seen, theories that have nothing in common with the research of Rudolf Steiner, apart from the terminology. And in the process he so overloads them with footnotes and quo-tations that it is by no means the case that every person can distinguish between what is borrowed from Steiner and what Prokofieff has thought up himself. Maybe he too, like Tomberg, finds it difficult to distinguish the one from the other.

In connection with the statement of Tomberg we quoted above, Marie Stei-ner wrote the following: „Herr Tomberg says in his first publication that he wishes to make it clear once and for all that he owes everything to Rudolf Stei-ner ... (cf. above). But what is the outcome of this? In Tomberg's work every-thing is built upon the foundations of Dr. Steiner's wisdom; this provides the firm basis enabling one always to make a deep impression, and where it suits one – or where one is driven to do so by unknown powers – one bends things

167

things round, gives them another direction, and no-one can tell any longer where Dr. Steiner's fund of wisdom stops and Tomberg's new inspirations begin. Is this a straightforward way of going about things? Is this honest towards Dr. Steiner?" (Marie Steiner, „Letters and Documents", Dornach 1981, p. 327). These questions could also be put to Prokofieff.

Tomberg goes so far as to defend the Catholic Church openly. It is conceivable that Prokofieff is trying to become the „Father" of a new „Church", which was founded at the Christmas Conference as the „General Anthroposophical Society"? This Society is preparing, for the sake of the fulfilment of what it calls the „Christmas Conference Impulse", to remain for all eternity in a rigidified, immobile form, outside of which a true Anthroposophy can no longer exist (cf. para. 7.3.), just as outside the Catholic Church there is said to be no true Christianity. Rudolf Steiner said: „The approach taken by Rome was such that it decrees: All that is connected with the Christ, all this was the content of a unique revelation at the beginning of our era, and this revelation was handed down to the Church; the Church has the task of carrying forward this revelation externally" (2.11.1919, GA 185). – Prokofieff's decree is as follows: The Anthroposophical Mysteries are the outcome of a single act: the founding of the General Anthroposophical Society (at the Christmas Conference 1923), and since that event only he/she can gain access to the impulse of the Christmas Conference as the „most important Christian impulse of our time", the „impulse of the New Mysteries", who is a Member of this „General Anthroposophical Society" (cf. I, Note 147, 149 [179, 182] to Ch. 3; and e.g. Note 76 [97] to Ch. 7).

The Roman Church stands immobile on (Peter) the Rock; the Church of Prokofieff is to stand equally immobile on its Foundation Stone (the new Grail), which will have been turned into a fetish, but whose essential nature he possibly does not yet grasp. He steps forward as the possessor of infallible knowledge of the deepest mysteries of the spiritual Cosmos, who looks down from the heights onto the events in the sinful earthly word; he is intimately acquainted with the intentions of the guiding powers of the world; he unveils the hidden paths of the great Initiates and the karmic secrets of the history of the nations; he explains to us in confidence and almost without end the true and deeper meaning of Holy Scripture and of the words of Rudolf Steiner; he enables us to recognize who is a genuine Anthroposophist, a Michaelite and a

Christian ... For what role is he preparing himself? With his many-sided zeal he even puts the Jesuits in the shade.

Marie Steiner spoke, again in connection with Tomberg, of the obligation „taken upon himself by the pupil of the Class ... to belong to no other esoteric stream, and if he wants to practise another form of esotericism, he must do this outside the Class and can no longer belong to this" (Marie Steiner, ibid., p. 321-322). But our question is: Do the Members of the High School n o t n o t i c e that Prokofieff is engaged in a quite different form of esotericism? – Why does he not found a School of his own and teach in his own name, and not in that of Rudolf Steiner's Anthroposophy?

Prokofieff bases his apologia for the General Anthroposophical Society, the „Church" of the Christmas Foundation, on the fact that at the Christmas Conference the Anthroposophical movement and the Anthroposophical Society became a unified whole. He raises this fact to a dogma, without saying what meaning he attaches to it. But this would need to be clarified, especially if one is basing one's activity upon it. Rudolf Steiner gave, in this connection, a number of indications which need to be interpreted thoroughly and from many sides, and should on no account be transformed into slogans.

With the term „Anthroposophical movement", Prokofieff offers a rigid and lifeless abstraction! What are we to understand by a general spiritual movement? Is it an object in the spiritual world which can be placed anywhere, at random? – Not at all. For it is a continuously flowing, self-renewing life, a weaving and becoming, whose components are constituted by the developing consciousness of the members of this movement. Rudolf Steiner sought a form in which the Anthroposophical moment could incarnate on Earth. In the lecture of 11.11.1904 Rudolf Steiner characterizes the reciprocal relationship between life and form, which can give us an idea of the necessary quality this form must have. „How does life become form?" – he asks. „Through its finding resistance; through the fact that it does not manifest all at once in a s i n g l e shape. Just consider how the life in a plant – a lily, let us say – hastens from form to form. The life of the lily has built up a lily-form ... When this form has reached its completion the life overcomes the form, passes over into the seed, to be reborn later as the same life in a new form. In this way, life advances from form to form. Life itself is without form, and in itself would be unable to come to visible expression ... That it appears in a limited form, is due to a constriction of this universally flowing life-element" (GA 93).

Thus the form is a hindrance placed in the way of the life; when it has reached completion it crystallizes and starts to dominate, to harden, to ossify – then the life departs from the form, with the consequence that renewal is no longer possible. The life metamorphoses the form of the plant from shoot to stem to the leaves, then to the bloom, to the seed, etc. Rudolf Steiner sought a form in which the flowing, ever-changing spiritual life could find its expression. At the same time he wanted to avoid the separation of the movement from the Society. For this reason the form of the Society was to be dynamic and mobile, capable of metamorphosis, of remaining fluid, of never ceasing to adapt itself to the life. The archetypes for such a form should be sought in the plant kingdom, not in that of the mineral.

Thus the Foundation Stone Verse, which speaks of the life that unfolds in the Anthroposophical Society, ought on no account to be a stone (mineral), or an object like the holy Chalice. An Anthroposophical Society that wishes to be one with the movement, cannot rest on an immovable „stone". Prokofieff's untiring effort to crystallize out the form of the Society, to make it eternal, will succeed only in driving the life of the movement out of it. But a holy place is never uninhabited – it will be filled with other contents. This is what happened with the Christian Church when an „eternally-abiding" form was impressed upon it, and the living stream of Christian life was thereby driven out. Anthroposophy is in danger of undergoing the same fate. If it is made into a „Church", institutionalized, then it will be transformed on the one hand into an exoteric, Church-like Anthroposophy, and on the other into a true, esoteric Anthroposophy represented by the „heretics". These will, in accordance with the dictates of the (negative) Zeitgeist, be driven out and persecuted by the „Church" Anthroposophists. – Indeed, history does repeat itself; the masks are new, the performers are the same! It is precisely this that the Jesuits were able to do with Freemasonry, when they introduced into its rigidified forms a foreign element, the modified „high degrees". And now it is the turn of the Anthroposophical Society – its form is to be deadened and then filled with other contents; any kind of pseudo-esotericism will do, wrapped up in Anthroposophical concepts.

Let us now turn again to Prokofieff's first book. Contained in it there are, in embryonic form, nearly all the themes that he later elaborated more fully. Seen thus, this book can be regarded as a kind of manifesto, a programme, in which the author makes known with considerable candour what he intends to do in the Anthroposophical Society. The schoolmasterly tone sounds across to the reader from every page; the impression can arise that the spirit-world is revealing itself directly through him, and that from this source a new message is being addressed to the Anthroposophists. The rigidified form of the Society is ideally suited for Prokofieff to instil into it a n e w content. His „programme" is regarded by the majority as Anthroposophy – and the tragedy takes its course. Wherein lies the secret of the success of his „enterprise"? Was no-one struck by the strange quality of his book, whose stylistic expression recalls the „masterpieces" of party-ideology, but which for this reason are out of place in spiritual, as in every other, science. And how was it possible that no-one asked the question: With what right and with what justification does the author impart instructions to the reader? Why did this not arouse suspicion? – Is Prokofieff actually right when he remarks that the Anthroposophists are still asleep?

We are inclined to attribute this to a s u g g e s t i v e i n f l u e n c e , as inspired texts possess a special power. It has been our task to follow up the traces of his source of inspiration and uncover the strategy of this source which does all it can to darken and confuse. It can make an author unable to find a way out of a not especially difficult situation, or, as one says in Russia, „lose one's way among three fir-trees". But it leaves behind quite clear imprints as it weaves its impulse not only into the content, but even into the general flow and the style of the text – a style that bewitches, and paralyzes the consciousness through countless repetitions and monotonous sentences. These sometimes extend down half a page, consist primarily of subordinate clauses subordinated to one another, and of the tables of contents of almost entire foregoing chapters periodically condensed into a single statement. The self-assured, lofty and solemn tone, rising at times to ecstasy, is that normally associated with the declamation of hymns; this book is actually not for reading – it needs to be sung! The reader is transported into a special, dreamlike, other-wordly consciousness – if he does not fall asleep, thereby risking following inwardly the peculiar rhythm of the text. This state of mind arouses pleasure, enchantment, enthusiasm, raises us above the earthly plane, and instils into us the feeling of our own elite status and special calling. One would like to return to it again and again.

On the other hand one is amazed by the poverty on the level of thought. The impression can arise that such a book was written only to hide within its bloated forms some of the teachings that we have analyzed, which are foreign to Anthroposophy. For the purpose of disguise a welter of quotations is used. If one could remove all the false teachings and the quotations, only the connecting sentences would be left, repetitions – and slogans or calls to action, with their suggestive force. In para. 4.4. we cited such a war-cry from the first book (I, p. 137). How wonderful and intoxicating it sounds, filling us with enthusiasm! For the understanding it remains devoid of meaning, but the greater the stultifying effect, the stronger the influence upon the feeling and will spheres. Every name and concept which occurs in this confusion is connected to an aggregation of mental images (Vorstellungen) and is summarized with great succinctness. The whole thing is an occult poison of „the highest quality" – narcotic for the 'I'-consciousness.

This is the way hundreds of pages are filled, enhanced with quotations and meditations of Rudolf Steiner as a seal of tranquillity.

The Jesuits want to use Jesus to block the path to the Christ. For this purpose specially-prepared imaginations of Jesus as a commander and King were applied in the training of the novitiates (the young monks). These specific and, as Rudolf Steiner says, saturated (saftig) imaginations strengthen the will of the pupil and, in accordance with the law of polarity, suppress the thinking. Instead of those thought-forms which would have been received by their school as an inheritance of Scholasticism and, in the event of their being developed, would have led to spiritual science, the pupils – says Rudolf Steiner – „were given dogma, which lets nothing come about, of what development would have caused to arise in the soul" (22.8.1920, GA 199). The Jesuit pupils felt that Jesus, their General, was in their midst, that they were his warriors. Shame on anyone who deserted!

Rudolf Steiner says that the will of a human being who puts himself in the service of any cause so unconditionally, without reflection, and with the corresponding devotion, is enormously strengthened. Such a will can work directly upon the will of another human being (cf. 21.8.1924, GA 240 and 4.10.1911, GA 131).

Similar to the way in which the Jesuits created a specific, new Jesus-picture to serve their purposes, Prokofieff creates a new picture of the Christmas Conference. He proclaims a future „… true Pentecost for the Anthroposophists when the impulse of the Christmas Conference is understood, accepted and brought to realization" (I, p. 355). Thus he proclaims to us now its hidden being and presents it as an act of suggestive mass-initiation. Selflessly and at the same time with fanaticism Prokofieff places himself in the service of this new reality propagated by him, and tries to arouse enthusiasm for it in his readers: „Therefore our task today is to strive for an ever better understanding (in his own sense) of the Christmas Conference ... and for the active taking up of its impulse ... as the source of living and effective supersensible forces, with whose help alone will we be able to fulfil that lofty task which is assigned to us Anthroposophists in the contemporary world" (ibid., p. 391).

Christ said: „Lo, I am with you until the end of the world" (Matth. 28, 30). Do these words not apply to us as Anthroposophists, as we are such a specially-chosen community? To believe Prokofieff, Christ would not be able to help us, as He is not the „source of the true, living supersensible forces".

Just as the Jesuits fought against the living, supersensible Christ through the figure of their „Jesus, our General", so Prokofieff banishes the living Christ from the life of the Anthroposophists, replacing Him with what he calls the „impulse of the Christmas Conference", and suppressing Him in Christology through over-emphasis of the Nathan Soul.

The Anthroposophists ought – according to Prokofieff – to concentrate, with an unyielding will, on preparatory work (this, too, is a Soviet ideological cliché) towards an understanding of the Christmas Conference and a taking up (Aufnahme; – also an „accepted" phrase) of its impulse. And just as the well-drilled Jesuit warrior exclaims in his enthusiasm: „Jesus, our King and General, is in our midst!" Or the Communists in their meetings: „Lenin lived, Lenin lives, Lenin will live!" or „Lenin (Stalin) is with us!", so Prokofieff exclaims ecstatically: „The Christmas Conference lives! It is here! It is in our midst and works on ..." (ibid., p. 297). And: „The Christmas Conference is among us! We ought to strive with all our forces to press forward to the place where it exists as an inextinguishable reality!" (ibid., p. 356). The Jesuits could well complain about us: Who do we think they are, actually? All these protestations can surely only apply to the shamans!

But can we also find in this endless declamatory frenzy that consistent effort of thinking which does not let itself be influenced by surges of feeling and by instincts, where genuine spiritual-scientific cognition leads to an u n d e r-s t a n d i n g of the Christmas Conference and a penetration of the concept of the Foundation Stone? In Prokofieff this is not to be found. He can only offer dogmas empty of essential content. In the relentless stream of consciousness (or rather of subconsciousness) it seems as through Prokofieff is singing; he brings together material that he has not understood, from Rudolf Steiner, breaks it down into separate words and word-combinations, and constructs out of them his dogmas and slogans; they slip unnoticed, because devoid of meaning, through our senses, and drop like lumps of lead into the region of our will, hardly touching the feelings. Still after so many years he is still propagating insistently and with unflagging will, in brochures, books, lectures, exactly the same picture of the Christmas Conference, contributing nothing whatever to its understanding.

Rudolf Steiner says: „In the cultural development of recent centuries there is hardly a greater contrast than that between Jesuitism and Rosicrucianism, because there is contained in Jesuitism nothing of what Rosicrucianism sees as the highest ideal ...; because Rosicrucianism has always wanted to hold at bay even the slightest influence from what can be termed a Jesuit element" (5.10.1911, GA 131). This fundamental opposition finds expression in the difference between the two paths of initiation: „The initiation of the Rosicrucians was a spirit-initiation. Hence it was never a will-initiation; for the will of the human being was revered as something holy in the innermost part of the soul ... No influence upon the will element was allowed to take place, because ... the Jesuitic path aims invariably to work directly upon the will, always wishes to take hold of the will directly" (5.10.1911, ibid.) And the Interested reader is not a little surprised to find Prokofieff speaking of the „modern will-initiation, the new Rosicrucian initiation" (I, p. 303). And this is written by someone who never speaks of the „usual", but always only of the „true" Rosicrucians, a modern variety to which he no doubt claims to belong himself. If one uses what has so far been said, to illumine this outrageous statement, then the explanation is plain to see. If one were to „tap him on the shoulder" in this connection, he would possibly make the excuse that he meant the carrying of the will into the thinking, etc. (Or perhaps he would be unable to find an excuse.) However, we are not trying to expose his excuses, but to investigate the spirit of his work in its totality, and to unmask the methods behind his falsifications.

To this belongs also his incredible assertion in relation to the 1st part of the Foundation Stone Meditation. Over several pages, assiduously, but without pretending to examine the theme in depth, he repeats what he has previously read in Rudolf Steiner in connection with the Rosicrucian initiation, and naturally speaks of work on „The Philosopher's Stone", etc. Finally he declares solemnly: „Thus the 1st part of the Foundation Stone Meditation contains [in a new form] both the most secret ideal of the striving of the Rosicrucians, and the [entire essence] of their path of initiation …, whereby the transformation of the human physical body into the new resurrection body through the [inwardized power of the] Christ-impulse [is the principal aim and the crowning] of the entire path of initiation" (I, p. 307 [p. 340]).

Here a sympathizer of Prokofieff will find enough material in his defence. Let him do this, if he so wishes. We, however, feel a certain sorrow on his behalf, and do no more than we consider necessary, First we must propose a simple analogy. When the child in Class 1 is being taught the elementary skills of reading and writing, one will, of course, amongst other things, consider his future: He/she will one day be able to read and write well, will study the basic elements of various branches of knowledge, leave school, maybe embark on a study of higher mathematics. In the light of all this, can we claim that the essential factor in the learning process of this child is the mastery of higher mathematics?

At the beginning of the last chapter we pointed out the amazing fact that Prokofieff tried for mysterious, unfathomable reasons to describe his spiritual development from the end backwards, and also recommends his approach to other people. And so he stood at the beginning of that path which, thanks to this enigmatic tendency, is at the same time its conclusion, and decided to impart to the world the knowledge of the „essential core of the Rosicrucian initiation". Now anyone who, today, in defiance of the necessity of the age, wishes to envelop this initiation in dense clouds of mist and make the entry to it inaccessible to the seeker – as was the custom in olden times – will be most grateful to Prokofieff for this. – Why then? Let us try, by beginning right at the beginning, to find our orientation.

In our view, someone who is about to describe the „essence" (Wesen), or indeed the „whole essence" of a certain path of initiation, needs first to know the basic, elementary principles, without which no step forward is possible. The Rosicrucians do not begin from the end, but from what is given in present reality; with the level of development of the person who is embarking on esoteric work. On this path very strict account is taken of the time factor, of natural laws, and of the sequence of stages of development. The path consists of stages which as a rule are pursued consistently, and sometimes parallel to one another, but never in leaps over several stages, and on no account facing backwards. Of course it can also be said that this whole path represents work done on the resurrection body, and it is also true that anyone who sets out on a study of spiritual science is, already by virtue of this alone, beginning work in this direction.

But we would emphasize that this is not what Prokofieff means. He connects his teaching concerning the will-initiation with the 1st part of the Foundation Stone Meditation, which speaks of the sphere of the Father, of World-Will; corresponding microcosmically, on the level of the bodily organization, to the metabolic-limb-system; and, with respect to the path of initiation, to the elaboration of the higher spiritual member – Atma. The assertion made in this context by Prokofieff is as follows: The essential factor of the Rosicrucian path of initiation is its seventh, i.e. final, stage (in our cycle of evolution). Now is that not absurd?

For whom is Prokofieff writing his book then? – Perhaps for the Masters, who have attained the Buddhi-stage? We hope that our readers will not reproach us for lack of respect for Prokofieff if we say that human beings of so lofty a rank do not need his teaching. Therefore we would return to the Earth, to human beings of our own kind, who are less advanced and have to fulfil elementary life-tasks – but also to Jesuitism. What, then, does the following gesture signify? In connection with the 1st part of the Foundation Stone Meditation, living in the here and now, and – what is also important – within a specific context in the work of our author, he states that the Rosicrucian initiation is a modern will-initiation, and announces that he wishes – God forbid! – to put it into practice. This would mean that on the path of occult learning one would appeal to the most unconscious part of the human being; in short, that one would train the will (of course he says – initiate it). At this point let us recall again what Prokofieff says in „The Occult Significance of Forgiveness" about the working of the (so-called) higher 'I' of one human being upon the (again so-called) lower 'I' of the other, right down to his „karmic foundations" – i.e. to the will-sphere (cf. para. 4.3.). This is what the mentors of the Jesuits are engaged in.

Here the imaginary defenders of Prokofieff could embarrass us with the question: „Don't you know what Rudolf Steiner says about the significance of the will in modern initiation, the will-exercises, etc.? (cf. e.g. 12.2.1922,

GA 210). Was he perhaps contradicting himself?" – This is precisely what one might assume, when one is reading the works of Prokofieff with their impossible theses. Let us try to bring forward a further distinction, in order to clarify the situation in greater detail to the „counsel for the defence".

What do we mean by saying, for example, that the thinking is penetrated by the will? Let us take any of the words of Rudolf Steiner that are intended for meditation, such as „Truth lives in the light". The pupil is supposed to shut out all other thoughts from his consciousness, and in the time allotted concentrate solely on this sentence. Must one repeat these few words in thought, imagine something at the same time, or do some other thing as well? Rudolf Steiner did not offer this exercise „on a plate", because one has to become active oneself. Some people despair, give up, because they are not able to satisfy the first condition – which is generally found to be difficult, namely, not to think of anything else. Whoever does not give up in spite of failure, shows strength of will in this alone.

Through the human consciousness there flow continually streams of thought, and the 'I' lets itself be led i n v o l u n t a r i l y in this or that direction. While this is going on, the human being can say – „I think". In reality he ought to say – „something thinks through me". Here an effort of the will is necessary: Out of the 'I' the human being says to this stream of scattered thoughts and thought-associations – „No!". This means coming to a kind of halt in the stream that has hitherto carried one along with it, and holding oneself on a firm inner ground; this firmness is one's 'I'. It grows stronger and b e g i n s i t - s e l f t o p r o d u c e t h e r e q u i r e d t h o u g h t s. It is then no longer an onlooker, but a creator of its thinking. Every moment of such a meditation proves to be an act of creation of thought, proceeding from the 'I', and is at the same time an act of productive will. In this one can understand Rudolf Steiner's words to the effect that thought and will are, in the final analysis, the same. Such a thinking-will is in the highest degree conscious activity of the 'I'.

Now there is another aspect of the will – that which lives in the instincts, in the darkness of the subconscious, in the metabolism. Behind this weaves the activity of lofty spiritual beings whose working remains beyond the reach of human consciousness. When someone carries out an activity with his limbs, these are set in motion by the muscles concerned, through the occurrence of certain metabolic processes of which the human being remains unaware. Here there unfolds at a barely observable boundary between the rarefied material world and the warmth-ether, the great mystery of the alchemy of material and spiritual substances which science calls the „disappearance of matter", that sulphurous combustion process which takes place both in the depths of the Earth and in the interior realm of the micro-structure of the physical body. This process is mentioned by Prokofieff in his reflection on „Will-initiation", but he calls it, entirely in the spirit of his own predilection, „the immediate sacrificial surrender to the high Gods (which ones?), self-sacrifice on the altar of the world" (I, p. 379).

Which „will", therefore, does Prokofieff want to initiate? – The one that is controlled only by the Spirit-Man who has attained the 7th stage, and „truly lives", in the sense of the 1st part of the Foundation Stone Meditation? „When human beings are one day able to master the forces of their own physical body – spoken of by the materialist as nature-forces – then he will have become a God" – say Rudolf Steiner (5.6.1905, GA 93).

Woe to the human beings who fall a prey to the temptation represented today by Prokofieff, but which for centuries has instilled weak and earlier immature souls with the hope of achieving, by simple methods and with the aid of various dubious tricks, an immortality of the body (even those in earlier times liked to call themselves „Rosicrucians"). The Earth risks being turned in this way into a haunt for monsters! But the world is – thanks to Almighty God – created out of wisdom and reason. There was built into it (as also into the esoteric exercises) a (to use a programming term) „fool-proof" system. Thus we see, instead of terrifying monsters, only strange, troubled shadows wandering over the Earth, who have long forgotten how a human being can laugh; following their subconscious, they wish to taste to the full the last remnants that glow in the depth of their metabolism, of old passions which are not yet lived out.

The price to be paid for the untimely igniting of the will is the extinction of individual consciousness. Our book describes, indeed, the „eternal recurrence of the same". Or should not, in the last resort, „every road lead to Rome"?

But now we wish to lead the romantic connection that Prokofieff has struck up with Jesuitism to a final conclusion. (The saying goes, that two lovers can only hide from one another their affection.) A quite remarkable phenomenon, which has a direct bearing on our theme, is Prokofieff's activity as a lecturer. People stream to his lectures in large numbers. If there are not enough seats in the auditorium, they stand crowded together in the entrance-hall for two hours, to listen. – What is it that draws people in this way? How is it they are prepared, in such conditions, to sacrifice their time and energy? If one inquires about the content of the lecture, one almost invariably gets the same answers: „Nothing special", „the usual", or: „the same as he says in the books". But there is a common element sounding like an ever-repeated refrain through all these replies: „It was so wonderful to hear him speak. What a pity you didn't come."

So: it was wonderful (schön)! Of course, seen from the artistic standpoint, Prokofieff's lectures are an aesthetic phenomenon. What he expresses of an erroneous or dubious nature in these lectures passes unnoticed; just occasionally his listeners recall such things after a lengthy interval of time (when they wake up), but in any case only if they are reminded of them. Then people are amazed to realize that such things could completely elude their conscious awareness.

On one occasion when a discussion was taking place about Prokofieff's errors, we had the opportunity to hear how one of his female listeners candidly admitted that she had noticed some of them, but that this did not concern her, because she was „enthusiastic about the lecturer". After one lecture the audience remained silent for a minute, as after an aria sung by a gifted singer; thereafter hesitant applause from single listeners, not accepted by the speaker; one person here moved to tears, another goes up to the lecturer to express his personal thanks … And all this happens after a lecture in which no-one has gained „anything in particular" by way of knowledge. What, then, had been going on?

Of course there arise in an atmosphere of this kind no questions as to the content. And even if someone were to raise a question all the same, this is treated as a special case (so that the others will not wake up). But if an independent effort of thought were to begin straight after the lecture, all the „enchantment" would vanish, a healthy discussion could start. But this is not allowed! The content must be received into the innermost soul regions in the form in which it was given, and from there pour itself into the will. Consciousness shall not be awakened after the lecture, for the „experience" must vibrate on for a period of time in the astral body. Only after the audience has already dispersed are questions and comments dealt with. Only when will the speaker and a few of those unfortunate individuals who ask questions because they suffer from sleeplessness, enter into a conversation.

Looking at Prokofieff's activity as a whole, the most outstanding factor is his capacity as a speaker. (When the present author met for the first time a person who was involved with Anthroposophy, and asked which personalities were then playing a leading role in the movement, two people were mentioned, one of them being Prokofieff. To the question: who was this Prokofieff? – the Anthroposophist replied: „Oh, what a voice he has! And he delivers lectures without ever stumbling!" But no further information was to be had.) The present author knows that Prokofieff also has listeners who have no idea of Anthroposophy, but enjoy his way of speaking. It is also a remarkable fact that they attend his lectures with unfailing enthusiasm, but show no interest in Anthroposophy as such.

Someone or other might ask: What is bad about the art of rhetoric – brilliantly delivered lectures that have a sublime influence on the soul? Nothing whatever, of course, if only they were not held in the halls of the Anthroposophical Society. For listening to such lectures can be regarded as a form of esoteric practice (whose first step is „study" – why else would it be necessary to hold them within the Anthroposophical Society?).

Of crucial importance is the fact that they have no right to be termed „Anthroposophical", as the Anthroposophical speaker is allowed to address only the waking 'I'-consciousness and the independent thinking of his listeners; the lectures should contain a wealth of spiritual-scientific content and provide nourishment for the understanding – of such a kind that will create, through the medium of knowledge, a warm echo in the heart.

Of this there is no trace in Prokofieff's lectures; instead we find a great deal drawn from that „arsenal" which – according to Rudolf Steiner – is especially characteristic for the Jesuits. He tells us that the Jesuits acquire through special methods a colossal power of the spoken word. Their speakers know how to build up an address so as to work upon the listeners: „All schooling given by Jesuitism aims to provide the Jesuit with the power to arrange his words, to fashion the manner of his speaking, in such a way that what he presents or what he does, creeps by stealth, one might say, into the astral impulses of the human being" (9.5.1916, GA 167; cf. also 4.4.1916, ibid.). For this reason there is contained in their lectures „nothing special" from the point of view of knowledge.

And if Prokofieff believes that the essential feature of the Christmas Conference is a suggestive mass-initiation, then he works – by his own testimony – consistently in their spirit.

In the phenomenon of Prokofieff we find other parallels to Jesuitism. It was already remarked that the over-stressing (Überspannung) of the Jesus-principle – as Rudolf Steiner calls it – corresponds in Prokofieff with the over-stressing of the Nathan Soul – with the single difference that the first is an earthly and that of Prokofieff is a heavenly human being; but in both cases the human being stands in the foreground, and the Christ has to retreat into the background. How strikingly oppressive is the contrast between, on the one hand, the lower, sinful 'I' of man (laden with every kind of vice), as depicted by Prokofieff in his book on forgiveness, and the all-forgiving, immaculate higher 'I', in the form of the angel who redeems the human being through taking control of his will (or the only living, heavenly Nathan Soul), on the other; all this corresponds to that disciplining of will, which is cultivated in the Jesuitic schools. There the pupil develops at the first stage the picture of the human being fallen into sin, who has turned away from God, and must now await terrible punishments; and at the second stage, that of the merciful God who redeems man (cf. 5.10.1911, GA 131).

In the News for Members in the weekly „Das Goetheanum" (No. 4 of 20.4.1997), Prokofieff published, as a continuation of the „accusation" against the Tomberg followers which he had begun in the first edition of the book „The Case of Tomberg", an article in which he charges them with having tried to demonstrate the similarity between the Rosicrucian and the Jesuitic paths of initiation. This „fight for the truth" looks like a strange misunderstanding on Prokofieff's part, when he declares quite openly that the Rosicrucian initiation is a will-initiation. He has therefore represented the two paths as being not merely related, but identical. But Prokofieff subverts the path of schooling not only with words, for by manipulating his readers and listeners with the seductive fruits of his atavistic clairvoyance and by means of suggestive methods, he subverts and destroys this path of schooling quite concretely.

But even the second point of his charge against the Tomberg followers, namely that they intend to divert the return of Christ in the Etheric on to Jesuitic paths, he must direct against himself. What else is he doing, when he steers the whole attention of his audience towards the so-called impulse of the

Christmas Foundation and declares this to be the impulse of the new Christian Mysteries? And as the highest goal and the highest ideal of these Mysteries he places at the focal point his „heavenly human being", the Nathan Soul.

The Tomberg followers sympathize with Jesuitism. Prokofieff criticizes it, but concealed behind this criticism he practises it with all the greater vigour and effectiveness. But the words of the Gospel proclaim in their wisdom: By their fruits you will know them (Matth. 7, 20).

This case is characterized in a particularly graphic way by the following words of Marie Steiner: „At the most varied points of the periphery there have often been mediumistic personalities who can offer minor demonstrations of clairvoyance and have initially impressed even prominent Members. Most of them have harboured the desire to come to Dornach and, as the emissaries of the Masters or 'out of the East', to rescue the Goetheanum. Until finally all the splendour that was built up on mediumistic faculties vanished into fog and mist and the eyes or most people were opened. But it has produced blooms of a ter- rible kind and borne fruits that resemble the deadly nightshade. And perhaps that which gives rise in the deepest and ultimate sense to our difficulties in the Society is the battle with those elements which try ever and again to break through the rigour and purity of Dr. Steiner's method of spiritual scientific work, and drive the Society onto the path of psychic sensationalism. In the 'Free Society' they have succumbed to this danger, the crass evidence for this being the still active case of Benthien,[*] which represents a summit of mischief of this kind. It came about because the young people received unsound advice. But the gates always stand open to every danger, as soon as vanity and ambi- tion strike up an alliance with uncontrolled psychic powers" (Marie Steiner, ibid., p. 326-327).

---

[*] A „clairvoyante" who, with her mystical utterances concerning incarnations, played a big part in certain circles of the Society in the 1920's and 1930's (Note from the book of M. Steiner).

Annexe

Review by Hellmut Finsterlin of the first book published by Sergei Prokofieff – „Rudolf Steiner and the Founding of the New Mysteries", Stuttgart 1982.

From „Erde und Kosmos" Nr. 2/1983:

There is not space in this issue to do more than mention this book, so we postpone a more detailed review until Issue Nr. 3. But we would like to say that the praise which has been lavished upon the author from all sides is not justified, unless one is willing to put knowledge of literature and the length of a text above its real cognitive content. This is the warning we wish to give, much as we would acknowledge the achievement of a 28-year-old Russian. Prokofieff, grandson of the famous composer, set himself, out of the full enthusiasm of his young, Slavic soul, a task which he could not fulfil: namely, to describe the genesis and the content of the modern Mysteries, in relation to the seven-year periods in the life of Rudolf Steiner.

From his knowledge of the seven-year rhythms described by Rudolf Steiner, he could himself have realized that from the third to the fourth seven-year period it is not possible to accomplish something which must, to a person who has matured through difficult life-trials, appear scarcely realizable or entirely unrealizable: to grasp to its very depths a life such as that of the great Teacher, and even - which is more ambitious still – the Mystery nature of Anthroposophy. Where a man who has grown wise would maintain a cautious distance – Goethe, for example, preferred to leave as a fragment a work for which his powers did not seem adequate – a young storm-trooper dashes headlong into many serious mistakes, errors and speculations.

Thus, for example, in 1925 Rudolf Steiner found that the Christmas Conference had failed (sei „nicht angekommen"). Not Prokofieff, however. This Conference could not fail, so he believes. Of course not; but to arrive on Earth („auf Erden ankommen") is something quite different. A „High School for Spiritual Science" requires not only sections, but three Classes, the second of which would consist of 36 Initiates, while the third would consist of 12. Where are the Classes, and where are the Initiates? Did the Christmas Conference really „succeed"? More details in the next Issue.

Issue Nr. 3/1983:

„We need only contemplate the sheer scope of the spiritual wisdom which came into the world thanks to the earthly activity of Rudolf Steiner. Where do we find anything similar in the entire outer history of Mankind's development? 'On the aesthetic level alone the spectacle of this world-view encompassing spirit and matter is something tremendous. One can have some knowledge of the spiritual history of Mankind and ask the question: Where has humanity ever experienced anything of this kind? Aristotle, Thomas Aquinas – here was still more ...' (F. Rittelmeyer, Stuttgart 1980. „My Meeting with Rudolf Steiner").

These words of Rittelmeyer indicate the place occupied by Rudolf Steiner in the spiritual and cultural life of Western humanity. All the fundamental expectations of Western humanity, the problems concerning the individual 'I', the freedom of the will, the nature of thinking, science, art, religion – all these questions we find drawn together in Rudolf Steiner as in an all-embracing centre, and from it they radiate into the world in six thousand lectures, dozens of books and essays. The entire picture of the spiritual life of mankind stands before us. It comes into the world for the first time, and we must ask: Where can it have come from, if not from those who in truth lead and realize this spiritual life of humanity and give it direction? We cannot inwardly regard ourselves completely as Anthroposophists if we do not fully comprehend that when, for example, Rudolf Steiner was speaking in his lectures on the Bodhisattva, the Bodhisattva was there beside him; when he spoke of Christian Rosenkreuz (sic), of Manes, Skythianos, Zarathustra, Buddha, all these great Teachers of humanity stood before his spiritual gaze, and blessed him in his service for them and for humanity, through revealing to him their own being. This is the spiritual reality which every Anthroposophist must absolutely recognize. But from this there follows the great responsibility borne by those who continue Rudolf Steiner's work on Earth. The responsibility of e v e r y Anthroposophist which he/she carries immediately before the spiritual world, and above all before those lofty spiritual Beings who, through their great representative, sent to the Earth the new spiritual revelation. The destiny of this revelation is now irrevocably bound up with the destiny of Mankind as a whole."

This perhaps somewhat verbose and, in its train of thought, not always quite logical (we find „questions" drawn together in Steiner's work) characterization of the spirit known to us under the name of Rudolf Steiner, one could very well imagine occupying a central place in a book dealing with the „Founding of the

New Mysteries". One could see it as an introduction, or as a result of the investigation. It was written by Prokofieff and it is found in his book, but only „en passant" as Note 40 to the third Chapter. It seems to me that the placing of it thus, speaks more loudly than many words, and one must ask oneself whether the author has really understood what he is writing. Could this be merely a resurfacing of things that he has previously absorbed with great zeal? – He is very well versed in Anthroposophical literature. Is it no more than a pouring forth of his own idiosyncracies, in the form of speculations, constructions which are shaped almost of themselves in his soul, as from an over-filled spring whose flow would need to be stemmed deliberately, in order to prevent an inundation? No doubt what Prokofieff says there is true. Whether he is able to do justice to this truth, only the content of the book will show.

The task undertaken by the author who at the time was aged 27-28, of describing the founding of the new Mysteries – the Mysteries of the 20th century – as seen in relation to the seven-year periods in Rudolf Steiner's life, is a formidable one! The hope that such a work might be accomplished is only justified on condition that the author has himself penetrated these Mysteries. This would mean that he had attained at least the degree of Journeyman on the path of initiation. A comprehensive work which is grounded in itself would not yet arise on this basis, but points of view could be presented which would prompt the reader to further study, and the sources of errors would be fewer than in the case of someone who has only read and studied.

If someone takes seriously the seven-year periods of development, then he must ask himself – when he has just completed the fourth seven-year period – to what extent the possibility is open to him to comprehend the Mysteries. The author must surely know something of these life-phases if he is taking those of Rudolf Steiner into account.

Rudolf Steiner himself, supremely gifted though he was, clearly did not find that he was in a position to come forward publicly with the content of the Mysteries before his 40th year. His first work pointing in this direction appeared in 1902. Its title was „Christianity as Mystical Fact and the Mysteries of Antiquity", a modest title compared to that chosen by this author. Did Prokofieff succeed in his aim? We think not. We would like to give our reasons for this with the help of a few examples.

Talkativeness – an Obstacle

What one meets – the further one advances in the text, the more unpleasant the feeling of one's mind being „steamed up" and pushed in the direction of thoughts which lead one away from realities rather than towards them – is the extreme wordiness. Every Anthroposophist who has trodden step by step his path of knowledge, working from the beginning and in an orderly fashion, knows that at an early stage he comes into the phase of the „runaway tongue". We know this phenomenon well, which many a person, even when he/she is old and grey, has never grown out of, although the 'chatterbox' period ought never to be more than a brief transitional phase. The nascent Anthroposophist – one who is just starting out on his/her Anthroposophical path of development – can only be advised to watch this initial phase with special attentiveness, and rein it in as energetically as possible.

Prokofieff knows no such restraint. He clearly found no teacher who urged him to pay attention to this phenomenon, which was already described by Rudolf Steiner in his basic writings on the theme of inner development. This weakness of the author shows itself in a particularly unfortunate way when he is speaking of the macrocosmic Prayer in connection with the laying of the foundation stone of the Goetheanum in 1913, and the lectures held by Rudolf Steiner later on the Fifth Gospel. This extends over many pages, and something happens that should never be done to one of the most profound words of the Mysteries: the author completely 'discusses it to death'. The reader loses sight of the text, and in its place has to take in one wordy speech after another. In this way one drives one's reader away from the substance instead of towards it, as the author would actually wish to do.

When in the course of his efforts and exercises the spiritual pupil comes close to the Threshold, the warning sounds across to him from the Guardian that he should avoid the thoughtless use of words. Every unconsidered word, every word too many – every one too few also – forms itself into a serious obstacle. The loquacious person is endangered to an extraordinarily high degree! He erases, so to speak, with a single verbal effusion, everything that strenuous effort may have brought him in the way of virtues. There are people who speak such an awful lot that they destroy not only what they have acquired in the present, but also good predispositions which they have brought into this life as a result of earlier earthly lives. The consequence of this, as one may well imagine, is that the pupil not only fails to progress, but actually retrogresses! It is often difficult, if not impossible, in such a case to transform this retrograde development into progress in the course of this lifetime. And for the person concerned, when he has once become aware of it, this is not only sad, but really tragic!

The reader of books which indulge in verbose discussion of the profound mysteries of humanity should be given this very emphatic warning. He can only absorb such writings without harm to himself if he does so with the use of wakeful, intensified forces of consciousness!

It is symptomatic that occasionally the author includes remarks which are supposed to be critical of others, and are not incorrect in themselves, but which actually apply to him. Such things arise from the subconscious, which is quite capable of self-criticism. On p. 118 he says the Anthroposophical daughter institutions have not only given rise to the 'most splendid fruits', but had also brought difficulties in their train. „These, however, arise … above all because many Anthroposophists who carried with enthusiasm the Anthroposophical impulse into important fields of life and activity, had not recognized, owing to insufficient preparation, the true nature of Anthroposophy. They had not understood that from the beginning Anthroposophy had a profoundly esoteric character, which it still has and will always retain in the future …" How true! The only question is: how great is the depth of the person who is judging the depths to be deep? Esotericism is the same as occult teaching. This does not allow, even in the age of the making public of the Mysteries, that one speaks of and around it more than is absolutely necessary. How much is necessary, this the esotericist, the occultist, must know precisely. If he does not know this precisely, then he must hold his tongue. In this sphere it is far better to say nothing than to say something incorrect.

Did Rudolf Steiner Sacrifice his Four Bodily Sheaths?
1. Sacrifice of the 'I'

The first part of the book deals with „The Mystery of Rudolf Steiner's Life-Path". Here the author puts forward the thesis that, between his 35th and 42nd year Rudolf Steiner had sacrificed his 'I', then in the next seven-year period his astral body, then his ether-body, and from his 56th year up to his death his physical body. The weakness of this line of thought is easily demonstrated. Steiner began, as we know, his teaching activity as an Anthroposophist after the turn of the century. According to Prokofieff it was, shortly after this, no longer he himself who was working at all, but the Being to whom he had sacrificed his 'I'. Something corresponding to this occurs in 1910 at the latest, when the astral body came into the possession of the Bodhisattva, who will attain the rank of Buddha after the lapse of three millennia. The uniqueness of Steiner's being has vanished. The Being to whom, according to Prokofieff, he sacrificed his ether body ought, if one takes it more exactly, to have considerably strengthened it. While the sacrifice of the physical body could only create an obstacle for the development of the Anthroposophical Society (so it turned out). One cannot help thinking of a Baba-yaga consisting of four dolls, of which one after the other is „sacrificed" until all four have gone. It seems that one imagines thus the four bodily sheaths of the soul and spirit being „Man", and the question what happened to the individuality of Rudolf Steiner becomes shrouded in uncertainty.

We do not want simply to dismiss such an idea, but will try to give more precise reasons why a „sacrifice" of bodily sheaths as here described, whether it be those of Rudolf Steiner or of any other personality, is a rather impossible conception.

The 'I', so Prokofieff argues, was sacrificed by Steiner in the sense of the words of St Paul, as an act of following in the footsteps – not of course an „imitation" (Prokofieff) – of the Christ. Now this surrender of the self before the higher, the true 'I', as the „World-I", is not something that the human being who has advanced in his development to the corresponding level can or should carry through on a permanent basis. There are certain actions which, if they are really to succeed, must take place with the surrender of one's own 'I' – e.g. the offering of the priest at the altar, the medical treatment of the sick, also the work with the bio-dynamic preparations, as I have often described.

The situation is somewhat different in the case of the cognitive processes, which rest – in the sense given this term by Steiner – upon intuition. An archetype of such processes is Goethe's becoming aware of the „Ur" (archetypal) – plant. The Goethean act of cognition comes about through the process whereby the knower himself becomes the Being he wishes to know. If this is, for example, a plant, then the knower will himself become the plant, but without giving up his self-consciousness. He must maintain this, otherwise the process has no meaning for him. The plant has a consciousness resembling that of our deep

sleep. The knower must become the plant, but maintain his waking consciousness at the same time. As a knower I must still be able to stand above my plant-
nature and observe my new (and temporary) being.

If, however, I now go on to make the result of my cognitive act ready for
printing on paper or for delivery in speech, then I cannot do without my usual,
lower 'I', for only this can handle paper, typewriter, and operate with spelling,
punctuation, syntax etc. There can be no question of a „sacrifice" of my instrument, my everyday 'I' – but rather of a „Lose yourself in order to find yourself". Rudolf Steiner has unquestionably been for us an outstanding example of
this, and in his writings on inner development he has described how the pupil
can himself come to ascend the stages of „losing oneself" in the „finding oneself". Now to put forward as an obvious fact that Rudolf Steiner had sacrificed
„his earthly 'I' to the Christ", „so that He could speak out of his physical
sheath", and to describe this as something quite exceptional which is especially
and uniquely characteristic of Rudolf Steiner – this is, if one enters more deeply
into the human striving for knowledge in the Rosicrucian sense, more a belit-
tlement than an honouring of the spirit of Rudolf Steiner, especially when this
happens in an exclusive (series of publications offering) „Stimulus to Anthroposophical Work".

2. Sacrifice of the Astral Body?

On p. 78 Prokofieff sums up his view of the second sacrifice of Rudolf Steiner
as follows: „Rudolf Steiner sacrificed as an Initiate his earthly astral body, placing it at the disposal of the lofty spiritual being, the Bodhisattva, who from then
onwards spoke through him. This deed is the second stage on the great path of
sacrifice of Rudolf Steiner. This took place between 1906 and 1907, around the
middle of the 7th seven-year period, which stands under the signature of the
forces of the Spirit-self. With this event the autobiography „The Path of My
Life" also reached its proper conclusion. For the word „my" can now be applied by Rudolf Steiner not only to himself as an earthly human being, but also
to the cosmic Beings who work through him." Appended to this impossible
statement is the Note which we used as our introductory quotation.

Firstly, what is an „earthly astral body"? An astral body is never „earthly",
unless in contrast to it there were such things as „heavenly astral bodies". We

do not wish to be pedantic, but merely look more closely at the very inadequate conception itself.

Wimbauer places the entry of the Bodhisattva in the 36th year, and now Prokofieff places the same event in the 46th year; while Steiner says that such a thing happens – if at all – between the 30th and 33rd year. But what are six or ten years to a young author? – A nothing in the great universe ... But what really happens is clear neither to the author nor to the reviewers who praise him. I will try to explain.

There are countless others too, but one help in orientation can be found in e.g. a brief summary of Steiner's on the theme of the three original degrees of the Masonic initiation (Berlin, 4.4.1916, in „Present and Past in the Human Spirit", Lecture 4; GA 167). For any kind of initiation there were definite stages, here called Apprentice, Journeyman, Master. The third degree, which one will certainly accord to Rudolf Steiner, is distinguished from the two lower degrees through the fact that whoever has attained it can voluntarily leave at any time his physical-etheric body, can ascend to higher worlds while completely maintaining his self-consciousness, and can then return of his own free will into the physical-etheric sheath. Thus a very lofty capacity has been attained. If it were necessary for such an initiate to come to an agreement with, let us say, the Bodhisattva who will rise to the level of Maitreya Buddha in 3000 years' time then he does not need, for this purpose, to „sacrifice" to him his astral body, but he will meet him in higher worlds. „Conferences" take place – and this occurs continually – of free spirits in higher worlds. Without them, nothing at all would happen on the Earth.

It should not pass unmentioned on this occasion that amateurishness in occult matters has been sprouting the most deplorable fruits for decades in Anthroposophical circles. It must strike the veteran as especially ridiculous when the claim is unmistakably being made by the person concerned that he knows everything much better.

So in what relation does the spirit of Rudolf Steiner stand to this Bodhisattva? In his Note to p. 134 (Nr. 136 on p. 420), referring to a later time, Prokofieff says the following: „At this time Rudolf Steiner rose in his individual development to that stage of initiation also, which was attained, though in a form corresponding to that time, by Christian Rosenkreuz (sic) in the 15th century, and which was later described in a more pictorial way in the book 'The Chymical Wedding of Chr. Rosenkreuz anno 1459'."

Incidentally, the name Rosenkreutz is spelled with a „tz". But who told our good Prokofieff when and how Rudolf Steiner completed his stages of initiation? Can one excuse such a thing with the rashness of youth? Who was at fault here? – The young man or his teachers? But it is not only for this reason that I quote the passage. For Prokofieff continues: „This also throws light on the following imagination given by Rudolf Steiner when, after the Christmas Conference, he was asked about the relation between the Anthroposophical and Rosicrucian streams: On the left stands Christian Rosenkreuz in a blue stole, and on the right Rudolf Steiner in a red stole; in t h i s imagination they stand side by side" (emphasis S.O.P.).

Prokofieff does not tell us where he got this from. It is described by E. Kirchner-Bockholt in „The Task for Mankind of Rudolf Steiner and Ita Wegman", Dornach 1976, in the chapter entitled „Rudolf Steiner's Mission". The theme under discussion is an initiation Mantram. It goes on: „To the second part of the verse Rudolf Steiner had said that one should imagine oneself advancing towards the altar wearing a white garment; on the left before the altar is standing Christian Rosenkreutz with the blue stole, and on the right Rudolf Steiner with the red stole. This altar must be imagined in the spiritual world. On another occasion Rudolf Steiner said that in the spiritual world the two stand side by side wearing these stoles."

Please note: Prokofieff says, „... in t h i s imagination they stand side by side". Why does he alter the statement so slightly that one hardly notices? – Because otherwise it does not fit into his scheme! This is supposed to be true only for o n e, for t h i s imagination. What is really the case, then?

In this respect the by no means infallible Hermann Keimeyer is far superior to his rivals H. Wimbauer, and now S. Prokofieff. He has been aware for a long time that, according to their stage of initiation, i.e. their hierarchical position, Christian Rosenkreutz and Rudolf Steiner stand on the same level. But on what level do these exalted spirits stand? We can grasp this at least in feeling when we learn from the Neuchâtel lectures of 1912 (GA 130) „The Mission of Christian Rosenkreutz, its Character and Task", that it is Christian Rosenkreutz who assigns to the Buddha – who rose to the rank of Buddha in the 6th century B.C. – a quite definite task. It follows from this that Rosenkreutz stands hierarchically on a higher level than the great Buddha. Let this fact impress itself upon us in its full significance! Then one will have a sense of the impossibility of Prokofieff's idea. Does the spirit who was incarnated in Rudolf Steiner really need to sacrifice its astral body to a Bodhisattva who will only attain the rank of Buddha in 3000 years, merely in order to partake of his inspiration?

Once one has awakened to it, one can find confirmation of this in many places in Steiner's lectures – e.g. also in „The East in the Light of the West" (lecture 9, GA 113) – assuming, that is, that one takes the trouble to read exactly, really quite exactly, and gets out of the bad habit of wanting to take in as much as possible as quickly as possible, even at the cost of the extremely important „love of the detail". Somebody might very well have had the idea some time, that a Buddha appears as member of a Lodge of 12 Bodhisattvas, when in fact the rank of Bodhisattva represents a stage prior to that of Buddha. Engaging with such questions, which look at first like incongruities, can make the striving pupil into a seeker for knowledge.

3. Sacrifice of the Ether-body?

Over no fewer than 25 pages (81-106) Prokofieff tries to persuade the reader to acknowledge that, from 1913, Rudolf Steiner sacrificed his ether-body to the Being whom one can call the „second Adam". Here, so much of the highest Mysteries is brought down to the level of the lower understanding and what it is able to offer by way of a horizon, that I would prefer not to go into it any further. At the beginning I pointed out that Prokofieff is lacking in a feeling for spiritual tact when he is speaking about the mysteries of the Fifth Gospel.

This supposed sacrifice of Rudolf Steiner is then brought into immediate connection with the building of the first Goetheanum. No-one will question that one must really speak here of an unparalleled sacrifice made by Rudolf Steiner, but this is not grasped if one reduces it to the surrender of the life-body of Rudolf Steiner, a surrender which, if it had really been a sacrifice of the ether-body, would have led to the instant death of the person concerned, unless we understand this sacrifice as being a descent of that chaste 'I' into this ether-body. But then the consequence of this would be that one could only have spoken of the spirit of Rudolf Steiner himself in a very restricted sense.

The logical consequence for Prokofieff is „that Rudolf Steiner had to give forces of his ether-body for the formation of a spiritual sheath around the hill of

Dornach – a sheath such as in ancient times surrounded all true Mystery centres – and which was to serve as a vessel for those sublime spiritual impulses which wanted to descend to this place, so that it could become the centre of spiritual life for Western humanity." This „mysterious relation between building and builder/architect (Baumeister)" is, as we shall see, for him the guarantee that Dornach was, is, and into the distant future will continue to be, that Mystery centre. What goes on there concretely, Prokofieff may have formed a fine picture of for himself. He did not receive an impression of this when he came to Dornach for the first time in Winter 1982/3 and got to know the building and the people who live in and inhabit it and fill it with their spiritual substance.

4. Sacrifice of the Physical Body?

With regard to the sacrifice of the physical body of Rudolf Steiner, the impression is given that here we have a quite natural and regular process which took place in connection with the previous sacrifices of the bodily sheaths in parallel with the seven-year periods. Steiner himself gave the cue to this sacrifice when he held the Christmas Conference, through uniting the errors, mistakes and inadequacies of the members with his own Karma (p. 133). The question whether after this Christmas Conference, after the laying of this Foundation Stone in the h e a r t of every single member, the spark should not have ignited, so that the taking upon himself of the karma of the Society need in no way have led to the destruction of the physical body of Rudolf Steiner, is not asked at all. For Prokofieff everything is perfectly in order: Steiner's sacrifice, Dornach as a Mystery Centre, and the human beings who form the membership of the Society. Those, however, who doubt that what lives today in the Goetheanum can justly be called a Mystery centre of the 20th century are, according to Prokofieff, Anthroposophists who consciously or unconsciously promote the impulses of powers who wish to prevent Rudolf Steiner from fulfilling his task. That a 28-year-old can come to such an opinion is understandable. That people who have grown old and grey as Anthroposophists can consider it correct, is less easy to grasp.

The Constitution of a Free High School for Spiritual Science elaborated by Rudolf Steiner envisages sections and three Classes. The existence and the work of these Classes depends upon at least 48 initiates of the second and third degree (Journeyman and Master degrees) being able to develop their activity to the full. With this fact in mind one should study Rudolf Steiner's „Last Address" of September 28th 1924, not just with one's understanding, but with an opening up of one's organs of cognition. But there can be no question of the activity of initiates in Dornach, for the members of the First Class – and the other two Classes do not exist – depend upon someone reading the Class texts of Rudolf Steiner; in other words someone reads out what Rudolf Steiner said in Class lessons held in the past. A leader of a living First Class ought – which should surely be easy to understand - to have the capacity to act as a „Bearer of the Word" to the extent that the inspirations for the holding of his Class lessons come to him at the right moment, and he is able to translate this into speech.

It is obvious that one cannot reproach a person because, although this is his task, he is not able to hold Class lessons. The reproach must nevertheless be made categorically when, in spite of this fact which can be neither evaded nor kept secret, the claim is made that Dornach should be recognized as a real „High School for Spiritual Science" – an institution which must have initiates as teachers. If Dornach is described in this way, then one is misrepresenting the facts. Jurists call it acting „under false pretences".

Prokofieff describes the „four sacrifices" of Steiner as though they are facts, in just the form he sees them. In so doing he forgets that one cannot think out facts, one cannot invent them. Facts need to be observed. Starting from the observation, one can describe them. Thus Prokofieff is also guilty of a misrepresentation of facts. And in the process of doing this he completely loses Rudolf Steiner - who is the central theme of the book. He no longer recognizes him as the individuality, the immortal spirit, the entelechy who, from 1861 to 1925, unfolded in the personality of Rudolf Steiner an earthly existence, and within this a definite, utterly amazing and unique activity, but sees „in him" other beings who made use of Rudolf Steiner's sheaths to be active themselves, whereby both Rudolf Steiner and these beings are seen in a false light. And for this the author receives praise from Anthroposophists, who most certainly would not wish this to be the case.

Allow me to draw attention to another symptomatic remark which can indicate one of the reasons why Prokofieff became so stuck in his point of view. On p. 119 it says: „It would have been necessary to connect oneself with Anthroposophy not only as a cultural-spiritual stream, but to receive it into oneself as a purely esoteric stream. However, this did not necessarily happen in every case at that time" (i.e. around the year 1919 – H.F.).

It seems to me that here, as if „en passant", a basic error is being formulated. Prokofieff regards Anthroposophy as a cultural-spiritual stream also, but actually as a purely esoteric stream – as a stream, therefore, which remains completely within the world of ideas, and does not wish to leave it. Interest in sense-appearance is for him tantamount to error. For him Anthroposophy is defined as the antithesis of materialism – it is spiritualism therefore. But Anthroposophy is not this, but, „esoterically speaking", it is a macrocosmic Being who connects the spiritual with the physical world. Anthroposophy weaves between materialism and spiritualism; it is a middle and mediating Being. It therefore comes to expression already before Rudolf Steiner in Goethe's way of viewing nature, in his „power of judgment in beholding"; namely, in the process of ascending from the sense-appearance which is all that is accessible to him at first, to the essence behind the appearance.

Because Steiner already found in Goethe a key to the development of Anthroposophy he was able to take his departure from him. People are so fond of describing the Weimar years of Steiner as almost wasted years, in which he only carried out what K. J. Schröer could not accomplish – something, therefore, that rather delayed than furthered Steiner's own activity. But one ought to realize all the same that in Weimar Rudolf Steiner made a crucial step in his own development, that in fact he laid the basis there for all his future creative work.

Whoever, starting like Goethe from the phenomenon, advances to a knowledge of the „Ur" (archetypal) phenomenon – starts from the single sense-perceptible object and works his way forward to its fundamental law. If he succeeds in this he is already in the spiritual world - namely, in that of the spiritual archetypes.

But whoever believes that the physical, the sense-perceptible world, is exclusively a world of appearance – and that is what the spiritualist believes, just as the materialist believes that only the world of matter exists – does not come to Anthroposophy, but he loses, at least in our age, the ground from under his feet. He comes to Lucifer.

On Dec. 24th 1923 Rudolf Steiner formulated the first paragraph of the „Statutes" as follows: „The Anthroposophical Society is to be an association of human beings who wish to cultivate the soul life in the individual and in human society on the basis of a true knowledge of the spiritual world."

We see, if we read with care, that here the soul element of the human being, i.e. his middle realm, is addressed, which appears on this Earth in a body arising from the Earth and in the society of his own fellow-men, as a being who forms a bridge to the spirit. Anthroposophy stands just as much in the middle between philosophy and occultism as it stands between anthropology and pneumatosophy. Rudolf Steiner has often described this, e.g. in „Riddles of the Soul", in „Anthroposophy – a Fragment from the Year 1910", in „Man in the Light of Occultism, Theosophy and Philosophy"; but in the widest and deepest sense in the Foundation Stone Verse of the Christmas Conference 1923/24.

There can be no doubt of the fact that whoever is striving for knowledge must disregard what he likes or dislikes, that he must rather ask at all times: how does this, how does that, Being speak? What is the true reality? Something one does not like at all can also be true. A truism, no doubt. But hardly anyone follows it in practice. The spiritual pupil must be confronted with very definite truths which are particularly hard to digest. There is no way around them, otherwise he cannot become a spiritual pupil. So long as this is not generally recognized among Anthroposophists, there is absolutely no possibility of our intervening in the immediate happenings on this Earth, so that we can do good; and this would mean that we really bring help instead of only making speeches – help which would benefit a humanity which stands at the edge of the abyss, not knowing which way to turn.

Postscript by the author: I can foresee that many readers will again find that what I say is „too harsh". It is not „harsh", but it is honest! It would be beneficial if people could find honesty and openness less distasteful! Truthfulness comes before amiability!